Chilton's
MORE MILES-
PER-DOLLAR
GUIDE

629.288
W
0049861

Ronald M. Weiers &
Chilton Automotive Editorial Department

CHILTON BOOK COMPANY
Radnor, Pennsylvania

ACKNOWLEDGMENTS

Chilton Book Company expresses appreciation to the following
for their assistance:

Cummins Engine Company
Columbus, Indiana

Champion Spark Plug Company
Toledo, Ohio

Motor Vehicle Manufacturers Association
Washington, D.C.

American Petroleum Institute
Washington, D.C.

Tire Industry Safety Council
Washington, D.C.

Rubber Manufacturers Association
New York City, New York

William A. Baxter
Firestone Tire and Rubber Company

Motorcycle Industry Council
Washington, D.C.

U.S. Environmental Protection Agency
Washington, D.C.

U.S. Department of Transportation
Washington, D.C.

Society of Automotive Engineers
New York City, New York

Mercedes-Benz of North America
Montvale, N.J.

American Honda Motor Company
Gardena, California

Contents

Introduction

Gasoline and maintenance costs are skyrocketing and show no sign of leveling off. *Chilton's More Miles-Per-Dollar Guide* can't lower the cost per gallon of gasoline, but it can show you how to use less of this expensive stuff. Actual tests by the Department of Transportation in a controlled environment using the methods outlined in this book have shown a typical reduction in fuel use of about 7%. This translates into $100 or more a year saved if you drive a standard American sedan. One chapter explains how to buy a new or used car that will provide economical transportation. In addition, it explains how to buy gasoline, oil, tires, and accessories that will give you the best results in miles-per-gallon. Chapter Ten gives you 125 ways to improve your gas mileage.

The second section of the book explains how the major systems of your car work and some things to look for when they don't. This is called troubleshooting. For instance, the quick troubleshooting section in the fuel system could save you the replacement cost of a new fuel pump if you follow the steps and find that your problem is a clogged fuel line. Each chapter first tells you how a system works and then provides step-by-step checks to make when it doesn't work properly.

A bonus section lists the official EPA gas mileage ratings for all 1977 cars, both domestic and import. These are the real figures, stripped of all advertising hoopla, to help you make an intelligent choice when buying a new car.

Chilton's More Miles-Per-Dollar Guide is just that, a guide to getting more miles for your inflation-ravaged dollar. How to drive for less money and how to maintain for less money—both are explained to help you reduce the high cost of owning a car.

1 · The Costs of Driving

For most of us, our automobile is the second-biggest purchase we will ever make. Besides costing a lot to begin with, it also consumes many of our hard-earned dollars just to keep it (and us) going. Before proceeding to the main purpose of this book—helping you to get more miles from each gallon of that expensive commodity called gasoline—let's take an overall look at the kinds of expenses your car involves.

Fixed Costs

Fixed costs are those over which you have relatively little control, and which don't change much regardless of the number of miles you drive your car or how well you take care of it.

DEPRECIATION

The used-car manager has consulted his little black book and explained that, since he needs to increase his used-car inventory, he's willing to go out on a limb and give you $900 for your three-year-old pride and joy. That's depreciation learned the hard way. The burden of depreciation can be reduced by purchasing used cars or by keeping your new car over a longer period of time. However, while you can significantly reduce the amount of gasoline your car consumes next month, there is relatively little you can do to lessen the amount it depreciates during the same period.

INSURANCE

Your yearly insurance premium, like depreciation, does not usually depend on the amount of driving you do. In most cases, the Sunday-mornings-to-church driver pays the same premium as the driver who logs 20,000 miles per year.

TAXES AND FEES

Sales tax is paid when you purchase your car, and once paid is gone forever. Likewise, state license and registration fees are the same regardless of the number of miles you drive.

3

Variable Costs

Variable costs are those which depend on the number of miles you drive, how hard you drive, and how well you take care of your car. Like the fixed costs just discussed, they are both considerable and real. However, unlike fixed costs, they are costs that you can do something about.

GASOLINE

Whether you drive a domestic V8 or a two-cylinder import, the more miles you drive, the more gasoline your car will consume. Figure 1-1 is derived from data developed by the U.S. Department of Transportation and demonstrates what you may have already guessed: gasoline represents the biggest variable cost in operating your car.[1] The illustration shown reflects the operating cost of a compact two-door sedan with six-cylinder engine, automatic transmission, averaging just under 16 miles per gallon, and being driven for 100,000 miles over 10 years.

NOTE: *This is even more impressive since the D.O.T. study assumed a gasoline price of 38¢ a gallon. Remember those days?*

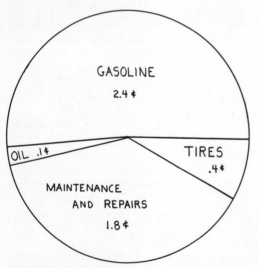

Fig. 1–1. Breakdown of operating costs for the compact sedan described in text. Skyrocketing price of gasoline has made driving even more costly than indicated here.

OIL

Don't let the .1 cents per mile price of oil mislead you into thinking that this is not an important item. Your car's health and efficiency depend very heavily on the oil you use and how often you change it. In general, the more miles you drive, the more oil your car will use, including changes and additions between changes.

TIRES

Besides being a variable-cost item themselves, your tires can help raise or lower your gasoline bill. As we'll see later, driving and maintenance practices which lead to more miles per gallon tend also to pay off in more miles per tire. As with oil, tires are often viewed in a too-narrow perspective, ignoring their influence on other aspects of the car, especially fuel economy and front-end wear.

MAINTENANCE AND REPAIRS

Maintenance and repairs make up the second-largest variable cost of operating your car. The "ounce of prevention" philosophy, though ignored by many, is a major key to lowering all of the variable costs discussed here. Reasonable maintenance, combined with the driving habits to be suggested later, should help you to get not only the most miles per gallon from your car, but also the most miles per dollar.

More Miles per Gallon

Getting more miles per gallon is not just a matter of memorizing a catchy jingle, buying a gadget, or even installing a sail on top of your car. There are no magic formulas, but rather a large number of hints, tips, and strategies which are supported by logic, common sense, and the laws of physics.

The emphasis here will be not only on what to do, but also on why the advice works. From time to time you may encounter a pep talk (to keep you thinking "economy") and a challenge (to persuade you to do something you didn't think you could do). However, when you finish this book, you should be a more efficient driver of a more efficient car and may even have thought of some ideas to add to those which follow.

RECORDING YOUR MILES
PER GALLON

Before proceeding to become the best economy driver on your block, there's one thing you need to do: prepare to keep accurate records of your progress. Forget that "I can drive to work for three weeks on a tank" chatter—let's talk about miles per gallon. For accurate measurements, keep the following in mind when you fill up:

1. Record the mileage reading, to the nearest tenth if possible—otherwise you may be off by as many as two miles in the distance covered between fill-ups.

2. Try to have the tank filled to the same level each time. Note that some attendants seem to squeeze gasoline into (or near) your tank until they get to the nearest half-dollar, while others don't go more than a dime beyond the pump's automatic shut-off. (Hint: carry change or a credit card to encourage odd amounts.)

3. Try to have the car in the same position each time. For example, if the filler pipe is on the left and the car is leaning toward the left, an air pocket may remain at the right side of the "full" tank. The more weight there is on the side of the car where the filler pipe is located, the better the chances of an air pocket in the tank and the better your latest gas mileage will appear to be. (Readers attempting to impress economy-minded friends, take note.)

4. If you really want to get picky, divide the cost of the fill-up by the cost per gallon to get a more accurate reading of the number of gallons consumed. However, for most purposes, the tenths wheel on the pump should be sufficient.

5. If the driving conditions between this fill-up and the last were unusual in any way, it will add more insight to your miles-per-gallon records if you make note of this with a short comment.

Figure 1-2 is an example of a record-keeping format you may wish to use in keeping track of your car's gasoline mileage. Remember that driving conditions have a lot to do with the number of miles you can get to the gallon. For example, open highway gas mileage is generally

Illus. 1–1. When you fill up, try to have your car in the same position each time and the tank filled to the same level. This will help ensure accurate gas mileage calculations.

Speedo Reading	Miles	Gals.	mpg	Avg. mph, Last Two Fills	Comments
1400	—	—	—	—	just bought book & haven't had chance to keep records yet.
1652	252	11.9	21.2	—	turnpike.
1800	148	18.3	8.1	13.2	hauled anvils to auction.
2045	245	14.8	16.5	11.9	commuting.
2235	190	9.2	20.7	18.1	Sunday drive.
2447	212	15.2	13.9	16.5	"Moose" Edwards joined car pool.

Fig. 1–2. A format you may wish to use in keeping track of your miles-per-gallon progress.

much higher than that obtained in slow-moving commuter traffic.

Since fluctuations from fill-up to fill-up are bound to occur, you can make a little more sense from the figures if you also calculate the average mpg for the two most recent fill-ups combined. Keep in mind that this is total miles divided by total gallons, not simply the average of the two mpg figures. In the records of figure 1-2, the average of the first two fill-ups is 252 + 148 = 400 miles divided by 11.9 + 18.3 = 30.2 gallons, or 13.2 miles per gallon.

CALCULATE YOUR SAVINGS

Depending on how economically you now drive and maintain your car, applying the ideas in this book can help your miles per gallon by anywhere from 0 to 30%—0% if you're already pretty good and 30% if you're a real leadfoot.

The Gas Savings Calculator in figure 1-3 makes the assumption that you will be able to improve your miles per gallon by 15%. Let's say you now get about 14 miles per gallon and drive 10,000 miles each year. A 15% improvement will take you up to 16.1 miles per gallon and save you the cost of 90 gallons that you now don't have to buy. The Gas Savings Calculator will tell you in an instant how many gallons you'll save with a 15% increase in your present miles per gallon. Just:

1. Place an X on your present miles per gallon (scale at left side).

2. Place an X on how many miles you expect to drive in the next year (scale at right side).

3. Connect the two X's with a straight line.

4. Read your gasoline savings at the center scale where the straight line has crossed it.

5. Multiply the gallons saved by the price you now pay for a gallon and find the number of dollars you'll save by improving your mpg 15%:

$$\frac{\text{Gallons}}{\text{Saved}} \times \frac{\text{Price per}}{\text{Gallon}} = \frac{\text{Dollars}}{\text{Saved}}$$

For example, if your present mpg is 16 and you drive 10,000 miles per year, a 15% mpg improvement will mean 82 gallons of gas that you won't have to buy.

The next chapter considers some of the scientific principles upon which gasoline consumption depends.

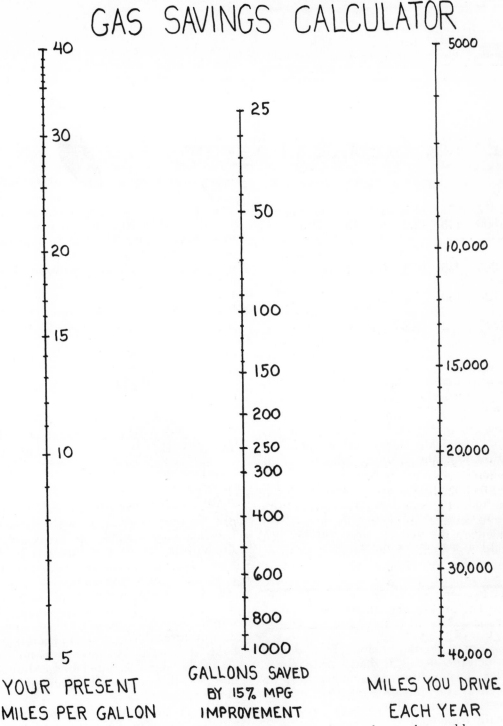

Fig. 1–3. Just connect your present mpg with the miles you drive each year, then read how many gallons you'll save by driving 15% more economically.

2 · The Science of Saving

If you saw a midnight thief siphoning gas from your tank, chances are that you'd quickly do something about it. However, the gasoline pirates in this chapter are not people, but invisible forces. They are not armed with a siphon hose, but with the laws of physics. Though you won't see them, they can pilfer your gasoline as surely as the best siphon man in the business.

Air Resistance

Conjure up an image of an engine which produces less than 1 horsepower. Next, imagine this engine powering a vehicle to a level-road speed over 138 miles per hour. Impossible, you say? No, it actually happened.

The "engine" in this case was a 29-year-old man named Al Abbott. The "vehicle" was a BICYCLE. Mr. Abbott pedaled his bicycle at an average speed of 138.674 miles per hour.[1] Naturally, his bicycle was hardly the kind you'd expect to find at your local department store. Its front sprocket, in order to provide the necessary gear ratio, was nearly as large as the bicycle's wheels.

What was his secret? In addition to a high degree of strength and skill, this feat also required a pace car with a special box-shaped rear section to break a path through the air. By pedaling closely behind his pace car, the rider experienced practically no air resistance.

If this seems insignificant, consider that a typical domestic sedan would require over 200 horsepower just to push its way through the air at 138 miles per hour. However, Mr. Abbott was able to attain the same speed with his human body, capable of producing perhaps a single horsepower.

NOTE: *"Horsepower" is the rate of doing work. One horsepower can move a 550-pound force 1 foot in 1 second. You can check your own horsepower by running up a flight of steps. For example, if you weigh 150 pounds and can run up a 20-foot-high flight of*

8

stairs in 10 seconds, you've generated 150×20 divided by 10×550, or .55 horsepower.

AIR RESISTANCE AND SPEED

If you've ever done a belly flop from the high dive, pushed your way through a crowd, or stuck your hand out the window of a fast-moving car, you've some appreciation of the fact that water, crowds, and air all resent your trying to move through them. And they return your movement with a force of their own.

When your car is traveling at even moderate speeds, the force exerted by displaced air can be quite considerable. Figure 2-1 presents the air resistance that a typical full-size car encounters at various speeds.[2] As the figures indicate, the air reacts quite strongly to increases in your speed. Doubling your speed from 20 mph to 40 mph actually quadruples the number of pounds of force which the air exerts against your car. (Note that the numbers in figure 2-1 are rounded off.)

Also presented in figure 2-1 is the horsepower it takes to overcome air resistance at the speeds shown. The horsepower required to overcome air resistance varies as the CUBE of your speed; so if you double your speed, you'll require eight times as much horsepower to overcome air resistance. The relationship is as follows: [3]

$$\left.\begin{array}{l}\text{Horsepower Required} \\ \text{to Overcome Air} \\ \text{Resistance}\end{array}\right\} = KDAeV^3$$

where:

K is a constant.

D is the vehicle's drag coefficient and is dependent on how aerodynamic the car happens to be. The more streamlined a car, the lower will be its drag coefficient and the better its fuel economy.

A is the frontal area of the car and is simply the area of a front view of the car. A rough approximation of your car's frontal area is 80% of its width times its

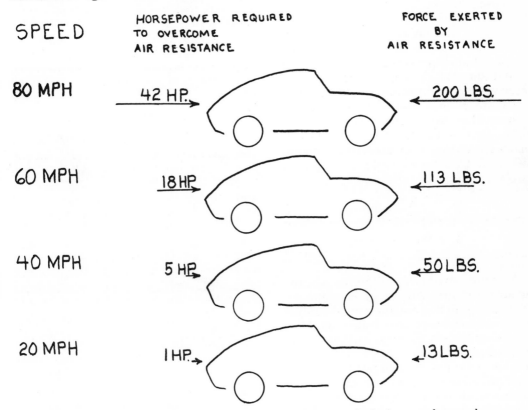

SPEED	HORSEPOWER REQUIRED TO OVERCOME AIR RESISTANCE	FORCE EXERTED BY AIR RESISTANCE
80 MPH	42 HP.	200 LBS.
60 MPH	18 HP.	113 LBS.
40 MPH	5 HP.	50 LBS.
20 MPH	1 HP.	13 LBS.

Fig. 2–1. Rapidly-increasing air resistance is the main reason why higher speeds mean lower gas mileage. Figures shown are typical of a full-size sedan traveling at these speeds.

Illus. 2–1. Passenger-car frontal areas don't vary much more than the three shown here. With other factors equal, the car with the smallest frontal area will get the best gas mileage.

height. Most passenger cars have a frontal area between 17 and 25 square feet.[4] Frontal area is one reason why low, narrow cars tend to get more miles per gallon—they don't need as much fuel to overcome air resistance.

e is the density of the air through which you're driving. The higher the altitude above sea level, the less air resistance you'll encounter at any given speed. Air density decreases by about 3% for every 1000 feet increase in altitude and drops by about 1% for every 10° F. rise in temperature.[5]

V is the speed at which you're traveling into the air around you. For example, you'll encounter the same air resistance under any of the following circumstances:

driving 50 mph through calm air, or driving 40 mph into a 10 mph wind, or driving 70 mph with a 20 mph wind.

In any of the above situations, you'll be moving into the air around you at a rate of 50 mph.

EFFECTS OF A CROSS WIND

Let's look at a certain 1700 pound import as it travels 75 miles per hour through a 20 mph cross wind. The air is subjecting the car to three different forces:[6]

1. A backward force of 106 pounds due to air resistance at this high speed.

2. An upward force (the same kind that makes airplanes fly) of 186 pounds. Most cars tend to get "lighter" as their speed increases, but stay grounded because they weigh more than the lifting force.

3. A sideward force of 166 pounds which tends to push the car toward one side of the road. By causing more friction between the tires and the road, a cross wind will actually reduce your gas mileage slightly.

Rolling Resistance

Whoever invented the wheel was probably to discover rolling resistance shortly thereafter. Your tires' reluctance to roll is another factor which affects your gas mileage. As a tire rolls, it squirms and flexes. This causes heat plus rolling resistance, which forces your engine to work harder.

Depending on its type of construction and the load it is supporting, a passenger car tire may require a force of 15 to 30 pounds just to keep it rolling at highway speeds. That means that your engine has to fight between 60 and 120 pounds of rolling resistance from all four tires.

In the 0–70 mph range where most of our driving takes place, the force required to keep a tire rolling is relatively independent of speed. Tests by Firestone provide the data presented in

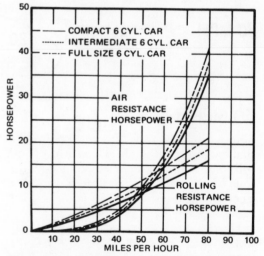

Fig. 2–3. Air and rolling resistance take their horsepower toll as speed goes up. When speed doubles, your engine must generate eight times as much horsepower to fight air resistance. *Source:* Jack C. Cornell, *Passenger Car Fuel Economy Characteristics on Modern Superhighways*, SAE Rept. No. 650862, Report to the National Fuels and Lubricants Meeting, Society of Automotive Engineers, Tulsa, Okla., Nov. 2–4, 1965 (New York: Society of Automotive Engineers, 1965.)

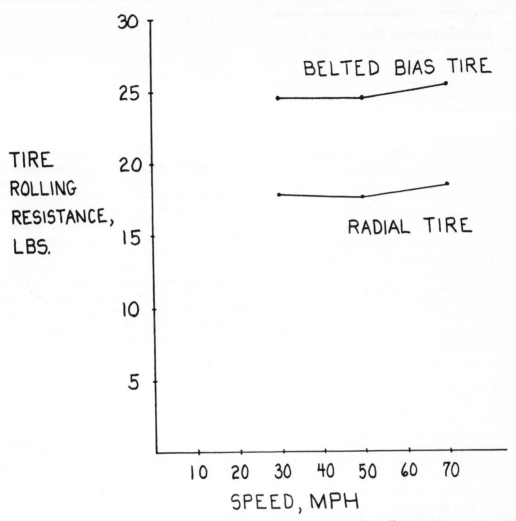

Fig. 2–2. Besides lasting a long time, radial tires save gas by rolling easier.

figure 2-2. At 50 mph, the steel-belted radial construction enables your tires to be rolled by a force of only 70 pounds, while four belted bias tires were found to have a combined resistance of 98 pounds at the same speed.[7]

Despite their practically constant rolling resistance, your tires will require more horsepower at higher speeds. This is because horsepower is a function of force and speed, not just force alone. Figure 2-3 combines air resistance horsepower and rolling resistance horsepower into a common chart involving 6-cylinder cars from the compact, intermediate, and full-size classes.[8]

To determine how much horsepower is required for you to cruise at a steady speed, add the rolling resistance horsepower to the air resistance horsepower. For example, for the compact car to cruise at 40 mph, approximately 10 horsepower is required—3 to overcome air resistance and 7 to overcome rolling resistance.

Your car's total resistance to rolling includes other parts of the drive train, such as the transmission, driveshaft, universal joints, rear axle, and wheel bearings. At lower speeds, automatic transmission torque converter slippage is also a factor. However, the primary component of rolling resistance is the combined reluctance of your tires to roll.

Acceleration Resistance

There's only one way to avoid acceleration resistance: never accelerate. However, this remedy isn't practical, since your car would sit forever in the driveway—whenever you're stopped and want to go, you simply have to increase your speed, or accelerate. A very good second-best strategy is to never accelerate when you don't have to and, when necessary, accelerate as gradually as possible. The amount of horsepower it takes to accelerate your car depends on three things that are summarized in the following equation: [9]

$$\left.\begin{array}{l}\text{Horsepower Required}\\\text{to Accelerate}\end{array}\right\} = KVWC$$

where:
K is a constant

V is how fast you're going when you decide that you'd like to be going faster. The higher your speed, the more horsepower (and gasoline) you're going to need for acceleration.

W is how much your car weighs. Accelerating a Cadillac is naturally going to be more expensive than accelerating a Volkswagen.

C is the rate at which you want to accelerate. Rather than blast from 40 mph to 60 mph in 5 seconds, your gas mileage will thank you if you have the patience to wait a little longer.

Figure 2-4 shows the general relationship between how fast you'd like to accelerate and the horsepower it will take to do the job. The graph holds true for any vehicle weight and any speed. The point is that horsepower required is proportional to the rate of acceleration and that an acceleration rate of zero will require zero horsepower. Remember that

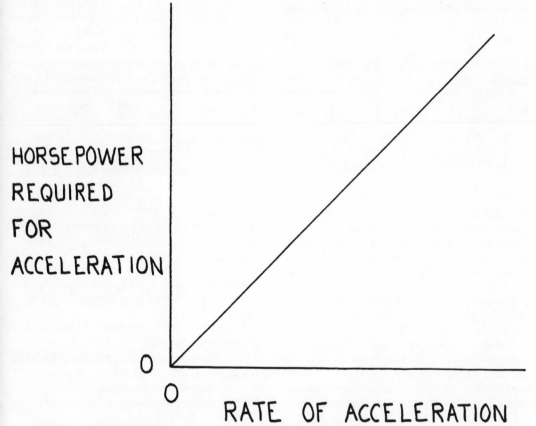

Fig. 2-4. The horsepower needed to accelerate goes up in proportion to the rate of speed increase, but zero acceleration means zero horsepower needed for that purpose.

we're talking about extra horsepower requirements, since your engine is already working to overcome air and rolling resistance.

MOMENTUM AND INERTIA

An object that's moving tends to continue moving and one that's stationary tends to remain stationary. This includes bowling balls, rubber ducks, and automobiles. It might take some gasoline to accelerate your car to 60 mph, but once you settle upon this, or any other constant speed, your only gasoline consumers are air and rolling resistance. When you keep your speed (and momentum) constant, you're eliminating acceleration resistance as a drain on your fuel supply.

Acceleration resistance is really no more than your car's reluctance to change its momentum. Changes in momentum use up energy, whether the direction of change is positive (accelerating) or negative (braking). However, since properly-operating brakes don't directly consume gasoline, we'll be concerned here with the effect of acceleration on your gasoline bill.

Gravity Resistance

If you've ever driven up Pikes Peak or followed a loaded coal truck up a Pennsylvania hill, you know that fighting the effects of gravity takes horsepower. On a mere 5% grade (5 feet of rise over 100 feet of travel), a 4000 pound automobile will experience a force of .05 × 4000, or 200 pounds. Assuming that this automobile is climbing the grade at 60 miles per hour, 32 horsepower will be necessary just to offset the effect of gravity. Add to this approximately 33 horsepower to overcome air and rolling resistance and you'll need 65 horsepower to make it up the grade without losing speed. On the other hand, if the same car were coming down this grade, the driver would need to apply just a touch of throttle in order to maintain 60 mph.

The maximum grade on most interstate highways is about 5 to 7%. To determine how much gravity resistance force your car must overcome in climbing a given grade, just multiply the operating weight of your car times the percentage of the grade. For example, a 7% grade will exert a force of 350 pounds on a 5000 pound automobile.

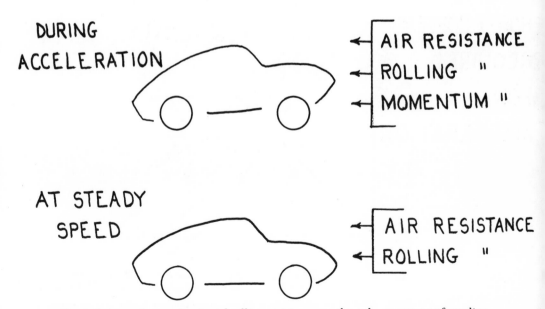

Fig. 2–5. At steady speeds, air and rolling resistance are the only consumers of gasoline.

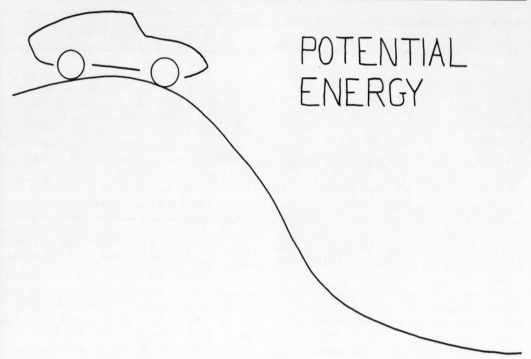

Fig. 2–6. The top of a hill provides your car with an abundant supply of potential energy.

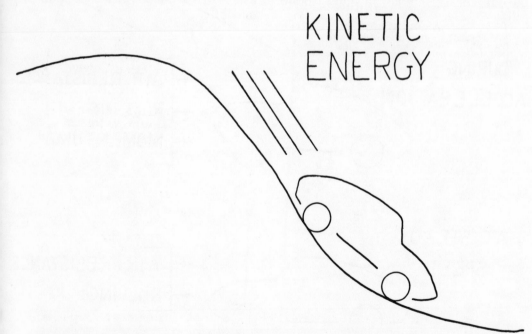

Fig. 2–7. Potential energy is transformed into kinetic energy as gravity provides you with extra horsepower.

POTENTIAL AND KINETIC ENERGY

Remember the carnival game where you used a sledge hammer to try and ring the bell, win a cigar and impress your friends? Well, when you raised the sledge over your head, the hammer gained potential energy because of its lofty position and the law of gravity. Were you to lose your grip and drop it, the hammer's potential energy would quickly be transformed into kinetic energy which would do considerable damage to any toes in the vicinity.

When your car has just puffed its way to the peak of a steep hill, it has potential energy because of the down-hill run which lies ahead. As you travel down the other side, the potential energy your car worked to obtain is converted into the kinetic energy of motion. Climbing a hill is like loaning energy to an old friend (gravity). You pay on the way up, but receive your repayment on the way down. Attacking hills is an important segment of economy driving strategy which we'll explore in a later chapter.

Engine Resistance

In the preceding sections, we've seen how outside forces make your engine

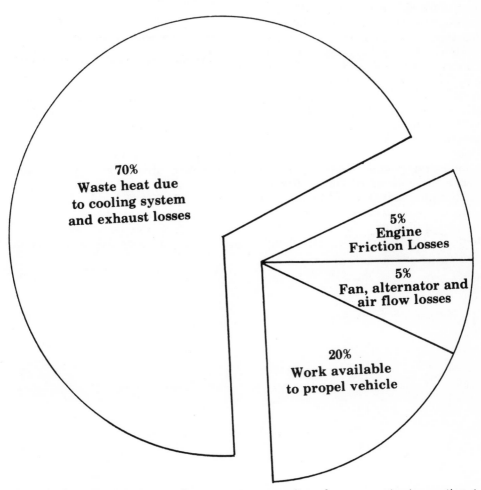

Fig. 2–8. This is what happens to the energy in your gasoline when your engine is operating at wide-open throttle. At part-throttle, this distribution changes and an even greater proportion of energy is lost to the cooling system and exhaust. *Source:* Carl E. Burke, *et al.*, "Where Does All the Power Go?" *SAE Transactions*, 65 (1957).

work harder. Add engine mechanical friction, air, gas and fluid flow resistance, the power necessary to turn the fan, water pump and alternator, and you have still another invisible man who is anxious to steal your fuel. These drains can consume 10% or more of the energy contained in each gallon of gasoline.[10]

Weather and Atmospheric Conditions

Colder weather lowers gas mileage by requiring a longer time for the various moving parts of your car to warm up. Lubricants don't flow easily when the temperature is low. However, once the moving parts are as warm as they're going to get, cold-weather fuel economy still suffers because of the cold air entering the engine. While some cars feed heated air to the air cleaner, this only reduces the penalty caused by the lower temperatures. At 50 mph, each 10°F. drop in temperature will lower your gas mileage by about 2%.[11]

As indicated in the discussion of air resistance horsepower, driving at 40 mph into a 10 mph headwind will lower your gas mileage to about what you would get when driving through calm air at a speed of 50 mph. The reverse is true of tailwinds, which allow you to drive faster while encountering less air resistance force than you would normally experience at the higher speed.

At higher altitudes, the thinner air will tend to trick your engine into burning a fuel-air mixture that contains too much gasoline and not enough air. Gas mileage can suffer by as much as 15% at an altitude of 4000 feet.[12] When you have your car "set up" to drive properly at high altitudes, the modifications made will often cause poor driveability at lower altitudes. The use of specially-designed carburetors, ignition systems and fuel injection all tend to reduce the loss in fuel economy which often accompanies high-altitude driving.

Road Surface Conditions

Poor road surfaces will increase your car's rolling resistance far beyond the smooth-road resistances already discussed. At a speed of 40 mph, a patched-up asphalt road will reduce your gas mileage by about 15%, a gravel road by 35%, a sandy surface by 45%, and a dirt road by 15–35%.[13] A road that is covered with water or snow also increases rolling resistance and reduces your fuel economy by as much as 1 mile per gallon.[14]

3 · Buying for Economy

With the possible exception of the expectant mother, nobody receives more advice than the new or used car buyer. In this chapter you'll find plenty of advice, but all of it will be directly or indirectly connected with the number one aim of this book: more miles per gallon of gasoline. In addition to carefully choosing your car and buying its gasoline, you should also be an informed consumer of the oil, tires, replacement parts, and various accessories which can help reduce your fuel bill.

Buying a New Car

THE BASIC CAR

Weight

The most important factor in your new car's fuel consumption will be how much it weighs. The heavier a car, the more energy it requires to climb hills, accelerate, and overcome rolling resistance. In addition, the greater frontal area of a larger, heavier car will mean more horsepower needed to fight air resistance at highway speeds. Figure 3-1 describes the relationship between weight and fuel economy as determined by the U.S. Environmental Protection Agency for automobiles of a recent model year.[1] The curve shows that a 500 pound gain in weight tends to reduce fuel economy by between 2 and 5 miles per gallon. Likewise, a 2500-pound car will tend to get twice the gas mileage of one weighing 5000 pounds.

The penalty for buying a larger, heavier car will be less severe if most of your driving is at highway speeds with relatively little stop-and-go operation. At these higher and more constant speeds, the acceleration resistance we discussed in the last chapter will have less influence.

Besides their weight disadvantage when stripped, heavier cars also tend to be equipped with larger engines and power-robbing equipment which are often necessary to offset their greater

17

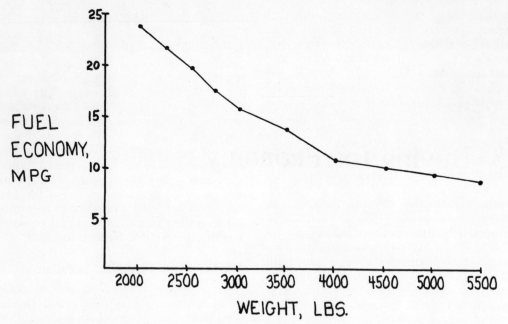

Fig. 3–1. Your car's weight is the most important factor in determining how many miles per gallon it will deliver.

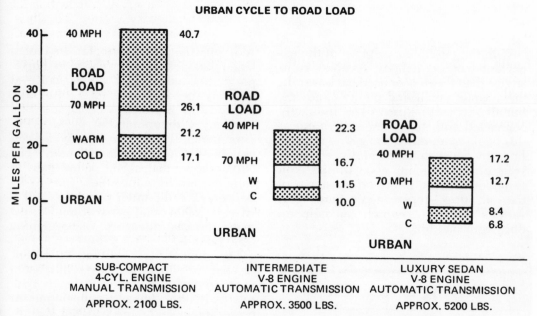

Fig. 3–2. Driving conditions can affect the gas mileage of any car, regardless of size. *Source:* G. J. Huebner, Jr., and D. J. Gasser, "General Factors Affecting Vehicle Fuel Consumption" (paper presented at National Automobile Engineering Meeting, Society of Automotive Engineers, Detroit, Michigan, May 15, 1973.)

bulk. Figure 3-2 summarizes the miles per gallon achieved by typical subcompact, intermediate, and luxury cars under various driving conditions.[2] The subcom-

pact model tested achieved 40.7 miles per gallon at a steady road speed of 40 mph, 26.1 at a steady speed of 70 mph, 21.2 when warmed up and operated in a typical urban driving cycle, and 17.1 when operated from cold in the same urban driving cycle. Comparable figures are presented for the intermediate and luxury models. Weight effect on gas mileage is the most important reason for you to buy the smallest and lightest car that will satisfy your driving needs.

Body Style

Choice of body style will depend largely on your individual requirements for carrying people and things. Again, keep in mind that the smallest car that meets your carrying requirements will generally be the most economical one for you to drive. My own choice is the subcompact or compact station wagon with its combination of versatility, economy, and load-carrying ability. This size wagon has about the same weight and frontal area of the sedan with which it is related, yet can haul more goods when the need arises. In a later chapter, you'll learn how the author, plus wife, three kids, and large German Shepherd managed to get 55 miles per gallon (with the dog riding, not pulling) from a subcompact wagon. Hatchback sedans are also handy, but sacrifice a bit of carrying ability because of their sloped rear deck. Naturally, if you intend to travel light, go the sedan or sports car route and get the same economy with a little more flair.

Illus. 3–1. The subcompact station wagon is one of the most economical buys around. It combines small frontal area and light weight with generous carrying capacity for highway trips.

Exterior Dimensions

Besides the obvious need for your new car to fit into your garage, there is another reason for checking the exterior dimensions of the models from which you're trying to choose—frontal area. With other factors equal, the car with the smallest frontal area is going to have the easiest time slipping through the air which surrounds it. As mentioned in the preceding chapter, you can get a fair approximation of a car's frontal area by calculating (Width) × (Height) × (.8). Longer, narrower cars will tend to have less frontal area than shorter, wider cars containing the same cubic footage inside.

Engine Size, Type and Location

Your miles per gallon will depend more on your car's weight and frontal area than on the size of its engine. With other factors equal, a 10% increase in the displacement of an engine will result in only a .1 mpg drop at a steady speed of 70 miles per hour and a .2 mpg reduction in a typical urban trip.[3] Figure 3-3 illustrates the steady-speed miles per gallon of comparable cars equipped with a small six-cylinder engine, a large six-cylinder engine, and a V8.[4] At higher speeds, where air resistance becomes the major force resisting progress, the various engines produced nearly the same number of miles per gallon. When two cars are otherwise equal, the one with the smaller engine will generally be more economical because conventional engines are more efficient when operating at a higher percentage of their full power. However, when compared to weight and frontal area, engine size is not a highly significant factor in determining the fuel economy you'll experience in everyday driving.

The type of engine also influences the number of miles you can expect from a gallon of fuel. Compared to conventional designs, the Wankel rotary may deliver 20–35% less fuel economy while a diesel can produce 40–70% more.[5] These estimates assume installation in a vehicle of the same weight, which is slightly unfair to the Wankel, which has the compactness and light weight to fit into

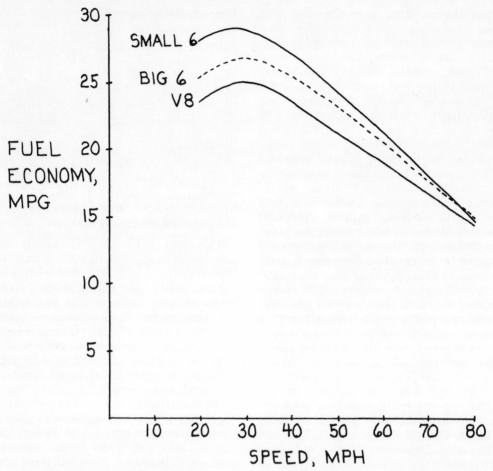

Fig. 3–3. At higher speeds, engine size has relatively little influence on gas mileage. *Source:* J. J. Cornell, "Car Size Chiefly Responsible for Low MPG at High MPH," *SAE Journal,* April, 1966.

smaller, lighter cars which have been designed around it.

Engine location may have a slight effect on your fuel economy if you live in an area where snow is a problem during the colder months. If the engine is located over the drive wheels (for example, front-engine/front-wheel-drive or rear-engine/rear-wheel-drive), you may not require the use of chains or snow tires as often as the person who owns a car with less inherent traction. The relationship of this to your miles per gallon is that snow tires and tires with chains tend to have very high rolling resistance compared to warm-weather tires.

Frequency and Ease of Servicing

Good fuel economy depends heavily on routine tune-ups and maintenance prescribed in the owner's manual which accompanies your new car. Whether you perform the work yourself or hire someone you trust, easy accessibility to the distributor, spark plugs, lubrication fittings, oil, air and fuel filters will tend to make your work less difficult or your mechanic's work less expensive. In either case, the quirks of human nature suggest that the easier it is to do something, the greater the chance that it will be done right. Don't be afraid to ask the salesman where the car's oil filter is located—in Chapter Five, I'm going to try to persuade you to change it yourself.

OPTIONAL EQUIPMENT

Optional Engines

For most of us, a standard engine will provide all the power we need. However, if you plan to pull a trailer or carry heavy loads, a larger engine may be required just to keep up with traffic under certain conditions. Remember that the larger engine will use more fuel, but that engine size is not as significant as weight and frontal area in determining gas mileage. While you may sometimes need a larger engine, consider how much extra fuel you're going to use during the majority of miles when you're not climbing 14,000 foot mountains or helping your neighbor pull out tree stumps. Except for very special needs, fight the temptations of "showroom fever" and settle for a standard engine.

Automatic Transmission

The fuel economy effects of an automatic transmission are negative, but not as bad as you may have thought. The loss will depend largely on the rear axle ratio and the kind of driving conditions you normally encounter. With other factors equal, the use of an automatic transmission can reduce fuel economy by up to 15%.[6] However, the automatic has advantages which can make its economy more comparable to that of a manual transmission, and in some cases better. First, most cars equipped with an automatic transmission are provided with a lower, more economical rear axle ratio than their manually-shifted counterparts. Second, because the throttle movement in shifting a manual transmission tends to increase hydrocarbon emissions, it is easier for a car with automatic transmission to meet the exhaust standards of the Environmental Protection Agency. At a given level of emission control, the car with manual transmission requires more strict engine adjustments, often in the form of a more retarded ignition spark.

When climbing hills or traveling at lower speeds, the torque converter of the automatic transmission will have more slippage and cause lower gas mileage. However, at steady highway speeds, the torque converter will tend to lock up and deliver fuel economy closer to that of an identical car equipped with manual transmission. Tests involving an intermediate size car have shown that automatic transmission costs between .5 mpg (steady 70 mph speed with a lower rear axle ratio than the manual model) and 1.8 mpg (urban travel cycle with equal rear axle ratios).[7]

Optional Rear Axle Ratio

The rear axle ratio is simply the number of times your driveshaft must rotate in order to make the rear wheels rotate once. Since top gear in domestic cars is direct-drive, the rear axle ratio is also the number of times your engine has to rotate in order to make the rear wheels turn one time. In general, a numerically-low (for example, 2.53) rear axle ratio means less engine wear, slower acceleration and more miles per gallon than a numerically-high ratio (for example, 4.11). Some imports have an indirect-drive top gear, in which case the rear axle ratio must be multiplied by the high gear ratio in order to compare different cars. For example, a Porsche has a rear axle ratio of 4.43 and a 5th gear ratio of .76 which, when multiplied together result in what amounts to a 3.36 rear axle which can then be compared to those of standard cars.

Standard axle ratios are, at best, a compromise. The 3.73 ratio that provides good hill-climbing ability in the mountains of West Virgina may be a little too short-legged for cruising the plains of Nebraska. For this reason, it is to your advantage to specify an optional (usually between $10 and $20) economy axle ratio which will allow you to maintain highway speeds while using fewer engine revolutions. Tests have shown that reducing the rear axle ratio by 10% (for example, from 3.00 to 2.70) can improve your fuel economy by between 2 and 5%.[8]

The following table compares the

engine speed (revolutions per minute) necessary to propel two cars at various speeds in high gear. The vehicles are equal except for their rear axle ratios.

Road Speed (mph)	Car A (2.73 axle) (rpm)	Car B (3.90 axle) (rpm)
30	1140	1630
40	1520	2170
50	1900	2710
60	2280	3250
70	2660	3800
80	3040	4330
90	3420	4870

At 70 mph, the engine in car A will be turning more slowly than that of car B when car B is traveling only 50 mph. Don't forget that the axle ratio effect is most important when other factors, such as weight, engine efficiency and design, and frontal area, are equal. For example, a small sports car with a 3.90 rear axle will easily exceed the miles per gallon achieved by a luxury sedan with a ratio of 2.73.

Be wary of the linguistics used by auto salesmen and mechanics: some mistakenly refer to the economy ratios as "high" and the stump-pullers as "low." A ratio is a numerical expression and should always be interpreted as such. If it's an economy ratio that you want, be sure that it is numerically low, not just verbally "low."

As the Scottish folk song says, you take the high ratio and I'll take the low ratio and you'll get to fuel up before me.

Overdrive Transmission

On a few models, generally of British origin, an overdrive transmission may be available. This consists of an add-on section at the rear of the transmission which provides an extra gear ratio to reduce the speed of the driveshaft to about 80% of the speed of the engine. In other words, it's sort of a transmission behind the transmission. With the overdrive in operation at cruising speeds, your miles per gallon can increase by 10% or more.[9] Because of high initial cost, lack of usefulness in low-speed driving, and compe-

tition from low rear axle ratios which accomplish the same purpose, the overdrive transmission is somewhat of a relic from the past.

Power Accessories

Accessories such as power steering, power brakes, power seats, power windows, and power sunroof reduce gasoline mileage due to the extra weight (up to 30 pounds for each) that they add to the car. In addition, they consume mechanical power directly from the engine or electrical power indirectly supplied by the engine through the alternator.

The loss in gas mileage because of power steering tends to decrease as you travel at higher speeds and the friction of the engine-driven hydraulic pump becomes less important relative to air resistance and other forces trying to impede your car's progress. You can expect power steering to reduce economy by about .7 mpg at a steady speed of 25 miles per hour and by .3 mpg at 70.[10] Despite its fuel penalty, power steering may be necessary if your choice is a heavy car that is frequently used in low-speed maneuvering in which the steering wheel would otherwise be difficult to turn or in highway driving where the quicker response of power steering provides better evasive ability in avoiding an obstacle. This is a case where the weight factor hits you twice—once for the weight itself, again for the power steering which you may need to handle it. Many smaller cars don't even offer power steering as an option. With lighter front ends and quicker steering, they can get along without it.

If you're strong enough to open your car door, chances are you've got more than enough strength to step on the brake pedal hard enough to stop your car with all the deceleration of which it is capable. Naturally, there will be exceptions to this statement, but the point is that power brakes are a needless luxury for most of us. The same applies to electric motors that raise and lower our windows, adjust our seats, and open our sunroofs.

Any electrical accessory will require power that—assuming you don't order an optional waterfall in your car—must come from the engine by way of the alternator. Tests on an intermediate car with automatic transmission showed that, with the alternator operating at its maximum output of 40 to 50 amperes, gas mileage suffered by between .9 and .5 miles per gallon.[11] As would be expected, lower electrical demands resulted in smaller reductions in economy.

Air Conditioning

Whether cooling or sitting idle, an air conditioning system adds about 100 pounds of weight to your car. In urban driving, this extra weight can be expected to decrease gas mileage by about .4 mpg for a subcompact car and about .1 mpg for a standard-size model.[12] As with any other source of weight, there is a larger penalty during stop-and-go driving than in steady-speed highway operation.

When the air conditioning unit is being used, power must be provided to drive the compressor and fan, thus leading to even greater losses in gas mileage. In one test, at an ambient temperature of 85° F., use of the air conditioner reduced economy by about 2.5 mpg at 20 miles per hour and by about .5 mpg at a speed of 80.[13]

As with other accessories, the gas mileage penalty of air conditioning is less at higher speeds because of the rapidly-increasing resistance of the air through which the car is moving. It's like forgetting about your toothache after you've dropped a bowling ball on your foot—at higher speeds, air resistance tends to overshadow all other sources of resistance and cause them to be relatively less important.

Automatic Speed Control

A speed "thermostat," this option will maintain any constant speed you desire without ever having to touch the gas pedal. Because there is never any acceleration when the device is in operation, the amount of fuel consumed by acceleration resistance will be minimized. The heavier your car, the more you can benefit from this option. The disadvantages of the device are its initial cost, generally around $80, and the possibility of your becoming inattentive from not having anything to do while you're driving.

Another negative consideration is that such an option is not useful during urban driving, suburban driving or any type of operation in which speed must vary or where interaction with other vehicles is frequent. In addition, the driving techniques described in the next chapter should enable you to get enough miles per gallon in steady-speed driving that such a device wouldn't allow you to do much better. Stated another way, if your best friend were to loan you the money to buy an automatic speed control device, it might be a long time until you could save enough to pay him back.

Disc Brakes

Optional front disc brakes are superior in so many ways—including directional stability, fade and moisture resistance, and ease of service—that it's difficult to evaluate them on a miles-per-gallon basis. However, the disc brake pads do press lightly against the rotor (disc) at all times instead of retracting as do the shoes of properly-adjusted drum brakes. To this extent, frictional losses on the road can be slightly greater than with drum brakes. One possible compensating factor is that the front wheel bearings need not be disturbed during the annual or semi-annual safety inspection required in some states. In order to inspect the brake linings of a front drum brake, it is necessary to partially dismantle the hub and wheel bearing assembly—a procedure which, if carried out by a careless mechanic in untidy surroundings, might result in a faulty wheel bearing adjustment or dirt entering the bearing lubricant. Besides wearing out rather quickly, a dirty or binding front wheel bearing isn't good for your health or your gas mileage.

The brake pads, besides being very simple to replace, can be moved very slightly away from the rotor by a simple driving strategy included in next chapter's discussion of driving for economy. For this and the reasons previously mentioned, my vote goes to the ordering of front disc brakes if they're optional, using them without regret if they're standard.

Radio and Sound Equipment

It would seem that optional equipment in this category is more hedonistic than economical. Naturally, a car radio can be useful in receiving helicopter reports of fuel-consuming traffic jams between you and the destination to which you may be commuting. However, fuel-economy-wise, an AM, AM-FM, or AM-FM-Stereo radio can do other good things. Likewise for a stereo-tape deck or short-wave adapter. To the extent that driving economically depends on your patience and state of mind, entertainment equipment, commercial-free music and short-wave broadcasts can help take the urgency out of your driving and the lead out of your foot. Long trips won't seem quite so long, traffic jams won't be as frustrating, and the kids can listen to music instead of fighting or playing count-the-cows.

Instrumentation

Like the radio, dashboard instruments can be a source of entertainment, alertness, and patience. In addition, they are useful sources of information on the status of what's happening (or about to happen) in your engine or electrical system. Some instruments and gauges which are available as aftermarket accessories are also useful in obtaining better gas mileage, and are included in a later section of this chapter.

Limited-Slip Differential

The limited-slip differential sees to it that both rear tires do their share when you're faced with a slippery road surface. While helpful in getting you to your destination under adverse traction conditions, and involving no added weight to the car, this is not an option that will save you gasoline. A possible exception would be if it means enabling you to travel without the use of snow tires during between-seasons driving, thus providing the same advantage as having the engine over the drive wheels.

Trailer-Towing Package

The trailer-towing option generally includes a number of heavy-duty and durability items, such as heavy-duty springs and shock absorbers, larger radiator, and special automatic-transmission oil cooler, among other things. However, these are accompanied by larger tires and a numerically-higher rear axle ratio. The larger tires won't hurt much, but if you're primarily interested in fuel economy, you may have to specify an economy axle ratio, if available, and try to get your heavy-duty and durability features separately. Naturally, if you plan to pull a heavy trailer, follow the manufacturer's recommendations and opt for the entire package. Like the limited-slip differential, this isn't an option that is generally useful in improving fuel economy.

Permanent Roof Rack

In addition to its usual role as shiny dead weight, a permanent roof rack does nothing to aid your car's fight against air resistance at high speeds. If you must use a rack often, its permanence will not be to your disadvantage. However, if you rarely need to carry roof-top items, consider a suction-cup or gutter-clamp removable rack instead. If at all possible, make do with the interior of the car as a storage location for bulky items, as roof-top loads tend to give your car the air resistance of a two-story bus when traveling at highway speeds.

Optional Tires

Various tire options include oversize tires, whitewalls, belted bias-ply tires, and radials. In case radials are not standard equipment, by all means specify them. In addition to lasting long enough to pay for their initial cost, they can deliver anywhere from 3 to 10% better gas mileage than conventional bias-ply tires.[14] Radials also provide better handling, traction, impact-resistance and high-speed performance than their bias-ply competitors.

Oversize tires will provide a larger rolling diameter, slightly greater ground clearance, and give the effects of a numerically-lower rear axle ratio. This latter gain may be partially offset by increased rolling resistance and slightly greater weight.

In general, any tire with belts under the tread will deliver better fuel economy than a non-belted design. This is due to less tread movement, lower heat build-up, and easier rolling. But the champion gas-saver is the radial ply type, with its combination of belts beneath the tread and easy-rolling radial construction.

OTHER NEW-CAR FACTORS TO CONSIDER

Color

Light colors tend to reflect heat and keep your car cooler. The choice of a lighter color should be considered if you live in a warmer climate, and regardless of whether you've decided to equip your new car with air conditioning. If you have air conditioning, a lighter color will help reduce the amount of cooling that the air conditioner must do, the proportion of time that it is operating, and the horsepower drain resulting from its operation. If you don't have air conditioning, a lighter color will make it less necessary to pay the air resistance penalty of lowered windows when traveling at highway speeds, and increase the probability that the flow-through ventilation will be able to keep you comfortable while cruising.

Dark colors, with their tendency to absorb heat, will help keep your car warmer in cold weather, thus reducing your use of the heater and its blower fan. Whereas light colors and tinted windows may be desirable in reducing the heat absorbed by an air-conditioned car, they can work against you in colder weather.

Seating Comfort

Like the radio equipment described earlier, seating comfort seems at first glance to be a luxury. After all, a car would be much lighter and more economical if it were equipped with orange crates instead of plush seats. Not quite true. You won't get good gas mileage while you're speeding in an attempt to reach your destination before your back breaks. While most cars you are considering will likely have comparable seating, be sure that your prospective model has enough leg and head room, and that the seat back, if not adjustable, is fixed at a

comfortable angle for you. Since your foot will spend a lot of time on the gas pedal, be sure that the angle is not awkward when the accelerator is pressed through its range of motion. Likewise for the clutch in a manual-transmission car—is it easy for you to depress it fully?

When you're sitting at home in your easy chair, you normally have the footrest in front of the chair, not offset to the right. Make sure that you won't require a knee operation in order to sit straight ahead and still be able to step on the throttle. On some smaller cars, the pedals may be drastically to the right of the straight-ahead position in which you're sitting, a fact that becomes more noticeable after 6 hours on the road than it may have been during the 10 minutes in the showroom.

Be sure you know whether you prefer the Italian-style arms-straight driving position or the steering-wheel-under-the chin stance. In some cars, you may not be able to easily reach the steering wheel when your legs are comfortable. A reasonable degree of comfort will aid your gas mileage by helping you enjoy the ride instead of clock-watching along the way. While you needn't sit in the showroom all day, don't be afraid to spend a few extra minutes trying on the seating package of each model you're considering.

Fuel Tank Size

If your trips are primarily short and local, a relatively small fuel tank may not be a handicap. However, if you often drive long distances, especially through areas where fuel is not in plentiful supply, the number of gallons your tank holds will be rather important. Determine the cruising range of a car you have in mind by multiplying its expected trip miles per gallon times the number of gallons the tank holds. Before making this calculation, you may wish to subtract one or two gallons from the tank size in order to allow for a safety margin. Unlike some older models, modern cars don't have a reserve tank to use as a crutch. When you run out today, you're out.

As an example of generous cruising range, consider the Porsche which has a fuel tank capacity of 16.4 gallons and probable gas mileage of 30 mpg on a trip. This combination would enable the car's driver to travel nearly 500 miles between fill-ups. On the other hand, another small car of equal economy may have only a six-gallon tank. Even at 30 mpg, the most daring driver would have to shop for gas every 150 miles. An optional, oversize fuel tank is offered on a few cars, and may provide a capacity of 30 gallons or more, depending on the size of the car and its normal fuel consumption. While the use of such a tank will greatly extend your range of operation, remember that you'll be increasing the weight of your car and thereby reducing its gas mileage. Not only will the larger fuel tank weigh more than a standard tank, but the extra gasoline it holds (assuming your use of the extra capacity) will further add to the car's weight. Every 10 gallons of gasoline you carry adds about 60 pounds to the weight of the car, decreasing your gas mileage by about .2 miles per gallon—not much, but consider that it costs gas to haul gas.

Buying a Used Car

When shopping for a used car, you should look for the same characteristics, features and options which were described as more economical under the various headings related to the purchase of a new car. The only problem is that there is very little chance that you'll find everything you're looking for in a single used car. However, you should still keep in mind the advice offered earlier so that you can better estimate the probable gasoline mileage of an individual used car with its particular combination of options, accessories, dimensions and weight.

A very important consideration in the purchase of a used car is the mechanical soundness of the car you have in mind. Whereas a new car has a reasonable warranty, a used car bought from a dealer may have only a short guarantee period, and one purchased from an individual owner will have none at all. Most of the

mechanical factors which can significantly affect gas mileage can be checked by you, if you're mechanically-inclined, by a mechanic in whom you have great faith, or by a diagnostic clinic. My recommendation is to take a proposed used-car purchase to a diagnostic clinic. Whether you're buying from a dealer or from an individual, if the car is as good as he says it is, the seller shouldn't mind your having a diagnostic center check it out.

At a diagnostic center—the Mayo clinic of the automotive world—technicians will connect everything but an IBM computer to the car in order to give it a complete "physical," determine what work may be necessary to bring it up to snuff, and advise you of the costs and consequences involved. Considering the benefits, the cost of having the used car checked at a diagnostic center is an excellent investment. Modern diagnostic equipment has the advantage of being able to test a car's key components while they are actually performing their critical jobs.

If there are no diagnostic centers in your area, the best alternative is to bring the prospective purchase to a *trusted* mechanic who you know will give you a reliable soundness report.

Armed with the center's test report or a mechanic's evaluation, you will be in a better position to decide whether the chariot you are considering is a gem or a lemon. If the tests uncover an expensive defect in the car, turn it down and you've saved a bundle of repair money, not to mention the sub-standard gas mileage its mechanical problems may have caused. If the tests are favorable, buy the car, then drive and maintain it intelligently to keep it in the good shape it's in.

Buying Gasoline

IMPORTANT GASOLINE CHARACTERISTICS

Octane

The octane rating of a gasoline is its ability to resist engine knock, which is a sharp metallic noise resulting from detonation or uncontrolled combustion within the cylinder. Among the least harmful effects of engine knock is an increase in fuel consumption. Other, less desirable, consequences may include cracked cylinder heads and damaged pistons. Octane measurements made under laboratory conditions lead to "Research" and "Motor" octane numbers for the same gasoline. In general, the Research octane number tends to be about 6 to 10 points higher than the Motor octane.[15] In addition, there is a "Road" octane which is determined by automobile road testing under standardized conditions. The Road octane rating is generally lower than the Research octane number and higher than the Motor octane. One commonly used anti-knock index is really the average of the Research and Motor octane numbers.

Your owner's manual will probably indicate the type and octane of gasoline recommended for use in your car. Since the 1971 model year, most cars have been designed to operate satisfactorily on 91 Research octane gasoline. However, octane requirements can vary according to the vehicle and the conditions under which it is operating. If you encounter sustained engine knock, wait until your tank is nearly empty, then try a gasoline with a higher octane rating. Don't overbuy—it's a waste of money to buy gasoline of a higher octane than your engine requires in order to satisfy its anti-knock need. As a new car is driven, combustion deposits build up and the octane requirement increases until an equilibrium level, normally between 4 and 6 octane numbers higher than the new-car requirement, is reached.[16] Other factors which can increase the octane an engine requires are higher air or engine temperatures, lower altitudes, lower humidity, a more advanced ignition spark timing, a leaner carburetor setting, sudden acceleration, and frequent stop-and-go driving which increases the build-up of combustion chamber deposits.

In deciding which gasoline has the proper octane for your car, the following guide developed by the American Society for Testing and Materials for informational purposes is a good starting point.

The grade designations and anti-knock index (average of Research and Motor octanes) are figures which may be appearing on gas pumps very shortly. The anti-knock indices will vary slightly according to geographic and atmospheric conditions.[17] Gasoline anti-knock designations range from 1 to 6 and are as follows:

Grade 1. This grade has an anti-knock index of 87 or less, and is for cars with low anti-knock needs.

Grade 2. This grade has a minimum anti-knock index of 87 and meets the anti-knock needs of most 1971 and later model cars.

Grade 3. This gasoline has a minimum anti-knock index of 89 and is suitable for most 1970 and prior models designed to operate on "regular" gasoline, and for 1971 and later models that require higher anti-knock performance than provided by grade 2.

Grade 4. This has a minimum anti-knock index of 91.5 and is a "mid-premium" or "intermediate" grade which meets the lower anti-knock needs of some cars designed to run on "premium" gasolines and the higher anti-knock needs of some cars designed to run on "regular."

Grade 5. This grade has a minimum anti-knock index of 95 and is suitable for most 1970 and prior models with high compression engines designed to run on "premium," and for later model cars with high-compression engines.

Grade 6. This gasoline has a minimum anti-knock index of 97.5 and is intended for cars with high compression engines designed to run on "premium" gasoline, but which require higher anti-knock performance than grade 5.

Lead Content

Older, higher-compression engines usually require a gasoline with a higher octane rating. The most efficient way of increasing the octane rating of a gasoline is to add a compound called tetraethyl lead. Therefore, if your owner's manual specifies the use of "premium" gasoline, you may have to use leaded fuels in order to avoid having your engine knock. However, should circumstances force you to use a low-lead or no-lead gasoline with lower octane than the car manufacturer specifies, you should temporarily retard the ignition timing very slightly in order to lessen the possibility of knocking. Some cars, though designed to operate on leaded gasoline, may be able to use the new low-lead and no-lead fuels. Again, experimentation is helpful in determining the gasoline octane which your car and your driving require. Don't automatically rule out a low-lead gasoline—if you haven't tried it, don't (sorry) knock it.

Volatility

The volatility of any liquid is its ability to vaporize, and gasoline must vaporize in order to burn. A highly volatile gasoline will help a cold engine start easily and run smoothly while it is warming up. However, the use of a highly volatile gasoline in warm weather tends to cause vapor lock, a condition in which the gasoline actually vaporizes before it arrives at the carburetor jet where vaporization is supposed to take place. This premature vaporization may occur in the fuel line, fuel pump, or in a section of the carburetor. When use of too-highly-volatile fuel leads to vapor lock, the engine becomes starved for fuel and will either lose power or stall. Although refiners vary the percentage of volatile fuel in their gasoline according to season and locality, vapor lock is more likely to occur in the early spring, when some stations may not have received supplies of lower-volatility gasoline.

Density

Density is another property of gasoline which can affect your fuel economy. It indicates how much chemical energy the gasoline contains. Density is generally measured in BTU's per gallon (the BTU, or British Thermal Unit, is a standard unit of energy), and usually varies less than 2% among most gasolines on the market. However, one study showed that six per cent of commercially-available gasolines varied by 4 to 8% in their BTU per gallon content.[18] This finding indicates that gas mileage could vary by as much as 4 to 8%, depending on the density of the gasoline you happen to choose.

Additives

Practically as important as octane rating and volatility are the additives that refiners put into their gasolines. Carburetor detergent additives help clean the tiny passages in the carburetor, thus ensuring the consistent fuel-air mixtures which are necessary for smooth running and good gas mileage. Winter additives include fuel line de-icers to reduce carburetor icing at the throttle plate. Carburetor icing, if it doesn't stall the engine, will at least restrict the carburetor opening and cause a richer fuel-air mixture which will lower gas mileage appreciably. Other additives are used to help control combustion chamber deposits, gum formation, rust, and wear.

WHEN YOU FILL 'ER UP

Know Your Gas Gauge

Learning to read your gas gauge is more than just knowing that "F" means full and "E" means walk. By noting the gauge needle position whenever you gas up, you'll soon become good at estimating how many gallons it will take to fill the tank in the future. This can be helpful when you're in a hurry and just want to get X dollars' worth instead of fussing with change and credit cards. In addition, knowing how to convert the needle position into gallons needed or gallons remaining will reduce the anxiety of wondering if you can make it from here to there on what you've got left. Remember that the gauge readings may change slightly if the car is going uphill, downhill, accelerating, braking, or traveling a sweeping curve.

At the Gas Station

One of the best practices in filling up is knowing when NOT to fill up. If you're on a trip and drive into a strange gas station only to find that the price on the pump is beyond reason, don't be afraid to ask for a dollar's worth (if you're shy) or for the directions to Punxatawney (if you're not). Driving out of an overpriced station may not be proper etiquette but, as a wise man once said, better them mad than you.

There are three sources of spillage which can reduce your miles per gallon. The most obvious is the careless station attendant who thinks he's doing you a favor by topping up your tank to the very limit and beyond. Another is a loose gas cap which has not been fully tightened down. The third source of spillage occurs when you fill up and allow your car to sit in the hot sun during a warm day—expanding gasoline may seep out of your filler neck and be wasted.

Either instruct the attendant not to squeeze gasoline into the tank after fuel appears in the filler neck, or buy your gas according to the number of dollars' worth you estimate will be needed. Don't trust the attendant to have tightened (or even to have replaced) your filler cap—it's unbelievable how many times a spot check will reveal a loose cap. Avoid warm-weather expansion spillage by not filling the tank completely when the car will be sitting shortly afterward. Unless you happen to drop your cigarette, you won't be traveling any miles on gasoline that's been spilled on the ground.

While at the station, especially if you're traveling, check your oil level and add a can from your trunk if a top-up is necessary. In case you never noticed, gas station prices for oil, anti-freeze, and windshield washer solvent are generally much higher than you'll find at your local discount or auto supply store. Naturally, you shouldn't expect the attendant to be cheerful about checking your oil when you're going to add a quart of your own. In addition to the obvious reason of courtesy, do-it-yourself checking and adding will ensure that you weren't "short-sticked," a practice in which a few unethical attendants push the dipstick only partially into its tube, then announce that you need oil when in fact you don't.

Buying Engine Oil

Three ways you can improve your car's mileage and insure that it delivers good economy for a longer time are: 1) under-stand the functions of oil in your engine, 2) choose the proper oil for various operating conditions, and 3) have the oil and filter changed at the recommended intervals.

THE FUNCTIONS OF ENGINE OIL

What does oil do in your car's engine? If you answered "lubricate," you're only partially right. While oil is primarily a lubricant, it also performs a number of other functions which are vital to the life and performance of your engine.

In addition to its role as a lubricant, oil also dissipates heat and makes parts run cooler; it helps reduce engine noise; it combats rust and corrosion of metal surfaces; it acts as a seal for the pistons, rings, and cylinder walls; it combines with the oil filter to remove foreign substances from the engine. In return for the performance of all these tasks, oil requires a modest wage—about a tenth of a penny for every mile you drive.

TYPES OF ENGINE OIL

Engine oil service classifications have been provided by the American Petroleum Institute and include "S" (normal gasoline engine use) and "C" (commercial and fleet) applications. The following listing compares the latest API oil classifications with those previously used: [19]

API Engine Service (Classification)	Previous API Engine (Service Application)
Service Station Applications:	
SA	ML
SB	MM
SC	MS (1964)
SD	MS (1968)
SE	None
Commercial and Fleet Applications:	
CA	DG
CB	DM
CC	DM
CD	DS

Service SA. For utility gasoline and diesel engine service. Oil in this classification must meet no performance requirements and is intended for use in engines operated under light and favorable conditions. Straight mineral oil falls into this category.

Service SB. For minimum duty gasoline engine service. This oil is satisfactory in gasoline engines which see mild service in which minimal extra protection is required. Oils in this classification have been in use since the 1930's and provide only scuff, oil oxidation, and bearing corrosion resistance.

Service SC. For 1964 gasoline engine warranty maintenance service. This oil, satisfactory for 1964 through 1967 cars protected by manufacturer's warranties during those years, is designed to control high and low temperature deposits, rust, corrosion, and wear in gasoline engines.

Service SD. For 1968 gasoline engine warranty maintenance service. Acceptable for warranty purposes by the manufacturers of 1968 through 1970 model cars, this oil may also be recommended in the owner's manuals of some 1971 and later models as well. Compared to the SC classification, it provides even more protection against high and low temperature deposits, rust, corrosion, and wear.

Service SE. For 1972 gasoline engine warranty maintenance service. Beginning with 1972 models and some 1971 models, this classification is required for engine warranty protection. Oil in this classification provides more protection against oil oxidation, high-temperature deposits, rust, and corrosion than the SC or SD oils. Regardless of the classification of oil that is called for, oil of the SE type may be used.

NOTE: *It is recommended that only oils identified as suitable for API service SE be used in your engine.*

Classifications CA, CB, CC, and CD refer primarily to oils for use in diesel engines, with CA, CB, and CD corresponding to light, moderate and severe duty respectively. Oil classified as CC is designed for diesel engines used in moderate duty and certain heavy-duty gasoline engines.

OIL VISCOSITY

In addition to meeting the SE classification of the American Petroleum Institute, your oil should be of a viscosity suitable for the outside temperature in which you'll be driving. Viscosity is defined as a resistance to flow—maple syrup has a high viscosity, sewing machine oil has a low viscosity. Proper oil viscosity is important for both maximum gas mileage and maximum engine life.

Oil must be thin enough to get between the close-tolerance moving parts it must lubricate. Once there, it must be thick enough to separate them with a slippery oil film. If the oil is too thin, it won't separate the parts; if it's too thick, it can't squeeze between them in the first place—either way, excess friction and wear take place. To complicate matters, cold-morning starts require a thin oil to reduce engine resistance, while high-speed driving requires a thick oil which can lubricate vital engine parts at temperatures up to 250° F.

According to the Society of Automotive Engineers' viscosity classification system, an oil with a high viscosity number (e.g., 40) will be thicker than one with a lower number (e.g., 10W). The "W" in 10W indicates that the oil is desirable for use in winter driving. Through the use of special additives, multiple-viscosity oils are available to combine easy starting at cold temperatures with engine protection at turnpike speeds. For example, a 10W-40 oil will have the viscosity of a 10W oil when the engine is cold and that of a 40 oil when the engine is warm. The use of such an oil will decrease engine resistance and improve your miles per gallon during short trips in which the oil doesn't have a chance to warm up.

Some of the more popular multiple-viscosity oils are 5W-20, 5W-30, 10W-30, 10W-40, 20W-40, 20W-50, and 10W-50. In general, a 5W-20 or 5W-30 oil is suitable for temperatures below 0° F, 10W-30 or 10W-40 whenever the lowest temperature expected is 0° F., and 20W-40 whenever the lowest temperature expected is 32° F. However, consult your owner's manual or a reputable oil dealer for the recommended viscosity range for your car and the outside temperature in which it operates.

ADDITIVES

A high-quality engine oil will include a number of chemical compounds known as additives. These are blended in at the refinery and fall into the following categories: [20]

Pour Point Depressants help cold starting by making the oil flow more easily at low temperatures. Otherwise, the oil would tend to be a waxy substance just when you need it the most.

Oxidation and Bearing Corrosion Inhibitors help to prevent the formation of gummy deposits which can take place when engine oil oxidizes under high temperatures. In addition, these inhibitors place a protective coating on sensitive bearing metals, which would otherwise be attacked by the chemicals formed by oil oxidation.

Rust and Corrosion Inhibitors protect against water and acids formed by the combustion process. Water is physically separated from the metal parts vulnerable to rust, and corrosive acids are neutralized by alkaline chemicals. The neutralization of combustion acids is an important key to long engine life.

Detergents and Dispersants use teamwork. Detergents clean up the products of normal combustion and oxidation while dispersants keep them suspended until they can be removed by means of the filter or an oil change.

Foam Inhibitors prevent the tiny air bubbles which can be caused by fast-moving engine parts whipping air into the oil. Foam can also occur when the oil level falls too low and the oil pump begins sucking up air instead of oil (like when the kids finish a milkshake). Without foam inhibitors, these tiny air bubbles would cause hydraulic valve lifters to collapse and reduce engine performance and economy significantly. Bubbles are OK in champagne, but not in engine oil.

Viscosity Index Improvers reduce the rate at which an oil thins out when the temperature climbs. These additives are what makes multiple-viscosity oils possible. Without them, a single-weight oil which permitted easy starting on a cold morning might thin out and cause you to lose your engine on a hot afternoon. If you use a multiple-viscosity oil, it's this additive that helps your gas mileage during those short trips in cold weather.

Friction Modifiers and Extreme Pres- *sure* additives are valuable in so-called boundary lubrication, where there is metal-to-metal contact due to the absence or breaking down of the oil film between moving parts. Friction modifiers, or anti-wear agents, deposit protective surface films which reduce the friction and heat of metal-to-metal contact. Extreme pressure additives work by reacting chemically with metal surfaces involved in high pressure contact.

That's the oil story. For best gas mileage and engine life, use a high-quality, multiple-viscosity, SE-rated oil. For a tenth of a cent per mile, you can afford to go first class. Like a marathon runner who wears cardboard shoes, a motorist who buys cheap oil will be unhappy in the long run.

Buying Replacement Tires

READING A TIRE

Practically everything you need to know about a tire is written on its sidewall. The tire pictured in figure 3-4 displays the following information: [21]

Size "F78-14 (replaces 7.75-14)" indicates the size of the tire in modern terminology as well as indicating the size of

Fig. 3-4. The sidewall of a tire contains important information, including the maximum pressure to which it should be inflated. *Source:* Rubber Manufacturers Association.

the equivalent bias ply tire which formerly applied. "14" indicates the diameter, in inches, of the wheel on which the tire must be mounted. "7.75" is the approximate width, in inches, of the inflated tire. "F" indicates the tire's size. Earlier letters in the alphabet correspond to smaller tires. "78" refers to the tire's profile, or height-to-width ratio.

Manufacturer. The tire's manufacturer and brand name will appear near the outside of the sidewall.

Maximum Pressure and Load. The tire in the illustration must not carry more than 1500 pounds when it is inflated to its maximum cold inflation pressure of 32 pounds per square inch. Since it will generally not be necessary to inflate the tire to its maximum pressure, consult your owner's manual for pressure requirements applicable to the tire as installed on your car.

Load Range indicates the number of plies at which the tire is rated. The "B" load range reflects the tire's 4-ply rating. Load range "C" corresponds to a 6-ply rating, while "D" describes a tire with an 8-ply rating.

Type of Cord and Number of Plies in the sidewall and tread. Each of these depends on the other, and both may vary according to the tire's construction.

Tube or Tubeless type design is indicated, though most of today's tires are tubeless.

Radial ply tires will have the letter "R" in the size designation and must have the word "Radial" written on the sidewall. For reasons described in other sections, this also says more miles per gallon.

Compliance with U.S. Department of Transportation tire safety standards is indicated by the "DOT xxxx xxxxxx." The first two characters identify the manufacturer of the tire and the others indicate the tire size, type, and date of manufacture. When you buy new tires, be sure that the dealer records your name, address and tire identification numbers—this is required by Federal law for recall and warning purposes.

TIRE CONSTRUCTION

Bias-ply is the conventional design which has been around for about half a century. This type of construction is low-priced, but wears out the quickest at the highest tire cost per mile. The bias-ply construction is illustrated in figure 3-5, which shows the criss-crossing cords which make up the tire body. The tire cords are in 2, 4, 6, or 8 layers and at a 30–40° angle to the center line of the tire. Although its many plies result in a relatively stiff sidewall and tread, a bias-ply tire will squirm and run hotter than either a belted bias tire or a radial. Because of these contortions and self-generated heat, its high rolling resistance will hold you back when you're trying for those all-important miles per gallon.

Belted bias tires also have their body cords arranged in a criss-cross pattern and are really just an improvement over the conventional tire. In addition to its conventional body, the belted bias tire also has special layers or "belts" under the tread. With this construction, a stiff

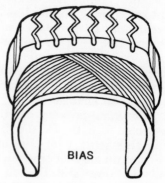

Fig. 3–5. Cross-sectional view of a conventional bias-ply tire. *Source:* Rubber Manufacturers Association.

Fig. 3–6. Cross-sectional view of a belted bias-ply tire shows the tread stabilizing belts that give it longer life and lower rolling resistance than the conventional bias-ply tire.

sidewall is combined with increased strength and stiffness in the tread. Having less tread squirm, the belted bias tire runs cooler, lasts longer, and has lower rolling resistance than a conventional tire.

Radial-ply construction, illustrated in figure 3-7, includes a body with cords running at a 90° angle to the center line of the tire. These body cords may be arranged in as many as three plies, or layers. The radial-ply tire also has between two and four very strong tread belts, which may be made of steel, fiberglass, or rayon. Because of its radial body and belted tread, the radial tire has a flexible sidewall and an extremely stiff tread. The bulging sidewall will cause a radial to look underinflated even when it isn't. The practically inflexible tread reduces squirming to a minimum, resulting in cool running, unbelievable tread life, and sharply lowered rolling resistance.

Fig. 3–7. Inflexible tread belts and radial body plies enable the radial tire to have lower rolling resistance than either the conventional or belted-bias types. *Source:* Rubber Manufacturers Association.

TIRE PROFILE

The profile of a tire is the ratio of its height to its width, and is shown in figure 3-8. The "78" series tire shown is 78% as high as it is wide. The lower the profile number, the fatter the tire. Wider tires will improve stopping and cornering by putting more tread in contact with the road. However, this larger "footprint" can make your car harder to steer and, with other factors equal, may have more rolling resistance than a narrower tire.

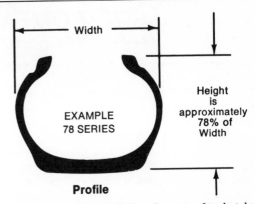

Fig. 3–8. A tire's "profile" is the ratio of its height to its width. *Source:* Rubber Manufacturers Association.

TYPES OF CORD

Sidewall

Sidewall body cords are usually made of rayon, nylon or polyester. Rayon is the oldest man-made tire cord material and is strong and smooth-riding. A weakness of rayon is that it tends to degenerate under continued exposure to water. However, unless a tire cut exposes the fabric to the elements during a long wet spell, this is not a disadvantage. Unlike nylon, rayon does not "flat-spot" after the car has been sitting overnight.

Nylon is resilient, resists heat and water, and is stronger than rayon. It is used in racing, aircraft and off-road tires as well as in those for automobiles. However, despite its merits, nylon's "flat-spotting" tendency causes a bumpy ride for the first few miles after the car has been parked for awhile. If much of your driving is of the short, errand-running type, the flat-spotting of nylon-cord tires may reduce your gas mileage slightly.

Polyester is becoming more popular as a body ply material. It is stronger than rayon, resists flat-spotting, and is not affected by exposure to water.

Belts

Belted bias tires and radial tires both have reinforcing belts beneath the tread. The belts in either tire may be constructed of steel wire, glass fibers, rayon, or polyester. Steel is generally considered to be the strongest belting material, will give maximum wear for a given tread

SIZE COMPARISON CHART
Interchangeability is **NOT** implied. See note below.

CONVENTIONAL (83) BIAS PLY		BIAS AND BELTED BIAS PLY				RADIAL PLY				
1965-On	Pre-1965	'78 Series	'70 Series	'60 Series	'50 Series	Metric	'78 Series	'70 Series	'60 Series	'50 Series
6.00-13						165R13				
		A78-13	A70-13	A60-13				AR78-13	AR70-13	AR60-13
6.50-13		B78-13		B60-13	B50-13	175R13	BR78-13	BR70-13	BR60-13	BR50-13
7.00-13		C78-13	C70-13	C60-13		185R13	CR78-13	CR70-13		
		D78-13	D70-13	D60-13			DR78-13	DR70-13		
						195R13	ER78-13		ER60-13	
						155R14				
									AR60-14	
6.45-14	6.00-14	B78-14				165R14	BR78-14			
6.95-14	6.50-14	C78-14	C70-14			175R14	CR78-14	CR70-14		
		D78-14	D70-14	D60-14			DR78-14	DR70-14		
7.35-14	7.00-14	E78-14	E70-14	E60-14		185R14	ER78-14	ER70-14		
7.75-14	7.50-14	F78-14	F70-14	F60-14	F50-14	195R14	FR78-14	FR70-14	FR60-14	
8.25-14	8.00-14	G78-14	G70-14	G60-14	G50-14	205R14	GR78-14	GR70-14	GR60-14	GR50-14
8.55-14	8.50-14	H78-14	H70-14	H60-14	H50-14	215R14	HR78-14	HR70-14		
8.85-14	9.00-14	J78-14	J70-14	J60-14		225R14	JR78-14	JR70-14	JR60-14	
	9.50-14		L70-14	L60-14				LR70-14	LR60-14	
					M50-14					
					N50-14					
		A78-15	A70-15				AR78-15			
	6.00-15	B78-15		B60-15		165R15	BR78-15	BR70-15		
6.85-15	6.50-15	C78-15	C70-15	C60-15		175R15	CR78-15	CR70-15		
		D78-15	D70-15				DR78-15	DR70-15		
7.35-15		E78-15	E70-15	E60-15	E50-15	185R15	ER78-15	ER70-15	ER60-15	
7.75-15	6.70-15	F78-15	F70-15	F60-15		195R15	FR78-15	FR70-15	FR60-15	
8.25-15	7.10-15	G78-15	G70-15	G60-15	G50-15	205R15	GR78-15	GR70-15	GR60-15	GR50-15
8.55-15	7.60-15	H78-15	H70-15	H60-15	H50-15	215R15	HR78-15	HR70-15	HR60-15	HR50-15
8.85-15	8.00-15	J78-15	J70-15	J60-15		225R15	JR78-15	JR70-15	JR60-15	
9.00-15	8.20-15		K70-15					KR70-15		
9.15-15		L78-15	L70-15	L60-15	L50-15	235R15	LR78-15	LR70-15	LR60-15	LR50-15
		M78-15					MR78-15	MR70-15		
8.90-15		N78-15			N50-15		NR78-15			

NOTE: Interchangeability between corresponding sizes of different construction tires is not always possible due to differences in load ratings, tire dimensions, fender clearances and rim sizes. or vehicle manufacturers' recommendations.

Fig. 3–9. A summary of which tires will fit on the same wheel. However, if the tire fits, your car shouldn't necessarily wear it—see text for precautions. *Source:* Rubber Manufacturers Association.

thickness, but is the most expensive. The presence of steel belts doesn't automatically mean that a tire is a radial—there are also steel-belted bias-ply tires.

TIRE SIZE COMPARISONS

Figure 3-9 presents a listing of tires that will fit the same wheels. Some radial tires may use a metric size designation in which the first number refers to the approximate cross section width in millimeters, while the second indicates the wheel diameter in inches. Although the tires listed in a given row will fit on the same wheel, there are a number of reasons why you shouldn't put a given tire on a given wheel. For example, although the tire may fit on the wheel, its width may cause rubbing against the body or fender well during turns. In addition, there are a number of cautions which should be observed when installing radial or belted bias tires. It is preferred that the same type of tire be mounted on all four wheels.

When installing radials, put them on all four wheels at once—mixing radials with other types of tires is asking for trouble. Some dealers recommend that if only two radials must be installed on a rear-wheel drive car, they should be placed on the rear axle. This advice also goes for snow tires, since combining conventional snow tires on the drive wheels with radials at the other end will give you the directional stability of a wounded goose.

If you mix belted bias tires with conventional bias tires, be sure that the belted bias tires are on the rear. Don't drive with two different sizes or types of tires on the same axle, be it front or rear. Consult your owner's manual or tire dealer for more specific instructions concerning the sizes, types of construction and other recommendations for your car and driving conditions.

WHICH TIRE FOR ECONOMY?

First Choice: Radial

If you can raise the higher initial cost of the radial tire, you'll be repaid with lower tire cost per mile as well as from 3 to 10% more miles per gallon. My personal choice is the steel-belted radial, on which I've been riding for most of my driving life. (The same steel-belted radials were once transferred from their original car to two subsequent vehicles over a total distance exceeding 60,000 miles.) Whether on the road or pushing the car back and forth to get through your crowded garage, the low rolling resistance of the radial tire will be evident to you and your gasoline bill.

The rolling resistance of the radial design has been shown in various tests to be only about three-fourths that required to roll a belted bias tire, and about two-thirds that of a conventional bias tire. In one study, the use of steel-belted radials reduced 50 mph rolling resistance by 28 pounds when compared to belted conventional tires.[22] Sure, 28 pounds doesn't seem like much—however, depending on the frontal area of your car, this can make a big difference. For example, let's say that a standard sedan is cruising at a steady speed of 50 mph. Its engine is pushing against about 170 pounds of combined resistance from air and rolling. If the switch to radial tires takes away 28 pounds of that force, the resistance the engine must fight is down to only 142 pounds, a reduction of 16%. Because of resistances in and around the engine itself (fan, alternator, etc.), the car's fuel consumption won't go down by 16%, but gas mileage will still increase by between 1 and 1.5 miles per gallon at that steady speed.

The effects of giving your car a 28-pound pat on the back are evident in the chart of figure 3-10, based on data collected by the Firestone Tire and Rubber Company during their testing of the company's original-equipment steel-belted radial tire against its comparable belted bias model.[23] The test involved a standard size domestic sedan driven at the steady speeds shown.

Other studies and estimates of the advantage of equipping your car with radial tires include miles-per-gallon increases of 3%, 6%, and 5–10%, depending on the source and the driving conditions assumed. The greatest mpg increase with radials will be evident at moderate, steady speeds during which rolling resistance is the main force holding you back. The smallest increases will be at high speeds, when air resistance is your main obstacle, and during stop-and-go driving, during which acceleration resistance due to inertia is your biggest enemy.

Belted Bias

As figure 3-10 indicates, the belted bias tire has more rolling resistance than the radial type this book strongly recommends. However, the drag of a belted bias tire will be a little less than the conventional tire from which it has evolved. If you don't want to invest in a set of radials, the belted bias tire will give you slightly better gas mileage and much

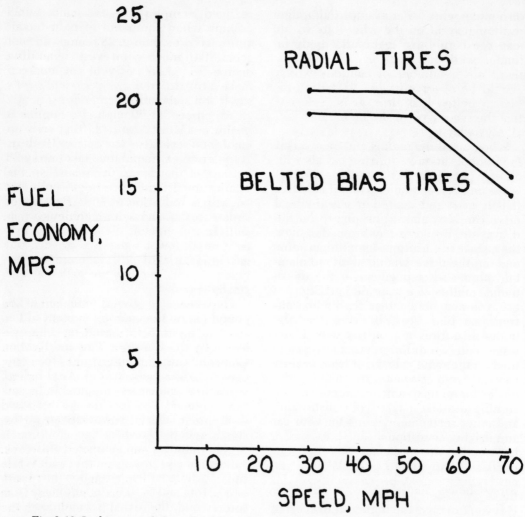

Fig. 3–10. In this test, radial tires enabled a full-size car to get about two more miles per gallon at the steady speeds shown.

longer tread life than a conventional design.

Conventional Bias

As you have sensed, the conventional bias-ply tire is not the tire to buy for maximum miles per gallon or minimum cost per mile. However, if circumstances, economics or old habits force you to buy a set of bias-ply replacement tires, all is not lost. Be sure to keep them properly inflated and balanced, then try a little harder to heed the other tips included in this book. With a little extra effort, you can beat the gas mileage of less enlightened folks who stop trying after they've bought their radial tires.

Buying Replacement Parts

Whether or not you do your own mechanical work and maintenance, it makes sense to buy high-quality replacement parts at the lowest possible price. Watch for special sales on oil, filters, spark plugs and tune-up kits. Inexpensive sources of supply generally include discount stores, department store automotive centers, auto supply stores and catalog mail-order houses. Be sure to follow your car manufacturer's recommendations in choosing replacement parts. Buying the wrong oil filter just because it's cheaper is like dropping your keys in the dark, then walking to the nearest street light so you can see better while you're looking for them.

Buying Accessory Items

ADDITIVES

Having discussed the various additives that refiners put into their gasoline and oil, it wouldn't make sense to say that additives aren't worth anything. However, if you already use good-quality gasoline and oil, make reasonable efforts to maintain proper mechanical tune and adjustments, and change your oil and filters at the recommended intervals, the benefits from increased use of additives should be minimal. Additives are often just concentrated versions of the same chemicals already employed in the higher-quality gasolines and oils.

Under certain conditions, it may be desirable to thicken your oil with a well-known viscosity index improver—for example, if your plans include high-speed, hot-weather driving when the oil in your crankcase happens to be of a lower viscosity than would be called for under these high-temperature circumstances. However, if you're already using the proper-viscosity oil, use of the additive becomes harder to justify.

When it comes to possible additives for increasing gas mileage, my choice would be an anti-friction additive, of which there are many types. I've used anti-friction additives in economy runs—partly because I thought they might help; partly because it didn't seem that they could hurt; and partly because the cost of the additive didn't mean as much as it would have in everyday driving. However, even for the anti-friction additive, when the manufacturer says that special additives are neither necessary nor desirable for its cars, my wallet suddenly becomes very hard to reach.

Instead of relying on additives to frighten automotive problems away, take the simple, time-tested approach of intelligent care, driving, and maintenance of your car. Just as one glass of tomato juice won't cure that hangover you worked all night to get, a can of additive won't cure 30,000 miles of negligence.

MECHANICAL DEVICES

The preceding advice also applies to many mechanical devices that are supposed to save gasoline by modified air-fuel mixtures, regulated fuel pressures, intensified ignition sparks and special spark plugs. Tests have been conducted in which the test car actually obtained better gas mileage without a device than with it.

ACCESSORIES

Electronic Ignition

One accessory generally thought of as a performance item rather than an aid to gas mileage is the electronic ignition system. By either eliminating the ignition points or reducing the current they carry, the electronic ignition system can extend the interval between tune-ups. Some cars have electronic ignition as standard equipment, which is an advantage for do-it-yourselfers who don't have the time or ability to do very much work themselves, but would like to do what they can. While most anybody can change the spark plugs, oil and filters, some shy away from attacking anything that has to do with the mysterious art of adjusting the ignition points or setting the timing. As your engine gets further away from its last tune-up, performance and gas mileage decrease. A principal advantage of an electronic ignition is not so much that performance and economy are increased, but that a given level of performance and economy can be maintained over a longer period of time without the necessity of a tune-up along the way. If you tend to be rather lax about periodic tune-ups, and if my pleas in Chapter Five don't sway you, you may be a candidate for an after-market electronic ignition system.

Keep in mind that some electronic ignition systems are highly geared for performance in the form of strong ignition sparks supplied all the way up to the uneconomical speeds of 6000 RPM and beyond. As a good economy-minded driver, you won't benefit greatly from the performance capabilities of such high-powered systems. Electronics, consumer, automotive enthusiast, and do-it-yourself magazines carry detailed tests and technical information on various systems that are available. Look before you leap.

Free-Flow Exhaust

If you're in the market for a new muffler, consider one of the low-restriction models available. With less back pressure, such systems require less engine horsepower to push the exhaust gases from the engine to the tail pipe.

Cooling Fans

The radiator cooling fan uses a significant amount of power, especially at higher road speeds when it isn't needed at all. Some cars are equipped with a friction-controlled fan which doesn't speed up as the engine speed increases. Others have an electric fan which cools the radiator only when water temperature reaches a given level. Aside from installing a friction-type or electrical fan in your own car, you may also benefit from a lightweight variable-pitch fan which varies its blade angle depending on the speed of rotation.

Even if you're very, very careful about your water temperature and travel only at high speeds, it's not a good idea to save gas by removing your fan from its hub. Although turning on the heater and switching the heater fan to high speed will help cool your engine in case you're stopped, the heater wasn't intended to substitute for the radiator.

Gauges

The ideal way to lighten both your foot and your fuel bill is to have a gauge that tells you exactly how many miles per gallon you're getting at any given time. Such gauges are now available, but are expensive since they require precise inputs from both the speedometer and the fuel line. In one miles-per-gallon gauge, a flowmeter divides each gallon of fuel into 110,000 electrical pulses while another sending device divides each mile into 16,000 pulses. To tie the fuel flow and

Illus. 3–2. Drivers of gas-thirsty vehicles are the ones most likely to benefit from the installation of a miles per gallon gauge.

speed together, an electronic module divides the gallons per hour into miles per hour and displays the miles-per-gallon that your car is getting at that exact moment.[24] While its benefit to the average driver will be less, such a gauge could really be a boon to drivers of trucks, recreational, and other thirsty vehicles.

The second-best way to get feedback on your car's fuel consumption is to install a vacuum gauge. These cost around $10–$15 and depend on the high vacuum which exists in the intake manifold during part-throttle operation. The vacuum gauge registers between 0 and 30 inches of mercury and can help you to achieve more economical driving habits and speeds. Remember the old-fashioned vacuum-operated windshield wipers that would flap back and forth when you were going down a hill, then die when you started climbing the next? The vacuum gauge works on the same principle, except that it will register your relative gas mileage a little more silently. By keeping the vacuum gauge needle in the upper ranges (actual numbers will vary depending on your car), you'll be getting as many miles per gallon as your car can deliver.

Vacuum gauges have been sold under more exotic names which imply that they indicate your miles per gallon rather than your intake manifold vacuum. However, they are still vacuum gauges. Besides the gauge possibility, some cars may be equipped with an "idiot light" which is activated whenever the vacuum falls below a selected level. Instead of constantly telling you the intake manifold vacuum, this arrangement would activate a warning light to remind you that you're wasting gas.

By keeping the vacuum in your mind, you'll be better able to think economy on the road.

4 · Driving for Economy

Whether you drive a Cadillac, a Volkswagen, a moving van, or a milk truck, you can improve your miles per gallon by remembering a few basic rules and applying them to the driving situations you encounter. While short formulas never tell the whole story, here is one to keep in mind the next time you fill up:

Travel at low, steady speeds
+ Maintain your car's momentum
+ Anticipate conditions ahead
+ Accelerate gently
+ Be patient

= MORE MILES PER GALLON

The forces you're up against don't know or care how much money you spend for gasoline. They've been described in chapter two and are listed below to refresh your memory:

Air resistance
+ Rolling resistance
+ Acceleration resistance
+ Gravity resistance
+ Engine resistance

= FEWER MILES
PER GALLON

Besides knowing the facts and opposing forces, inspiration will also be important. Like pole-vaulting, in which one's opponent is the crossbar, or sprinting, where the runner fights a stopwatch, driving for economy is an individual event in which you're competing both with yourself and with the miles per gallon figure calculated from the speedometer and gas pump. By approaching driving for economy as a challenge, and not as drudgery, your gas mileage may even exceed that of less-inspired friends who happen to own smaller cars. Economy-run reporters who confide that "you won't approach the gas mileage of Mr. XYZ, but here are some little tips for you" imply that Mr. XYZ has some magical abilities which you lack. Don't believe it—give that little extra effort and you'll see.

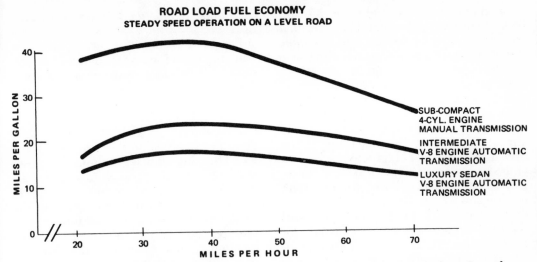

Fig. 4–1. Speeds of 35–40 mph are best for maximum economy. *Source:* G. J. Huebner, Jr., and D. J. Gasser, "General Factors Affecting Vehicle Fuel Consumption" (paper presented at National Automobile Engineering Meeting, Society of Automotive Engineers, Detroit, Michigan, May 15, 1973.)

Smooth and Steady Wins the Miles Per Gallon Race

LOW SPEEDS SAVE GAS

The expense of driving at higher speeds is evident in figure 4-1. When traveling at a constant speed, each model was most economical at about 30 to 40 miles per hour.[1] At speeds over 40 mph, higher air resistance attacks a car's frontal area and causes economy to drop sharply. When you double your speed, you need eight times as much horsepower to fight air resistance. At speeds below 40, tire rolling resistance is the major factor causing low gas mileage. Another study revealed that a car getting 19.7 miles per gallon at 40 mph delivered only 18.3 at 50 mph, 16.2 at 60 mph, and just 14.2 at a speed of 70.[2]

Your car will deliver its best gas mileage at moderate speeds in the neighborhood of 35–40 miles per hour. When it's not possible to maintain this most economical speed, do the next best thing and travel as slowly as possible without becoming a safety hazard. A 10% increase in your speed (e.g., from 50 to 55 mph) will require a 33% increase in the horsepower you need to overcome air resistance. Greater increases are even more costly and are shown in the following table:

Increase in Speed	Increase in Horsepower Required to Overcome Air Resistance
10%	33%
20%	73%
30%	120%
40%	175%
50%	240%
60%	310%

Regardless of the vehicle, higher speeds mean less economy. However, don't feel too sorry for the driver of a diesel-engined car. For example, the fuel mileage of the diesel-powered Mercedes-Benz 220D drops from 50 miles per gallon at 30 mph down to 25 mpg at a speed of 70.[3]

MAINTAIN A CONSTANT SPEED

By keeping your speed as steady as possible, you'll conserve your car's momentum and reduce its fuel consumption. Unnecessary changes in speed can be quite wasteful. For example, by letting your speed fluctuate between 55 and 65 mph, instead of maintaining a constant 60, you can lose between 1 and 1.5 miles per gallon.[4] When you're traveling at a steady speed, acceleration resistance isn't present and it doesn't matter as much how heavy your car happens to be. If your car doesn't have a cruise control device, you can practice until you can do almost as well as the machine. When driving on an open highway, glance at your speedometer every 10 seconds or so. If your spot-checks show, for example, readings of 57, 60, 65, 59, 56, you're not doing very well. Keep practicing until the readings are very nearly constant, for example: 60, 60, 61, 59, 60. This type of practice is an excellent application of the little extra effort we talked about earlier.

ACCELERATE GRADUALLY

A "jackrabbit" start may be good for bunnies, but it's very expensive for your car. A rapid getaway can use twice as much gasoline as a more moderate, gradual start. In moving off from a stop, try to get into a high gear as soon as the engine will accept the load. With an automatic transmission, this means a very light foot on the throttle so that high gear will be chosen as early as possible. With a manual transmission, don't over-speed the engine in the lower gears—learn to shift up at the minimum speed that the engine will accept in the next higher gear.

If you drive an emission-controlled car equipped with a transmission-controlled ignition spark retard mechanism (see Chapter Five), it's even more important for you to get into high gear as soon as possible. In these cars, unnecessary use of the spark-retarding lower gears will keep your engine running inefficiently for a longer time.

BRAKE SPARINGLY

The world's most expensive magic trick is the one you perform when you change gasoline into brake lining dust. Every time you step on the brake, you're dissipating momentum that the engine worked hard to build up. Don't use the brake more often than is really necessary. Just as a polite cowboy might tip his hat to ladies on the street, some drivers touch

their brake at practically every turn in the road.

Frequent panic stops are a sign that you aren't driving as economically as you could. While panic stops are necessary at the time they're made, most of them reflect that the car was traveling too fast in the first place. Although you don't hear much about "jackrabbit stops," they aren't economical either. Some of the worst braking offenses include charging a stop sign only to screeech to a halt; braking unnecessarily while traveling uphill; rushing into a turn, then applying the brake; not releasing the handbrake completely; and "riding" the brake. As an indication of how little the brakes can be used, consider that two men once drove from Detroit to Los Angeles without once touching their specially-sealed brake pedal.[5] While you needn't go to this extreme, remember that hitting the brake isn't free—it's paid for by your gasoline dollar.

PASS SMOOTHLY

If you're driving for maximum miles per gallon, you probably won't be passing anything except gas stations. However, when you must pass, accelerate as gradually as possible and increase speed only to the level that safety requires. This may be difficult to do, as we all have a bit of race-driver within us that tempts us to whip right out there and show the other guy what a real car can do. Making an impression on the person you're passing will also make an impression on your fuel bill.

MERGE SMOOTHLY

We've all been in the sidewalk or doorway situation where we meet another person and play the guessing game of who goes first. Its baseball counterpart is the "I've-got-it-you-take-it" outfield catch. When merging onto an interstate or other major highway, the same thing happens. Interaction with other cars tends to upset the smoothness of your economical driving. If you simply blast onto the highway with eyes straight ahead, you've wasted gasoline as well as risked your neck. If you timidly creep up to the highway itself, you'll be forced to accelerate for all you're worth just to keep your car at its present length. Either strategy will reduce your miles per gallon. By trying to "fit in" with the traffic with which you're merging, and by making use of the full acceleration distance provided by the highway engineers, you can maintain your momentum, speed up more slowly, and save gas.

Some Little Things that Mean a Lot

STEADY AT THE WHEEL

By keeping the steering wheel as motionless as possible, you'll minimize the side-to-side movement that increases both the distance you must travel and your tires' rolling resistance along the way. Each little change in direction interrupts your car's considerable momentum and causes the front tires to be paid just a little more horsepower for their work.

A DRAG ERASER

If your car is equipped with disc brakes, and if you sometimes drive for long distances on a very straight road, here's a tip that can make a slight reduction in your rolling resistance. Disc brake pads, instead of retracting away from the rotor, will drag lightly against it after you've released the brake pedal. Your front wheel bearings, if adjusted properly, will have a very small amount of looseness, or "play." If you were to keep your foot off the brake, then make a left turn followed by a right turn, play in the wheel bearings would move the rotor just enough to push the brake pads very slightly back into their housings and reduce their drag on the rotor. Once you're on that straight piece of road, the normal act of passing and returning to your lane can provide enough sideward force to retract the pads ever so slightly.

DON'T PUMP THE GAS PEDAL

It wouldn't help your gas mileage if the neighborhood kids decided to refill their squirt guns from your gas tank. However, every time you press down on the gas pedal, you activate a squirt-gun-like device called the accelerator pump. Thinking that you want to accelerate, the faithful gadget shoots some raw gasoline into the engine. The purpose of the accelerator pump is to smooth the transition from steady speed to acceleration. Some economy run drivers have been known to disconnect the accelerator pump in order to avoid the squirt-gun effect—however, this is neither necessary nor safe for everyday driving purposes. By moving the gas pedal very slowly when you decide to accelerate, you can fool the accelerator pump and save the gas it would otherwise squirt into the engine. After turning the engine off, removing the air cleaner, and holding the choke valve open, you can manipulate the throttle and see for yourself how much gasoline is being wasted. With the help of someone observing the carburetor throat, you can even practice pressing on the gas pedal until you have a better feel for how fast it can move before the accelerator pump goes into action. For safety, make sure you have the engine turned off and are not smoking when either observing or practicing. Because raw gasoline squirted into a stopped engine will thin the oil, it's also advisable to do your accelerator-pump practicing just before you change oil.

RULE OUT THAT BARREL

On most foreign cars equipped with a two-barrel carburetor, one will do the work under normal conditions, while the second will operate only at high speeds or when extra power is needed. When in the same gear, pressing to a certain point of the accelerator pedal movement will cause a slight surge in the engine's power and a change in the sound it's making. By becoming familiar with the point at which your second barrel is activated, you can avoid the drop in economy that accompanies its use. (Note: the preceding advice goes double for readers driving four-barrel carburetors.)

However, most American cars with two barrel carburetors (except Pintos and late model Vegas) do not have this progressive opening sequence. Therefore, both barrels are always operating, which requires the driver to have a very light foot.

OPEN WINDOWS WASTE GAS

At highway speeds, an open window will increase your car's air resistance and lower your miles per gallon. On a warm day, it's better to crack the vent windows slightly and use the flow-through ventilation with which your car may be equipped. If you don't have flow-through ventilation, crack open as many windows as necessary and use cool air from the conventional heater-defroster air system. If it's too hot, don't turn on the fan—open more windows. Economy run drivers have been known to swelter inside their cars in order to avoid opening a window and suffering the penalty of increased air resistance. At very low speeds, air resistance is less important and it's not as expensive to lower the windows. However, you can leave them up and your friends will think you have air conditioning.

TURN OFF THE HEATER FAN

When traveling at speeds over 40 miles per hour, you're wasting gasoline by turning on the heater-defroster fan. At these speeds, normal air resistance will force plenty of air through the intake of your heating-ventilation system. Unnecessary use of the fan places an extra load on the alternator, which in turn places an extra load on the engine. The electric fan, depending on its size, design, and running speed, may consume between 4 and 24 amperes of electrical current. An alternator forced to supply 40 to 50 amperes will lower gas mileage by .5 to .9 miles per gallon.[6] As with so many other consumers of your gasoline dollar, the electric fan should be used only when you need it.

SPARE THE AIR

If your car has air conditioning, use it sparingly. The fan in an air-conditioned car will tend to draw electrical currents in the higher parts of the 4–24 ampere range just mentioned. Use of the air conditioner will also require engine horsepower to operate the compressor unit and to activate the magnetic clutch which keeps the compressor engaged. Figure 4-2 compares the average miles per gallon of test cars with and without their air conditioning units in operation.[7] Depending on the speed traveled, drivers lost between 1.0 and 2.2 miles per gallon by turning on the air conditioner.

AVOID UNNECESSARY IDLING

That breakfast-table warm-up might make your car warm and toasty by the time you've finished your pancakes, but you've been getting zero miles per gallon in the process. It's much more economical to start out from cold and warm up the entire car at the same time—at least you'll be getting miles from gasoline otherwise wasted in a standing car. The same advice applies to drive-in banks, movies, ice-cream stands, churches, hamburger stands and gas stations. If you know that you're going to be stationary for more than a minute, you'll save gas by shutting off and restarting instead of allowing the engine to idle.

WHILE YOUR CAR WARMS UP

Any professional athlete knows that it takes a gradual warm-up before going full tilt. Arm-conscious baseball pitchers don't take all those warm-up tosses just so the management can sell more popcorn. Your car also needs to warm up before it can run most efficiently—in cold-weather driving, this may take over five miles.

After sitting in the driveway during a wintry night, your car is as stiff as an arthritic statue—engine oil is like molasses, wheel bearing grease has the consistency of window caulking, and other lubricants are also too thick to properly flow between the moving parts to which they're assigned. After you've started the engine, wait until the oil pressure warning light goes off, then move off and drive more slowly than usual for the first few miles. Rolling resistance during this period will be very high, and you'll save gas by going slower against the extra drag.

When starting a cold engine, don't speed it up to the point where it sounds like pistons are about to come bursting through the hood. Besides wasting gasoline, this can damage moving parts that

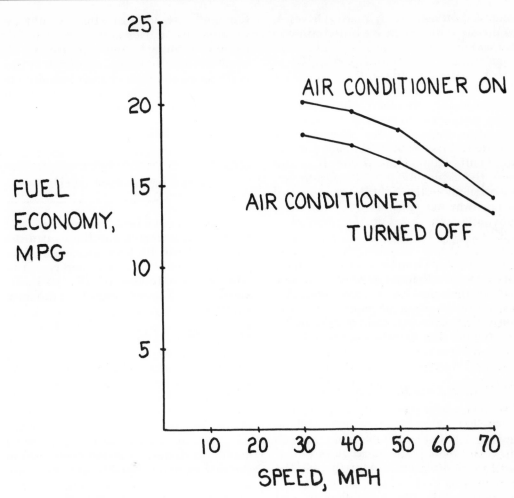

Fig. 4–2. While air conditioner use hurts economy at moderate speeds, at 70 mph there isn't much difference.

are not yet fully lubricated. Instead of racing a balky engine, let it idle for a minute or so until it is smooth enough to move the car.

WHEN YOU'RE GOING THE WRONG WAY

When you're traveling down a busy two-way road and discover that you're headed in the wrong direction, there's an economical answer to your problem. Figure 4-3 shows two ways of handling this dilemma. You can turn right, as driver B did, then attempt to turn left in order to get going in the desired direction. However, driver B has a problem: before he can turn back onto the highway, he must wait until two lanes of traffic are clear—a

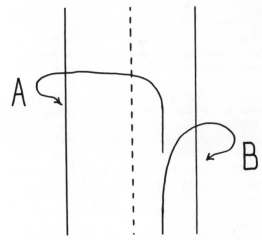

Fig. 4–3. Two possible ways to turn around when you discover you're headed in the wrong direction. Text tells why driver A saves gas.

long wait on many busy roads. Driver A, on the other hand, drove a little further in the wrong direction until he could make a convenient turn into a parking lot or street on the left side of the road. Once there, he only needed to wait until one lane of traffic was clear, which is more probable than two lanes being clear at the same time. If the road is very crowded, driver A will be headed in the proper direction while driver B is still back there playing the "It's-OK-to-the-left-what-about-the-right?" game and idling away his gasoline.

MAKING THAT DIFFICULT LEFT TURN

It's all but impossible to turn left onto a four-lane road that is crowded with cars, but uncontrolled by a stop light. Yet many drivers sit at the intersection and waste their gas while they're praying for an opening that stretches across all four lanes at the same time. A safer and more economical approach is to turn right and go a short distance until you can turn left into a street or lot, then come back in the direction you wanted to go in the first place. Through a little creative thinking and going with the flow of traffic, you can often find more economical ways of getting to your destination. As in this and the preceding section, it can be more economical to "use" the traffic flow instead of fighting it.

WHEN YOU REVERSE

When you want to back up, use the brakes to stop the car completely, then shift into reverse and apply the gas. It's more economical to stop the car with the brakes than it is with the engine. Likewise, if you're already traveling backward, use the brake to stop before you shift into First or Drive and step on the gas. Reversing a car's momentum in either direction takes energy, of which the engine is an expensive source. With today's automatic and synchromesh transmissions, it's all too easy to use the engine to do a job more efficiently done by the brakes.

If you have enough room, and if laws and safety conditions permit, making a U-turn will help you maintain your momentum and use less gas than would be required by a back-and-forth reversing maneuver. Since highway U-turns are almost universally illegal, U-turn reverses of direction can save you gas primarily in parking lots, service stations and other areas where the reverse gear might otherwise be used.

Taking to the Hills

In getting the best gas mileage that your car and driving conditions can deliver, hills can be very important. Like the stock market, they either go up or down—and, as the successful stock trader knows, each direction calls for a different strategy.

THE DOWN START

When starting from rest on your way down a hill, let gravity give you a hand. With a manual shift, allow the car to drift a few feet before you engage the clutch. Depending on your car and the steepness of the hill, you may even be able to start off in Second instead of First. Allowing gravity to change your momentum from stopped to moving will mean less wear on your clutch and more miles to your gallon. If you drive an automatic, you can also make use of gravity's pull on your car. Just keep a soft touch on the gas pedal and gravity will help you get into your economical high gear in a very short time.

The greater ease of accelerating downhill is one reason why it's a good idea to stop on the right side of a downhill road whenever you need to read the map or stop for gasoline, food, or whatever. Your engine is at its thirstiest when you ask it to accelerate up a hill.

SKIPPING A GEAR

Though something more likely to be done by a novice driver, skipping a gear when accelerating downhill can reduce wasteful throttle manipulations (remember the accelerator pump) involved in the ritual of shifting through all the gears when they're not really necessary.

Going from 1st to 3rd or from 2nd to 4th can save gas when you're accelerating downhill—but be careful not to lug the engine.

THE UP START

Starting from rest on an uphill road calls for your foot on the brake until the very instant that you begin to accelerate. Otherwise the engine will have to reverse the car's momentum from downhill drift to uphill acceleration. For an automatic transmission, this is relatively easy—all you have to do is keep your left foot on the brake until your right foot has begun to press the gas pedal. With a manual transmission, the problem can be a little harder on both your clutch and your gas mileage. If you're driving a stick shift, keep the handbrake applied until the clutch is almost engaged and the engine is just starting to move the car. With a little practice, you should be able to start on a hill without drifting back at all. The secret is correct timing in releasing the handbrake—too soon and you'll drift, too late and you may stall the engine. Needless to say, the stick driver is going to waste both gasoline and clutch lining if he rides the clutch in order to hold his position on a hill.

DRIVING THE UPS AND DOWNS

Except for the most extreme circumstances, don't ever accelerate while climbing a hill. You'll be using gasoline far out of proportion to the little speed you may pick up. If acceleration is inefficient on a level road, it's downright wasteful on the way up a hill.

If you drive a heavy car, especially one with an automatic transmission, don't poke along on your way up a hill. Gradually press the gas pedal in order to maintain your momentum, but remember not to accelerate. Automatic transmissions tend to "lock up" and become more efficient at higher speeds, so it pays to climb quickly. Learn not to approach a hill with any more initial speed than you need in order to easily maintain momentum on the way up. Likewise, don't put your foot to the floorboard in an impossible attempt to maintain speed on a very steep grade. If a hill starts to win the momentum contest, be a good loser—slow down as it dictates and continue climbing at a rate that feels comfortable.

In a small car, allow your speed to drop slightly as you climb. Keep the gas pedal steady if you're not slowing down too quickly, press down gradually if you are. If you're driving a manual transmission, don't be afraid to downshift if necessary—you'll get better gas mileage by allowing the engine to run at a more efficient speed. Don't worry about traveling slowly as you reach the peak. This speed is easily picked up as you gradually accelerate on the way back down.

Regardless of the car you're driving, let gravity help you gain speed on the downhill side. Any extra gas you use here may well be wasted by a sharp curve on the way down or by a stop sign at the bottom. Follow the stock trader's example and don't invest good gasoline into a hill that's on its way down.

For some readers, placing the transmission in Neutral and coasting downhill may be a strong temptation. However, don't do it—for a number of good reasons:

1. It's illegal in many places.
2. In today's steering-lock-equipped cars, a driver coasting with the engine off might remove the ignition key by force of habit, thus locking the steering wheel when the car is moving at high speed.
3. It can damage the internal parts of an automatic transmission.
4. It increases the load on the brakes and makes them more likely to overheat and fail on a steep hill.

Your Driving Environment

Knowing what's going to happen before it does is an asset in any business and likewise with driving for economy. The sooner you know what's ahead, the quicker you can prepare for it in order to use less gasoline along the way. Don't just think about where your car is right now. Consider the conditions you'll be facing in a few feet, in fifty yards, or maybe even a couple of miles. By anticipating upcoming conditions, you can immediately react with gas-saving actions that will enable you to maintain your momentum, accelerate more slowly, drive more steadily, or avoid a wasteful sudden stop. While your "messengers" of advance warning can take many forms, the following are among the most important:

READ THE SIGNS

"Stop sign ahead" should automatically tell you to get off the gas pedal and gradually slow down. Ignore this advance notice and you'll be just another magician who turns gasoline into brake lining dust. Other such warnings are "Traffic signals ahead" and "Toll booth ahead." Whenever a sign tells you that *anything* is ahead, it's bound to have some effect on what you should do if you're driving for economy.

"Hill next two miles, trucks gear down" practically screams that any gas you use between here and the steep hill is going to be wasted on the way down. Another hint that you should lighten up on the gas is the presence of a mountain elevation or summit marker.

"Curves ahead" isn't advertising a girlie show, but describing a driving con-

dition where you can save gas by flowing slowly and smoothly, instead of rushing from one curve to the next. If you happen to be following someone you'd like to pass, back off and forget about it as soon as you see this sign.

Illus. 4–2. If you were thinking about passing that driver up ahead, relax for a few curves and enjoy the scenery.

Illus. 4–1. When you see a sign like this one, your car has valuable potential energy—don't use any more gas than necessary in getting from here to the down-hill slope.

Illus. 4–3. Sign at right tips off the fact that this hill is going to start down very abruptly once you get to the top.

"Merge ahead" tells you that you're going to have to interact with cars going in the same direction, and that you'd better check your speed, traffic spacing, and length of acceleration lane if you're going to get through the experience while using the least possible amount of gasoline.

"No passing zone," "School zone," "Narrow bridge ahead" are all signs which can increase your miles per gallon. By anticipating stops, slow-downs, and other special conditions, you can take your foot off the gas pedal earlier and slow down more gradually. Whether a sign warns of a rough road, a troll under the bridge, or a nudist colony crosswalk, chances are it's something for which you'll have to slow up. After all, there aren't many signs urging that you drive faster.

USE YOUR SHARE OF THE ROAD

By anticipating successive curves and how you can stay in your lane in order to get through them in the shortest distance, you can shorten the length of a trip, better maintain your car's momentum, reduce your tires' rolling resistance, and get better gas mileage. Not much better, but remember that all these little things add up. In general, by keeping to the inside of curves, you'll minimize the length of any trip. But be sure to stay in your own lane while you're doing it.

READING THE RED LIGHTS

On frequently-traveled roads, learn to "read" the red lights ahead. If the lights are synchronized to encourage a certain speed, try to maintain that speed. If you see that a light is going to turn red before you reach it, ease up on the gas and approach the light as slowly as you can. If the light turns green, you've maintained your momentum and can accelerate more economically. If it's still red when you arrive, you've saved some gasoline during your gradual approach. Hurry-up-and-wait isn't good for your gas mileage. If you know that a certain stop light stays red for a long time, don't ruin your gas mileage by rushing to it when it's green,

but you're still far away. Even if you do have to stop for a seemingly perpetual red light, you can save gas by turning off the motor while you're waiting.

CHANGING LANES

Just as an airplane pilot likes to travel at the altitude where the winds happen to be most favorable, you should try to "read" the flow of the various lanes available to you in congested driving situations. Observation of the lane patterns in your everyday driving can help you pinpoint exactly where lane 1 begins to slow down and lane 2 begins to speed up. It's not economical to zig-zag down the road, jumping into every open spot that arises, but you should likewise not limit yourself to one lane and ignore the others. Race drivers practice courses until they know the precise location where they must hit the gas when coming out of each turn. While driving to work in the morning is a little less thrilling, you can still profit from the race driver's example and practice different strategies until you find the one that works best for you in the lane patterns you're up against.

When travelling in traffic, always watch the red lights and traffic flow ahead so that you can maintain your car's momentum by moving into the lane with the least congestion. Through awareness of the cars around you and allowing acceleration room between you and the car ahead, you can make a smooth change-over without the need to stand on the gas pedal. Temporarily switching to a slower lane can sometimes be advantageous. For example, if a heavy truck is stopped at the red light near the bottom of a hill, the natural tendency is to choose the passing lane so that you won't have to creep up the hill behind him. However, since other drivers will share this tendency, they may have the passing lane backed up a long way. Under these circumstances, you're better off behind the truck—at least he and you will be through the intersection by the time the light turns red again, while the backed-up drivers may end up waiting for the same red light twice. Don't ignore a possible strategy just because it seems unconventional.

DON'T TAILGATE

Whether driving in traffic or on the freeway, tailgating wastes gas. In addition to its safety hazards, tailgating ruins the tempo of your driving and leads to jerky, momentum-wasting changes which become necessary in order to avoid rear-ending the car ahead. When driving for economy, you can't afford to change speeds every time the brake-tapper in front decides to accelerate, decelerate or swerve, depending on how he's doing in the card game he and his passengers might be playing. If possible, pass the slower driver; if not, drop back and try to find a relaxing song on the radio. Don't let the driving behavior of others anger you into losing sight of your miles-per-gallon goal.

USE THE REAR VIEW MIRRORS

Proper use of the mirrors will enhance the smoothness of your driving by keeping you aware of the changing conditions around you. When driving for speed, you're passing everything on the road and most of the action is taking place up front—in this case, the mirrors are slightly less important. However, when you're driving for economy and the people around you aren't, there will be more activity behind you than if you were driving faster.

Many a middle-distance runner has been "boxed-in" while running on the inside lane of a tiny indoor track. With a runner in front of him, a runner beside him, and a runner directly behind, there's no way he can improve his position. He's forced to follow the pace of the man in front, which may be the exact opposite of the pace that is best for him. The same situation can come up in driving on any multiple-lane highway. If you're approaching a slower driver at the same time that a faster driver is approaching you, be sure to pace your pass so that you aren't boxed-in behind the driver ahead and forced to slow down. Anticipation of who-is-going-to-be-where-and-when is a key to economical driving, and frequent glances at your rear-view mirrors can help immeasurably.

YOU'RE WATCHING THE WRONG CAR

Everybody knows that, in traffic, the most important car is the one directly in front of you. After all, if you make a mistake, he's the one you're going to hit. That's a fine rule of thumb for safe driving, but when driving for economy we should take this for granted and try to go one step further. In this case, it's really one car (or more) farther ahead. Instead of concentrating entirely on the car directly ahead, look also at the car that's ahead of him.

If you were to watch commuter or other heavy traffic from the air, it would look like a giant screen-door spring expanding and contracting as it wiggles down the highway. Cars spread out as each takes its turn to accelerate, then bunch together as they take turns slowing down. The normal reaction is to accelerate as soon as the person in front of you begins to accelerate and to slow down as soon as he begins to slow down. This alternate hurry-up-and-wait and wait-and-hurry-up activity detracts from the smoothness which driving for economy demands. However, unless you're driving a bulldozer, it will be impossible for you to maintain a steady speed.

The next best thing is to reduce the amount of speeding-up and slowing-down you have to do, and the secret is to watch cars that are further ahead than the one in front. Whenever the second car ahead begins to accelerate, anticipate your own movement by taking your foot off the brake and starting to accelerate very slightly—by the time your turn comes, you'll already be moving and won't have to accelerate as quickly to keep up with the flow. Likewise, as the cars ahead start slowing down, begin to reduce your own speed before you really have to. By looking further ahead and beginning your speed changes earlier, you'll be able to enjoy the economy of smoother driving and smaller momentum changes. As you practice this strategy, you'll continue to get a better feel for the acceleration and deceleration "countdowns" which can give you gas-saving advance notice of necessary changes in your speed.

Even better advance notice is possible when driving in traffic through a tunnel, on a wet road, or at night. The shiny walls and roof of the tunnel will reflect the brake lights of cars further ahead, giving you a slow-down cue even when you can't see the cars themselves. Likewise, the successive switching off of brake lights gives you advance notice that you need in order to accelerate sooner and more slowly. Like the tunnel walls, a shiny or wet road surface will reflect the brake lights of the second car in front, except from underneath the car ahead. Likewise for night driving, in which anticipation is naturally more difficult because of lower visibility.

If you happen to be directly behind a truck or other large vehicle, your looking-ahead strategy will not be possible. In this case, it's appropriate to do a courteous turn for your fellow drivers—back off and let a few of them in front of you.

BEND WITH THE WIND

With today's engines, wind doesn't have much effect on how fast you can go. However, it can be a factor in deciding how fast you *should* go. By watching flags, factory smoke, bushes, trees and skinny telephone poles, you can determine if the wind is for you or against you. Drive a little more slowly when the wind is against you—air resistance depends on the relative speed between you and the air, not just on your speedometer reading. With the wind at your back, higher speeds will be much less expensive. Recall once again that the increase in air resistance is far out of proportion to the increase in your speed, and that a 10% increase in speed means a 33% increase in the horsepower your car needs to overcome air resistance.

In one gas mileage study, a standard size car was driven at high speed with and against a stiff wind. Going 70 mph into the 18 mph wind, the car was able to achieve only 11.6 miles per gallon. However, when driven 70 mph with the wind at its back, the car's mileage increased to 16.6 miles per gallon.[8]

Driving an Automatic

If you're driving a car with an automatic transmission, don't despair. Look at the bright side—by increasing your miles per gallon by 15%, you'll save more money than the stick driver who makes the same improvement. If that's not bright enough, consider the following:

Most cars with an automatic transmission are provided with a lower, more economical rear axle ratio to help compensate for economy lost through torque converter slippage. In addition, since the torque converter dampens uneven running which often occurs with lean air-fuel mixtures, an engine used with an automatic transmission can use a slightly leaner carburetor mixture than the same engine hooked up to a manual transmission. Another compensating factor is that high speeds tend to lessen the disadvantage of an automatic transmission. This is because greater air resistance lowers the economy of any car, regardless of transmission type, and because the torque converter becomes more efficient at higher speeds.

Besides applying the general techniques discussed so far, you can get more miles per gallon from your automatic by doing the following: Keep the car in high gear whenever possible. This may sometimes require a very light foot in order to avoid the selection of a lower gear. In some situations, it may be advantageous to use your left foot for braking. When you're trying to maintain your momentum by avoiding the brake, yet feel that a sudden stop or slow-down may become necessary, having your left foot in position near the brake will reduce your reaction time. Any time you are traveling downhill or decelerating, it's a good idea to keep your braking foot poised near the pedal—however, be sure not to "ride" the brake. Since your automatic transmission "locks up" and is more efficient at higher speeds, make a strong charge at the hills which lie ahead. Maintain or gradually build up speed as you approach the hill, then gradually press the gas pedal to maintain it on the way up.

Attitude is Important

Driving for economy requires a certain state of mind. You should be relaxed enough that you aren't in a hurry and are free of the temptations of tail-gating, lane-jumping, and race-driver passing techniques. On the other hand, you must be alert to your driving environment and possible changes in it which may affect your speed, acceleration, and braking decisions. In short, driving for economy requires that you think economy. Every time you move the gas pedal, brake pedal, steering wheel or shift lever, one of the main thoughts in your mind should be—how is this going to affect my gas mileage?

RELAX IN THE "PIPELINE"

You'll encounter some situations where your speed is sharply reduced and in which you may become totally frustrated. It's morning rush hour and there are 5000 cars in front of yours; or you're following a cement mixer on a one-lane road; or you're stuck in the crowd that's taking a 14-mile detour. In these circumstances, it's sometimes hard to think sanity, let alone economy. But try. Whether you curse the mayor, sing Christmas carols, or play tic-tac-toe on the windshield, it isn't going to make one minute of difference in the time at which you'll arrive at your destination. When in these "pipeline" situations where you're trapped and can't do anything about it, try to relax and let the pipeline carry you at its own rate. However, along the way, get the best gas mileage you can by anticipating the movement of the cars in front of you and by applying various other tips presented here. This situation is one in which the AM-FM radio, stereo-tape outfit or shortwave unit can be a handy gas saver. If listening to the radio or tape deck calms you down, you're going to drive more economically. However, don't pump the gas pedal in tune with the music.

ENJOYING THE TRIP

Though sometimes more boring than frustrating, long trips can benefit from the same philosophy that is useful in the "pipeline." Radio equipment and gauges can help fight fatigue and impatience, as can keeping track of your average speed or competing with yourself to improve your gas mileage from one fill-up to the next.

Illus. 4–4. If your windshield view looks like this, you're in the "pipeline" and shouldn't yield to the temptations of uneconomical driving.

How Fast Are You Really Going?

When you're driving for economy, it helps to know how fast you're going. Your speedometer may not be as accurate as you think, especially if you have over-size or snow tires on your car. Snow tires, which are larger in diameter than their summer counterparts, can fool your speedometer into reporting that you're going as much as five miles per hour slower than you really are. Thinking that you're going 55 when you're really going 60 may not seem like much, but it can be important to air resistance as well as to the radar cop down the road. At 60 mph, you'll require almost 30% more horse-power to overcome air resistance than you would at 55.

You can easily give your speedometer a lie detector test while driving on any highway equipped with mile markers. In addition, some roads have special mile-marked sections for the specific purpose of testing your speed. Drive at a constant speed which is comfortable, and which you can easily maintain over a distance of either one or two miles. Have a passenger time how long it takes to complete the course, then refer to the following table to determine your actual speed:

Two-Mile Time min.	sec.	Actual Speed mph	One-Mile Time sec.
1	40	72	50
1	44	69	52
1	48	66.5	54
1	52	64	56
1	56	62	58
2	0	60	60
2	4	58	62
2	8	56	64
2	12	54.5	66
2	16	53	68
2	20	51.5	70
2	24	50	72
2	28	48.5	74
2	32	47.5	76
2	36	46	78
2	40	45	80

For example, if you maintain a constant speed over the one-mile course, a time of 68 seconds would indicate that your average speed was a very economical 53 mph. Be sure to check your speedometer accuracy from time to time, especially after you have switched to a new set of tires.

A Poor Man's Tachometer

A tachometer is an instrument that measures engine speed in revolutions per minute (RPM). While most engines operate at 500 to 5000 RPM, depending on how fast you're going and the gear you're in, they're not equally efficient at all speeds. Torque and horsepower, the two most common measures of engine output, both depend heavily on the speed of the engine.

The torque of an engine is the twisting effort it is able to exert, and is generally expressed in foot-pounds. If you couldn't open the pickle jar this morning, it was because your torque wasn't high enough. Torque drops off at very high and very low engine speeds, with most engines reaching their maximum torque some-where between 2000 and 4000 RPM. Your engine's "breathing" ability, tech-nically referred to as volumetric ef-ficiency, is highest at the same RPM where the torque output peaks out.

Torque is important in driving for economy, especially if your car has a manual transmission. If you're accelera-ting and shift into a higher gear too soon, the engine will be unable to generate enough torque to efficiently do the job you've given it. On the other hand, wait-ing too long before upshifting wastes gas because of the unnecessary use of the lower gear. If you have an automatic transmission, you're less likely to be able to shift too soon, but a heavy foot could cause your transmission to shift too late for best economy. You can influence the automatic upshift by lifting your foot slightly at the time you'd like to have the higher gear selected.

The other common rating of engine

output is horsepower, or the rate at which the engine is capable of pushing against a load. Where torque is a measure of an engine's twisting force, horsepower is a measure of the speed at which the engine can exert that force. Unlike torque, horsepower keeps going up as engine speed increases, and usually peaks at higher speeds in the 4000 to 5000 RPM range.

The SAE "net" torque and horsepower ratings and speeds are the most important, since they are measured with the engine equipped as it is in your car, with air cleaner, alternator, emission-control, cooling, and exhaust systems in place. Your owner's manual will specify the maximum torque and horsepower of your engine and the RPM values at which these peak efforts are reached.

You can buy a tachometer to tell you when your engine is operating in the area of its maximum torque or horsepower RPM. However, if you're not interested in that kind of expense or accuracy, and simply want some idea of how fast your engine is turning at various road speeds in different gears, you can use a tape measure and some simple arithmetic to tell you your RPM. Here are the steps involved in making your "poor man's tachometer":

1. First you need to find out how far your tires will carry you in one rolling revolution. Lightly dab some white shoe polish or other marking liquid near the center of the tread of one of your rear tires. (Use a front tire if you have front-wheel drive.) Next, drive the car straight forward or backward until the tires have made at least two complete turns. Now measure the distance between any two white spots on the ground.

2. Look in your owner's manual for your car's overall drive ratio in high gear. For most cars, this will be the same as the rear axle ratio. In case your car has an indirect-drive top gear (i.e., not 1.00:1), just multiply the rear axle ratio times the top gear ratio. If your car is equipped with an optional rear axle ratio, or you think it may be, check with your dealer. Using the wrong axle ratio will give you inaccurate RPM figures in the steps to follow.

3. Using figure 4-4, place one end of a ruler or other straight edge at the number of inches you measured in Step 1. Place

the other end at the final drive ratio you looked up in Step 2. Along the way, the straight line will cross the center scale at the number of miles per hour your car travels at 1000 RPM in high gear. For example, if the measurement in Step 1 was 80 inches, and your overall drive ratio in high gear is 3.00, this means that your top gear will deliver 25 miles per hour from each 1000 engine RPM. If you're arithmetically inclined, you can calculate this yourself from the following formula. For any gear:

$$\text{Miles per hour per 1000 engine RPM} = .944 \times \frac{\text{inches covered in one tire revolution}}{\text{overall drive ratio}}$$

4. Now comes the tachometer part of the operation. Look up the other gear ratios in your transmission and divide each gear ratio into the figure you got in Step 3. For example, if the car in our example had a Third gear ratio of 1.40, a Second gear ratio of 1.95 and a First gear ratio of 2.70, we would divide 25 by each of these to get mph per 1000 RPM figures of 17.9, 12.8, and 9.3 for the other gears. (Note: If your car has an indirect-drive high gear, you'll need to use the formula in Step 3 to get your mph figures for each gear.)

Now that you know the long-leggedness of each gear, you can use these mph figures to find out how fast you're going at any RPM in any gear. Multiply each mph figure times the number of thousands of engine RPM and you can make a tachometer similar to this one, which happens to reflect the RPM-mph relationship of the car in our example:

	1st	2nd	3rd	4th
mph/ 1000 RPM	9.3	12.8	17.9	25
Engine RPM:				
1000	9mph	13mph	18mph	25mph
1500	14	19	27	38
2000	19	26	36	50
2500	23	32	45	63
3000	28	38	54	75
3500	33	45	63	88
4000	37	51	72	100

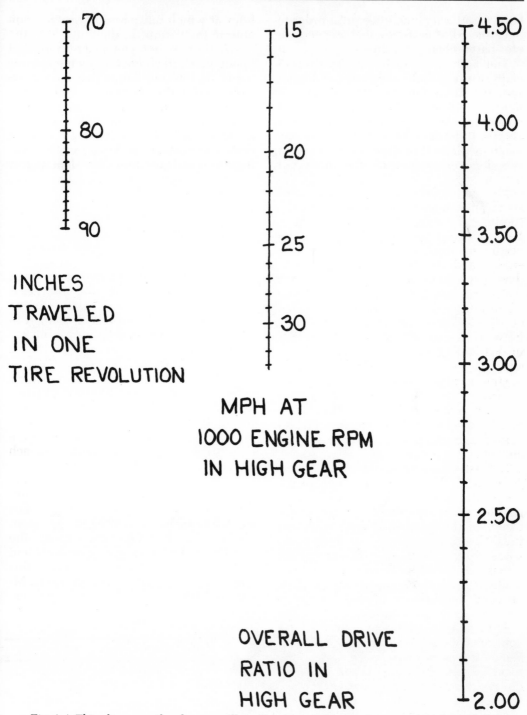

INCHES
TRAVELED
IN ONE
TIRE REVOLUTION

MPH AT
1000 ENGINE RPM
IN HIGH GEAR

OVERALL DRIVE
RATIO IN
HIGH GEAR

Fig. 4–4. This plus a pencil and paper will enable you to make your "poor man's tachometer."

When using your own RPM chart, remember that it depends on the size of your tires and the accuracy of your speedometer. Whenever you switch tires, your old chart may no longer apply. In addition, your speedometer may not be equally accurate (or consistently inaccurate) at all speeds, especially in the lower end of the scale—for this reason, don't rely on a tachometer chart for an upper limit of speed in each gear. If you're looking for maximum acceleration, you'll have to get a real tachometer in order to have the RPM accuracy that a speedometer-based chart can't provide.

The normal expansion of tires (especially the non-belted variety) at higher speeds will tend to make the actual mph figures slightly higher than the ones you've calculated. In order to make your chart a little more operational, you may want to place thin tape strips on your speedometer to indicate the miles per hour at which maximum torque is available in the various gears.

Whether or not you make your own "poor man's tachometer," remember to apply the driving habits that have been described in this chapter. By making use of as many of them as you can, you'll be sure to improve your gas mileage. Above all, think and drive for economy. When it comes to adding up those gasoline savings, you can count on your right foot.

5·Maintaining for Economy

Whether you're a do-it-yourselfer or a fugitive from the customers' lounge, attention to your car's mechanical needs will help it to join you in your efforts to get more miles per gallon. For the average car, a simple tune-up will increase gas mileage by 6%—for a badly neglected car, the improvement can be 20% or more.[1]

The operations described in this chapter are important in determining and maintaining your car's gas mileage performance. While other maintenance requirements should not be ignored, they will not have as great an effect on fuel economy in the short run. Be sure to consult your owner's manual for periodic maintenance recommendations made by the manufacturer.

Because of the increasing popularity of do-it-yourself, some of the tune-up and maintenance steps are described in greater detail than others. In order to help you decide how much you'd like to take on yourself, any special tools or instruments required will be mentioned, along with their approximate cost. In general, you should find that investments in do-it-yourself equipment will be quickly repaid through lower maintenance and fuel costs.

The Engine

MECHANICAL CHECKS

Compression

Before tuning the engine, it's a good idea to check cylinder compression in order to get an idea of how successful you're likely to be. If the engine has one or more weak cylinders, smoothness and economy will be impossible to achieve through normal tuning, and mechanical repairs may be necessary. An accurate compression gauge will cost in the neighborhood of $5–$10. Warm up the engine to its normal operating temperature, then turn it off. Stick numbered pieces of tape onto the spark plug wires so that you'll be able to put them back where they belong.

57

Fig. 5–1. Checking compression.

Carefully disconnect the wires from the spark plugs—don't pull on the wires themselves, because you might separate them from their insulating boots. Using a spark plug wrench (cost: about $1–$2), and being careful not to drop any dirt or particles into the cylinder, remove each spark plug.

At this point, you'll need an assistant to floor the gas pedal and switch on the starter. With the compression gauge held firmly in the spark plug opening, crank the engine until the needle reaches its highest reading. This will generally take less than 4 seconds.

CAUTION: *When working under the hood, be sure to avoid the fan, drive belts and other moving parts. Neckties, loose clothing, jewelry, and long hair*

Maximum Pressure Pounds/ Sq. Inch	Minimum Pressure Pounds/ Sq. Inch	Maximum Pressure Pounds/ Sq. Inch	Minimum Pressure Pounds/ Sq. Inch
134	101	186	140
136	102	188	141
138	104	190	142
140	105	192	144
142	107	194	145
144	108	196	147
146	110	198	148
148	111	200	150
150	113	202	151
152	114	204	153
154	115	206	154
156	117	208	156
158	118	210	157
160	120	212	158
162	121	214	160
164	123	216	162
166	124	218	163
168	126	220	165
170	127	222	166
172	129	224	168
174	131	226	169
176	132	228	171
178	133	230	172
180	135	232	174
182	136	234	175
184	138	236	177
		238	178

Fig. 5–2. Compression pressure minimum-maximum chart. Pressure in weakest cylinder should be at least 75% of that in strongest.

are all hazardous when you're working around a moving engine. Make sure that the handbrake is firmly applied.

After taking and recording the readings in all cylinders, compare the lowest with the highest. If the compression of any cylinder is less than 75% of that recorded by the highest, the low cylinder is likely to have either burned valves or worn piston rings. Check your compression readings with those specified as acceptable from various manuals or from dealer service departments.

It's a good idea to check and record cylinder compression readings at periodic intervals. Although readings will vary with temperature, oil viscosity and other factors, knowing how readings tend to vary between cylinders can give you early notice of advancing ring and valve wear. Since compression testing involves the flow of gasoline into an engine that isn't running normally, it can cause dilution of the engine oil. For this reason, it's advisable to schedule your compression test just before an oil change. In addition, compression pressures may also vary with the altitude of different geographic areas.

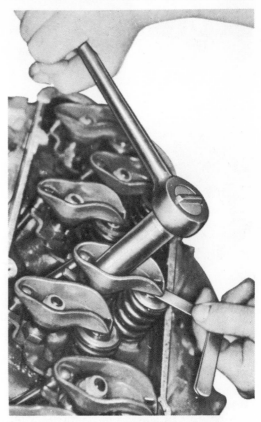

Fig. 5–3. Adjusting mechanical valves.

Valve Clearance

Since most cars are now equipped with hydraulic valve lifters, you probably won't need to bother with routine valve clearance checks. Hydraulic lifters do the same job as a mechanical lifter, but are self-adjusting, operate with no lifter-to-valve-stem clearance, and use normal engine oil pressure for their operation.

If your car has mechanically-operated valves, their clearance should be adjusted either hot or cold, depending on the manufacturer's specifications. Valve clearance will change slightly with changes in engine temperature. For each cylinder, the valve clearances can be checked and adjusted when the piston of that cylinder is at the very top of its compression stroke and the distributor rotor is pointing to that cylinder's spark plug wire connection in the distributor cap. At this point, both the intake and exhaust valves will be closed. A feeler gauge (cost: $1–$3) leaf may then be inserted between the valve stem and the lifter (or,

for some overhead camshaft engines, between the cam and lifter) to check the clearance. After making the necessary adjustment, be sure to recheck the valve clearance to be sure it is correct. The simple tightening of a rocker arm locknut can change the clearance significantly if you're not careful.

If clearance is too small, the valve will be opened for longer than necessary and won't have enough time to transfer its great heat (up to 1200° F.) to the cylinder head and cooling system. This may cause the valve to warp or burn, leading to reduced compression in the cylinder involved. A valve that has too much clearance won't open completely and will cause the engine to run rough and deliver poor gas mileage. You can't rely on valve train noise to warn you of badly adjusted valves—while a valve with excessive clearance will click loudly, one with too little clearance may bear its burden in complete silence.

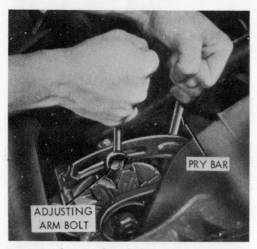

Fig. 5–4. Adjusting drive belt tension.

Fig. 5–5. Manifold heat control valve.

Drive Belts

Inspect the drive belts for wear, cracks and tension. A belt that is too tight will reduce gas mileage and lead to rapid wear in the bearings of the device it's operating. In general, a belt will have correct tension if you can use firm thumb pressure to depress it one-half inch in the middle of its longest travel between pulleys. A preferable method of checking is to use a special tension gauge as recommended by some manufacturers. Be sure to check with your owner's manual for the proper tension specifications for your car. To adjust a drive belt, loosen the bracket nuts of the accessory involved and rotate the bracket slightly.

Exhaust Manifold Heat-Control Valve

The often-neglected manifold heat-control valve controls the flow of gas through the exhaust manifold and normally aids fuel economy by helping the engine to warm up more quickly. When the engine is cold, the valve directs hot exhaust gas through a passage in the intake manifold to heat the incoming air-fuel mixture, helping it to vaporize more easily. As the engine warms up, the valve rotates to enable exhaust gas to follow its normal route through the exhaust system. The presence of this valve in your car is indicated by a shaft and counterweight below the exhaust manifold.

A valve stuck in the "cold" position will cause hot exhaust gas to circulate even when the engine is warm, leading to overheating of the engine and spark plugs, knocking, and loss of power and fuel economy. A valve stuck in the "hot" position will reduce gas mileage by extending engine warm-up time and fouling spark plugs. If your car has this valve, check its freedom of movement when the engine is cold—the counterweight should move easily. Should it be sticking, tap it lightly and apply a special penetrating oil to the ends of the shaft. To help prevent future problems, it's best to use an oil that won't leave high-temperature deposits which can cause further sticking.

COOLING SYSTEM

Hoses and Clamps

A collapsed or leaking radiator hose will, at best, reduce your gas mileage. If you're less fortunate, the resultant overheating could ruin your engine. Check all heater and cooling system hoses for cracks, and their clamps for tightness. Use a water pump lubricant and rust inhibitor to lower water pump friction and reduce the formation of rust scales which could lower cooling efficiency.

Thermostat

If your engine never warms up completely, or warms up very slowly, you may be losing miles per gallon to a faulty thermostat. Besides helping the engine to warm up quickly, the thermostat has the job of seeing that economical running temperatures are maintained. Within reasonable limits, higher temperatures result in better gas mileage. When a car is traveling at 30 mph, increasing the water temperature from 120° F. to 190° F. can improve gas mileage by 3%.[2] In addition to lowering fuel economy in the short run, a bad thermostat can cause dilution of oil, accelerated wear and the formation of sludge in your engine.

Wear of the cylinder bore and piston rings at lower temperatures is very high. At a water temperature of 100° F. the cylinder bore and top piston ring will wear out at the rate of about .001 and .002 inch, respectively, each thousand miles.[3] However, at temperatures over 170°, their rate of wear is practically zero. Owners who make the mistake of removing the thermostat in order to increase gas mileage are making a big mistake. Besides actually reducing fuel economy, the absence of a thermostat keeps the engine in the low-temperature, high-wear zone where engine lifetime suffers considerably.

The heat range of a thermostat is usually described by two temperatures—the one where it starts to open, and the one at which it is fully opened. A 180–200 degree thermostat will begin to open at 180° F. and be fully open at 200°. With increased emphasis on engine emissions, thermostats in recent models begin opening near 190 degrees, opening fully at about 210 to 215 degrees.

If you suspect that your thermostat isn't providing the quick warm-ups and proper running temperature for maximum economy, you can easily check and replace it. To remove the thermostat, drain the cooling system until the water is below the level of the thermostat housing, then remove the housing and thermostat. With the thermostat and a high-temperature thermometer in a pot of water, heat the water to boiling and observe the expansion of the thermostat to

Fig. 5–6. Replacing the thermostat.

determine the exact temperatures at which it begins to open and is fully open. (Note: If the thermostat is supposed to open fully at a temperature above 212° F., it may not reach this temperature in an open pot of boiling water.) When replacing the thermostat, be sure to use a new housing gasket.

Heater Control

Be sure that, when the heater is turned off, the control valve at the engine is fully closed. Otherwise, the engine will have to pump some water through the heater core even when the heater isn't turned on. As an aid to finding the location of the heater control valve, look under the hood while someone inside the car turns the heater temperature control between the off and warm positions. In some cars, heater temperature is controlled by the amount of air flowing through the heater core rather than the flow of water through it. In this case, there will be no heater control valve to check or do anything about.

Radiator Cap

The radiator cap is necessary to pressurize the cooling system in order to increase water pump efficiency and pre-

Fig. 5–7. A radiator pressure cap.

vent boil-over at higher temperatures and elevations. For example, in the mile-high city of Denver, water will boil at only 200°F. A 4 psi (pounds per square inch) radiator cap will increase water's boiling point to about 215°F. at this altitude. Visually check the radiator cap for cracks, damage or a worn gasket. A better test is to have your local service station or dealer pressure-test it to measure the pressure at which it allows air to escape. If the cap can't hold the pressure at which it's rated, replace it.

FUEL SYSTEM

Carburetor

The two most common carburetor adjustments are the idle speed and idle mixture. For either adjustment, a dwell-tachometer (cost: about $30, but useful in ignition tuning as well) is desirable. The idle speed is adjusted by turning the throttle valve stop screw, and should be set to the manufacturer's specifications. The engine must be warm for all cars, with manual transmission in Neutral and automatic transmission in the gear specified. Other idle speed setting requirements may include operation of the headlights and air conditioner while the speed is being adjusted. Refer to your owner's manual or read the label in the engine compartment for the correct RPM and setting conditions. If the idle speed of an automatic transmission-equipped car is set too high, the car will waste gasoline by trying to "creep" when it is stopped. The idle mixture adjustment is a matter of history for 1968 and more recent models. The idle mixture screws on these cars are provided with a locking cap to limit the range of adjustment. For 1967 and earlier cars, turn the idle mixture screw in or out until the tachometer reading is at its peak, then reset the idle speed if necessary. For owners of post-1967 models, follow the same advice and do the best you can within the range provided by the limiter cap. Tampering with or removing the limiter cap is against the law if done by a commercial service facility. However, the vehicle owner may remove the idle limiter caps for adjustment provided that he does not exceed the emission levels for that model car.

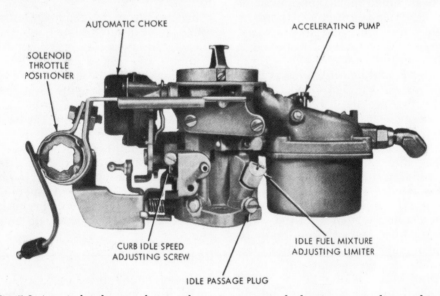

Fig. 5–8. A typical carburetor showing the various parts and adjusting screws discussed in this chapter.

Other carburetor adjustments which can affect gas mileage are the fast-idle speed, the stroke of the accelerator pump, and the float level. The fast-idle setting causes the engine to idle a little faster when it is warming up, while the accelerator pump stroke adjustment determines how much raw gas gets squirted into the engine when you push on the gas pedal. If the carburetor float is set too low, leaks, or is too heavy, the rich mixture which results will sharply lower your fuel economy.

An automatic choke that's not working right can cost you 3 miles per gallon.[4] With the engine cold, the choke plate should be completely closed. As the engine warms up, it should gradually approach the vertical position. If the choke sticks, use a special cleaner to remove deposits from the plate pivot points. The use of engine oil could cause future sticking by attracting dirt to these critical locations. Be sure that the choke is set to the leanest possible setting for proper starting and operation of the car. The best way to find out is to gradually adjust it in the lean direction until starting becomes difficult, then back off slightly for less choking and more miles per gallon.

Be sure that there are no leaks at the carburetor base or intake manifold. These leaks can reduce your gas mileage and may be detected by applying engine oil to the edges of the surfaces involved. Clean and lubricate the carburetor linkage so that it will move smoothly and easily when your educated right foot is coaxing the pedal downward during a driving-for-economy start.

Fuel Lines

In addition to being dangerous, leakage in the fuel lines and connections can waste gas before it has a chance to get to your engine. Check the integrity of the fuel lines between the carburetor and fuel tank, and between the tank and filler cap. While you're at it inspect the tank, too—the seams of an older fuel tank might have weakened over the years. Carefully tighten the various carburetor and other bolts and screws along the way but don't be heavy-handed or you could strip their threads.

Fuel Filter

There are various types of fuel filters in use and various locations in which they are installed. The important thing is that you clean or replace yours at the recommended intervals. A clogged fuel filter can allow dirt to enter the carburetor and

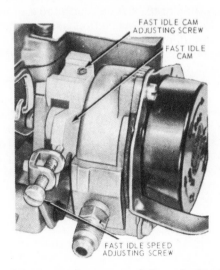

Fig. 5–9. A typical automatic choke and adjusting screws.

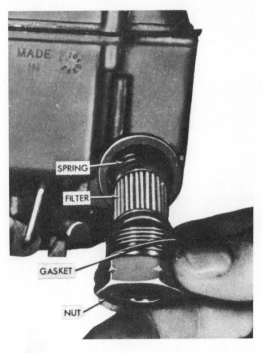

Fig. 5–10. A typical paper fuel filter.

Fig. 5–11. A typical air cleaner filter element.

narrow passages which are critical for the proper air-fuel mixture.

Air Filter

If your car has a clogged air filter, it can cost you 1 mile per gallon.[5] Every gallon of gasoline you use requires up to 9000 gallons of air to do the job. Whenever the air filter becomes even partly clogged with dirt, the result is the same as if the automatic choke were in operation. The passage of incoming air is restricted and the air-fuel mixture becomes rich, resulting in lower gas mileage. Because this loss of economy is gradual, the air filter is easier to ignore than other gasoline robbers which are more obvious, but less important. For example, a clogged air filter may waste 5 times as much gas as a 200-pound set of weights carried in your trunk.

For most cars equipped with the paper-element type of air filter, replacement of the element involves removing the wing nut which secures the top of the air cleaner, taking out the old element, and replacing it with the new. The oil bath air cleaner used in some cars requires removing the entire filter body, rinsing the base in gasoline, then refilling the base with fresh oil. Always change or clean the air filter according to the manufacturer's recommendations, and more frequently if dusty driving conditions are encountered.

One air filter which often escapes attention is the small oil-wetted gauze filter in the oil filler cap of some cars. It cleans air which is drawn for crankcase ventilation, and should be removed, washed in gasoline, dried and re-oiled at periodic intervals.

Fuel Pump Pressure

Excessive fuel pump pressure has the same effect as an improper carburetor float setting. In some cars, the fuel pump pressure is even more important. For example, cars equipped with electronic fuel injection usually require a very high and constant fuel pressure to accompany the electronic brain's decision on how long to hold the injectors open under various operating conditions. However, any car, regardless of the fuel system with which it happens to be equipped, will suffer a loss of fuel economy when operated under excessive fuel pump pressure. A combination vacuum gauge and fuel pump pressure tester (cost: about $7) can be used to check whether your fuel pump is working too hard. The higher fuel line pressures of electronic fuel injection systems will generally require a special gauge with a range up to 35 psi.

LUBRICATION SYSTEM

Engine Oil

In the miles you cover between oil changes, your engine oil gradually becomes contaminated with dirt, dust, metal particles, acids, soots, water, gasoline, oil oxidation products and various other unfriendly substances. If the oil is used too long, additives discussed in Chapter Three become depleted and can no longer offer protection against these contaminants. In addition, a dirty or clogged oil filter can offer no assurance that dirt and metal particles will be removed from the oil. When a filter becomes clogged, oil will flow directly to your engine by way of a filter by-pass designed to protect against loss of lubrication when the filter is blocked or the oil is too thick to flow through it.

By ignoring periodic oil changes which remove contaminants that the old oil has collected, you'll only hasten your car's journey to that great highway in the sky. Secondarily, your gas mileage will suffer in both the long and short run—over-extended oil increases engine resistance as well as wear, thus ensuring that neglect will haunt you both now and later. The

American Petroleum Institute recommends that you change oil every 3000 miles or 3 months, whichever comes first, but never to exceed the time or mileage intervals which the car manufacturer recommends for the conditions under which you drive. Short trip, stop-and-go, cold weather, heavy duty and extended idling conditions, all make it advisable to change oil more often than you may think necessary. Under ideal conditions, such as turnpike driving or other sustained operation, engine oil will last longer and be less contaminated by the acids, water vapor and other substances which tend to form during cold-engine, low-speed operation.

Before changing the engine oil, warm the engine to normal operating temperature so that the oil will carry more contaminants in suspension when it is drained.

CAUTION: *When changing the oil, be sure that the tires are blocked and the emergency brake firmly applied. An automatic transmission should be in Park and a manual transmission in Neutral whenever you have changed the oil and are checking for possible leaks with the engine running. Be sure that there is adequate ventilation and that you are careful of moving engine parts.*

Place a suitable container under the oil pan—be sure that it will hold the number of quarts you're draining. While a one-gallon can may seem plenty big, a five-quart crankcase makes it small in a hurry. Loosen the oil drain plug and try to remove it without getting hot oil on your hand. Don't worry about dropping the plug into the container—you can get it later when the oil cools down. Allow 5 or 10 minutes for the oil to drain from the crankcase. This will minimize the amount of old oil left to mingle with the fresh stuff you're going to add. If this is one of the oil changes during which an oil filter change is made (If you're changing oil every 3000 miles, you can replace the filter at every other oil change), take care of the filter replacement while the last drops of old oil are on their way out.

After the oil has drained, retrieve the drain plug, check its sealing washer, then install and tighten it into place. Don't lean on it too hard—if you have a torque wrench, about 15 foot-pounds should do the job. When adding fresh oil, remember that a new oil filter will require the addition of a little extra, usually a quart. Check your owner's manual for refill requirements and be sure not to add too much, especially if you happen to be using a 10-quart can. Oil is a lot easier to add than it is to remove. After you've added the proper quantity of oil, start the engine and check for leaks at the drain plug and oil filter. Tighten further anything that leaks. If it continues to leak, remove it and determine the source of the problem.

Oil Filter

Your oil filter will probably be of the disposable canister type, which screws on and can be removed either by hand (cost: $0) or by oil filter wrench (cost: about $1–$2). While a filter that has been in place for many miles may require the use of the wrench, the use of a clean rag for a better grip should enable you to remove it by hand. After removing the old filter, wipe the dirt from the area where the new filter will contact the engine. Spread a light layer of engine oil on the gasket surface of the new filter. Before installing the filter, read the tightening instructions on its side, then use hand pressure to screw it on tight. Don't use the wrench on a new filter.

Fig. 5–12. Removing an oil filter with an oil filter wrench.

Other filters may employ a replaceable cartridge. In this case, instead of replacing the entire filter, you need only buy a new cartridge. Before removing this type of filter, check to see if a drain plug is provided to drain oil from the filter housing—if so, use it and thank the designing engineers. Remove the housing bolt or nut, take out the housing and cartridge, then clean the housing and other permanent parts with gasoline. Install the new cartridge into the housing, lubricate its gasket, and replace the housing to its base. Replace the drain plug, if any. Tighten down the center bolt or nut.

After installing an oil filter of either type, add the necessary quantity of oil, then start the engine and check closely for leaks.

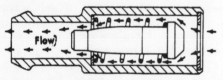

Fig. 5–13. Flow of crankcase ventilation gases through a typical PCV valve.

PCV Valve

The positive crankcase ventilation system "freshens" the crankcase with a current of clean air and recirculates crankcase fumes back into the engine for more complete burning. In addition to preventing crankcase fumes from entering the atmosphere, the PCV system helps reduce oil contamination caused by combustion by-products. The heart of this system is the PCV valve, which prevents an unbalanced air-fuel mixture by metering the amount of crankcase fumes allowed to enter the intake manifold. A typical PCV valve is shown in figure 5-13. If the PCV valve is clogged, there will be two major results. First, the unbalanced combustion mixture will provide poor engine performance and economy. Second, the lack of crankcase ventilation will lead to heavy sludge formation and possible engine damage.

Periodic changes of oil and filter will help keep the PCV valve clean and functioning properly. However, because of its low cost (about $1–$2) and important

function, it should be replaced at the intervals recommended by the manufacturer, typically every 12 months or 12,000 miles. You can check your PCV valve by pulling it from its housing and putting your finger over the end. With the engine idling, you should notice a strong suction. If not, the valve is defective and should be replaced.

IGNITION SYSTEM

Electrical Connections and Wiring

Before tuning the ignition system, you should check the electrical connections at the distributor, coil, and spark plugs. All connections should be clean and tight. Examine the high tension coil and spark plug wires for fraying, cracks, softness, and oil contamination. When the engine is running in the dark, it is possible to visually inspect for leakage from the spark plug and coil wires and for induction cross-firing of plugs served by adjacent spark plug wires. While the wires may all have a very slight glow, serious leaks from a wire to the car body or from wire to wire will be evidenced by lightning-like sparks.

Spark Plugs

Although it's a stranger to the biology lab, a spark plug like the one dissected in figure 5-14 can cost you 2 miles per gallon if it's not adjusted or working properly.[6] To get the best gas mileage, it's a good idea to clean and gap your spark plugs every 6000 miles. While spark plug replacement is generally recommended every 10,000 or 12,000 miles, they can last longer if you pay attention to them and to the other maintenance operations described in this chapter. The only parts of the spark plug that require normal maintenance are the electrode gap, shown in figure 5-2, and the cleaning of deposits from the sparking end of the plug. If you want your do-it-yourself time to be spent as profitably as possible, it's difficult to recommend a more gas-mileage-rewarding project than the simple cleaning and adjusting of your spark plugs.

When servicing your plugs, label the wires with chalk or tape and grasp them

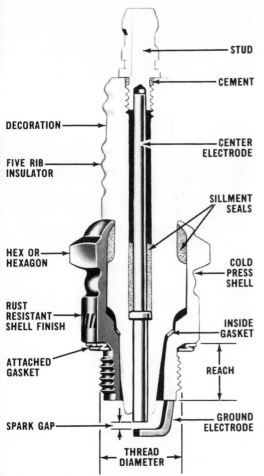

STUD

CEMENT

DECORATION

CENTER
ELECTRODE

FIVE RIB
INSULATOR

SILLMENT
SEALS

HEX OR
HEXAGON

COLD
PRESS
SHELL

RUST
RESISTANT
SHELL FINISH

INSIDE
GASKET

ATTACHED
GASKET

REACH

SPARK GAP

GROUND
ELECTRODE

THREAD
DIAMETER

Fig. 5–14. Cross-sectional view of a spark plug and its components. *Source:* Champion Spark Plug Company.

Fig. 5–15. Your spark plugs should look like the normal one shown here. *Source:* Champion Spark Plug Company.

Fig. 5–16. A worn out spark plug. *Source:* Champion Spark Plug Company.

by the insulating boot when pulling them from their plugs. After you've removed the plugs, read what they have to say about your engine, your driving, and your maintenance habits. The most talkative parts of an engine, the spark plugs can give you an "insider's" view of why your car may not be giving you the gas mileage you'd like. After you've pulled your plugs, these conditions are the ones most likely to greet you:

Normal. Hopefully, your plugs will look like the one in figure 5-15. This spark plug has no evidence of electrode burning and contains the usual brown and gray deposits. Under normal conditions, the plug gap will not increase by more than .001 inch every thousand

miles. When a plug is functioning normally, it can be cleaned, filed, regapped and put back to work in your engine.

Worn-Out. The spark plug shown in figure 5-16 is just plain worn out. Its eroded electrodes and pitted insulator tell you that your gas mileage will benefit from installing a new set of plugs.

Carbon-Fouled. If your spark plugs look like the one in figure 5-17, you've

Fig. 5–17. A spark plug that has been carbon-fouled. *Source:* Champion Spark Plug Company.

Fig. 5–18. An oil-fouled spark plug can mean costly engine work ahead. *Source:* Champion Spark Plug Company.

probably noticed that your gas mileage hasn't been too good lately. Those fluffy black deposits indicate that you're being victimized by one or more of the following gas thieves: a faulty carburetor; a too-rich mixture adjustment; an automatic choke that's over-doing its job; a clogged air cleaner; a sticking exhaust manifold heat valve; defective ignition points, coil condenser or high tension wires; or use of a spark plug that is too cold for the engine in its normal use. If you usually drive at very low speeds, or if your engine spends a lot of time idling, spark plug temperatures may not be high enough to burn off the normal products of combustion. If so, check with your dealer about the suitability of a hotter spark plug for your engine. A carbon-fouled plug that is in otherwise good condition may be cleaned and re-used.

Oil-Fouled. An oil-fouled spark plug (figure 5-18) will look similar to one that is carbon-fouled, except that the deposits will be wet and covered with oil. Oil-fouling is usually caused by oil entering the combustion chamber through worn pistons and rings or by way of worn valve guides and stems. While the use of a hotter spark plug will reduce oil-fouling, its presence tells you that your engine is in need of major repairs. Oil-fouled spark plugs will further reduce gas mileage in an engine that is already hard-pressed to

perform at a satisfactory level. A plug in this condition may, if otherwise OK, be cleaned and re-used.

Overheated. The presence of a burned or blistered insulator nose and badly eroded electrodes indicate that a spark plug has been subjected to excessive

Fig. 5–19. This spark plug may have been overheated by an excessively lean mixture. Other possible causes are discussed in text. *Source:* Champion Spark Plug Company.

temperatures. If your spark plugs look like the one in figure 5-19, check for incorrect ignition timing, the use of a fuel of too-low octane which has caused knocking, an excessively-lean air-fuel mixture or a blockage in the cooling system. If you normally operate your car at high speeds or with heavy loads, you may wish to switch to a colder spark plug. If any of your spark plugs show signs of having been overheated, it's a good idea to replace them with a new set.

Splash-Fouled. Splash-fouling (figure 5-20) occurs when long-accumulated combustion chamber deposits are suddenly melted and thrown against the plugs, generally during acceleration or at high engine speeds. A plug that is splash-fouled may, if otherwise sound, be cleaned and replaced.

Fig. 5–21. This plug isn't as bad as it looks. It has been hit by fuel scavenger deposits and may be cleaned and re-installed. *Source:* Champion Spark Plug Company.

Fig. 5–20. A plug that has been splashed by melted combustion chamber deposits. *Source:* Champion Spark Plug Company.

Fig. 5–22. If ignition current is going in the wrong direction, the result could be lower voltage, less gas mileage, and spark plugs that wear like this one. *Source:* Champion Spark Plug Company.

Scavenger Deposits. The deposits shown in figure 5-21 are normal with the use of some gasolines. The addition of so-called "scavenger" compounds to these fuels chemically changes combustion chamber deposits so that they are more readily vaporized and blown out. These flaky deposits are generally white or yellow and, despite their appearance, are easily removed. Plugs in this condition may be cleaned and re-used.

Reversed Polarity. The presence of the dish-shaped ground electrode wear pattern in figure 5-22 indicates that the ignition spark may be traveling in the wrong direction and requiring more voltage than it should. This reversed travel not only reduces fuel economy, but can also

Fig. 5–23. Besides lowering your fuel economy, pre-ignition can be very hard on your spark plugs. *Source:* Champion Spark Plug Company.

cause hard starting, missing under load and shorter spark plug life. If you discover this wear condition, your low-tension ignition coil leads may be reversed. To find out for sure, have a tune-up oscilloscope connected to your engine.

Pre-Ignition. If any of your plugs have melted electrodes like the one in figure 5-23, hot combustion deposits in the cylinders have caused severe pre-ignition of the air-fuel mixture. As evidenced by the spark plug in the illustration, this condition can be both violent and damaging. Check for leaks at the intake manifold, induction crossfire of plugs attached to adjacent wires, and worn distributor parts. Make sure that you are using the proper fuel for your engine and that your spark plugs are not too hot for your normal driving conditions.

Depending on the results of your spark plug inspection, you may want to check with your dealer about the advisability of installing either hotter or colder spark plugs to better suit your engine and your type of driving. Remember that, while a hotter plug will tend to raise fuel economy and carbon up less, it will also be more prone to pre-ignition and overheating.

If you intend to re-use the spark plugs you've just examined, scrape all deposits from the electrodes, body and insulator, then use an ignition file (cost: about $1) to clean up the electrodes. Whether installing new or used plugs, check the gap with a round feeler gauge (cost: about 50¢). Don't use a flat leaf gauge on used plugs—you'll get an inaccurate measurement. With the gap tool portion of the gauge, bend the ground electrode until the proper gap is obtained. Never try to adjust the gap by bending the center electrode. If the manufacturer specifies a range for the spark plug gap, try to stay near the center of the range, since normal wear will increase the gap by about .001 inch every 1000 miles. Don't go too narrow to compensate for the expanding gap which occurs over the miles, as a too-small gap won't be able to supply a strong spark. If you're interested in the maximum possible economy at the cost of some of your time, gap the plugs as wide as specifications allow, then re-gap at this setting every 2000 miles. Clean the spark plug hole and apply a drop of oil to the plug threads. Being careful to avoid cross-threading the plugs, screw them in firmly with hand pressure, then tighten beyond the hand-tight position. Don't twist too hard on the wrench, as this could damage the threads in the cylinder head. If possible, use a torque wrench and tighten the plugs to the manufacturer's specifications.

Fig. 5–24. Checking spark plug gap.

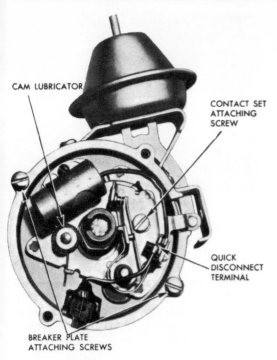

CAM LUBRICATOR

CONTACT SET
ATTACHING
SCREW

QUICK
DISCONNECT
TERMINAL

BREAKER PLATE
ATTACHING SCREWS

Fig. 5–25. The inside of a distributor.

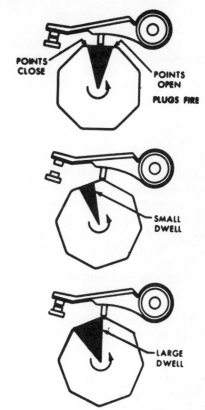

POINTS
CLOSE

POINTS
OPEN

PLUGS FIRE

SMALL
DWELL

LARGE
DWELL

Ignition Points

The distributor contact points are the heart of your car's ignition system. In performing their job of controlling the spark to each cylinder, they may have to open and close as often as 300 times each second. (If you tried to clap your hands that fast, your elbows would disintegrate.) When the points are closed, they conduct an electrical current that allows the coil to build up an intense magnetic field. Then, as the points open, the interruption in current causes a rapid drop in magnetism which creates the 20,000 volts available to spark your plugs.

Naturally, since the points open and close, they must be open part of the time and closed part of the time. The part of the time that they are closed is called the dwell angle, and is illustrated in figure 5-26. If the points are not closed long enough (too little dwell), the coil won't have time to build up a strong magnetic field and the resulting spark will be weak. If they are closed too long (too much dwell), electrical current will heat up the coil, increase its resistance, and likewise result in a weak spark. In order

Fig. 5–26. Shaded area shows the distributor dwell, or angle during which the points are closed. This has to be just right in order to get the best spark and gas mileage.

to give the coil enough time to build up voltage, but not enough time in which to lose it, the dwell angle must be—like Goldilocks' porridge—just right.

The time-honored way of measuring ignition point dwell has been the flat leaf feeler gauge. It relies on the fact that dwell decreases when the points are set further apart and increases when they are closer together. The feeler gauge measurement is, at best, an approximation of the actual dwell angle specified by your car's manufacturer. Not only is it an indirect measure of the actual degrees of dwell, but it's often not even a good measure of the gap between the points. While not too bad for brand new points, the feeler gauge will always underestimate the actual distance between used points. This is because of the pits and craters which develop on even recently-installed points. Because of the inaccuracies of the feeler gauge, if you're going to do your own ignition point setting, it's recommended that you invest in a dwell meter (cost: about $15) or combination dwell-tachometer (cost: about $30). With the dwell meter hooked up, you'll know exactly what the dwell angle is and how it compares with the setting that will give you the best spark and the most miles per gallon.

You can examine your ignition points by removing the distributor cap and rotor, then using a small screwdriver to spread the points apart. If they're excessively burned or pitted, replace them. If not, file them smooth and re-adjust them. The job of the condenser is to reduce the electrical arcing which causes transfer of metal from one point to the other. If one point has a large peak which matches the other's crater, the condenser should be replaced when new points are installed. Figure 5-27 shows the effects of a condenser having too little or too much capacity.

In order to get the moving point into its wide-open position, operate the starter for brief spurts. An alternative is to turn the engine by hand until the moving point is at the peak of a cam lobe. (Depending on your engine, you may need to give your hand an advantage by removing the spark plugs.) With the moving point riding on the peak of a cam lobe,

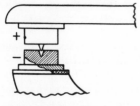

Pitting caused by low capacity

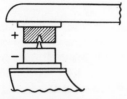

Pitting caused by high capacity

Fig. 5-27. The ignition point that gets the crater will reveal whether your condenser is of over or under capacity.

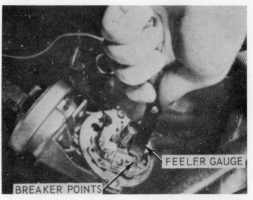

Fig. 5-28. Checking the breaker point gap with a feeler gauge.

use a feeler gauge to make an initial setting of the point gap according to the manufacturer's specifications. If you don't have a dwell meter, this will also be your final setting so skip the next paragraph. When tightening the screw which locks the stationary point, be careful not to give it the King Kong treatment. The plate below is rather thin and its threads are easily stripped. In case you should manage to strong-arm the screw and strip the threads, you can use a small sheet-metal screw to hold the points until you're able to get another plate. Before leaving the points, pull a piece of lint-free paper between them in order to remove traces of oil or grease which might cause poor performance and rapid wear.

If you have a dwell meter or dwell-tachometer, you can improve on the rough setting provided by the feeler gauge. The recommended dwell angle will appear in your owner's manual or on a label in the engine compartment. If, with the engine idling, the dwell meter indicates that the actual dwell angle is greater than that specified by the manufacturer, stop the engine and move the stationary point so that it is further away from its partner. If the dwell angle is too small, move the points closer together.

CAUTION: *Be careful when working around the running engine. Loose clothing, long hair, and jewelry are hazardous when you're working under the hood. Work outdoors or where there is plenty of ventilation to carry away deadly exhaust fumes.*

If your distributor is provided with an

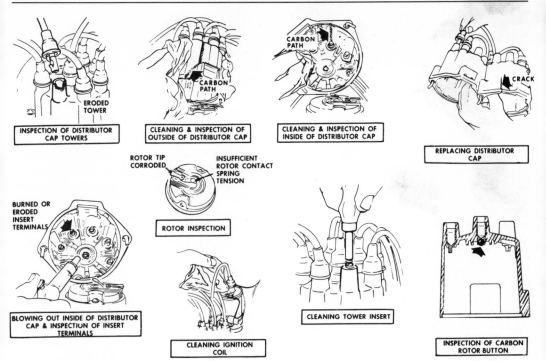

Fig. 5–30. What to look for when cleaning and inspecting the distributor cap, rotor, and coil.

Fig. 5–29. Adjusting the dwell angle with an allen or "hex" wrench.

access cover (most AMC and GM V8's), you can use an allen (or "hex") wrench to adjust the dwell angle as you watch the meter. This is the easiest and quickest way to adjust the points. If you have no access cover, you can save the trouble of constantly removing the distributor between checks by just leaving the cap off and cranking the engine with the starter until you're close to the desired setting. Because of the current drawn by the

starter, the meter may register a slightly larger angle than it should, so be sure to make your final check with the engine idling. After you have the points adjusted, increase the engine speed up to about 2500 RPM and observe the dwell angle. It will probably be a few degrees less than it was at idle. This is due to contact point "float," and is normal. However, too much float (e.g., over 5 degrees) indicates that you may have a wobbly distributor shaft.

Before leaving the distributor, check the distributor cap for cracks, carbon tracking, terminal erosion and excessive wear of the center contact button, shown in figure 5-31. Inspect the rotor for physical damage and erosion of the tip, shown in figure 5-32. The presence of any of the preceding conditions can lower the voltage available to your spark plugs and hurt your gas mileage.

If you're thinking about buying a dwell-tachometer to help you in your pursuit of better gas mileage and lower maintenance bills, lean toward a unit that provides two RPM scales. For example, 0–1000 RPM and 0–5000 RPM scales have their own specialties, the former for

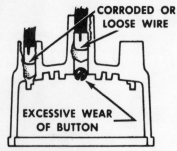

Fig. 5–31. Check your distributor cap for voltage robbing problems like the ones shown here.

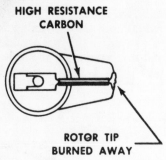

Fig. 5–32. An eroded rotor tip can reduce your gas mileage.

idle accuracy, the latter for higher speed checks. Some meters try to squeeze all 5000 RPM into a narrow band only a few inches wide, thus making small RPM changes difficult to see.

Whether you've used a feeler gauge, a dwell meter, a dwell-tachometer, or a surveyor's transit to set the point gap, you'll now need to adjust the ignition timing. Any change to the contact points automatically requires that the ignition timing be checked.

Ignition Timing

Now that we have a spark of the proper strength, we need to make sure it arrives at the proper time. A spark that gets to the cylinder just 5 degrees too late can cost you 1 mile per gallon.[7] Ignition timing is best done with a stroboscopic light (cost: about $5–$25) and must be carried out after the dwell or point gap has been adjusted. While any stroboscopic light will do the job of glowing at the right time, the more expensive ones plug into a 115 volt wall socket and make it much easier to see the timing marks that you're supposed to be lining up.

CAUTION: *In using the stroboscopic light to time the engine, you'll be working near the fan and fan belt. Loose clothes, jewelry, neckties, and long hair are hazardous under these conditions. Be sure to have adequate ventilation to prevent carbon monoxide poisoning.*

Conditions and specifications for setting the timing are in your owner's manual or on a label under the hood. The timing marks are generally found on the vibration damper or crankshaft pulley, with a pointer located on the cover of the timing chain or belt. Figure 5-33 shows a typical timing mark scale and pointer. The position in the inset of figure 5-33 shows that the engine is at top dead center ("DC"). The 10 degree mark in the direction of engine rotation (arrow) from "DC" indicates 10 degrees before-top-dead-center.

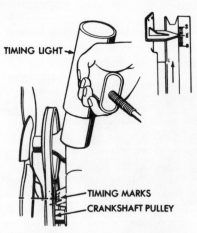

Fig. 5–33. Typical timing mark arrangements. The stroboscopic timing light makes the marks "freeze" like the wagon wheel spokes in a western movie.

Put a chalk mark on the pointer and on the specified timing mark on the scale. Unless the manufacturer has specified otherwise, disconnect the hose from the vacuum advance and plug it with a blunt pencil. Hook up the timing light according to the instructions which accompanied it, then aim the light at the timing pointer or scale, whichever is stationary. With the engine warmed up and idling slowly, the timing light will flash each time the spark plug in number one cylinder fires. The light should "freeze" the motion of the pulley or damper so that the chalk marks line up perfectly. If they don't line up, loosen the distributor clamping bolt and gradually rotate the distributor until they coincide. (If your first try moves the marks further apart, turn the distributor in the other direction.) After tightening down the distributor, re-check to ensure that the setting has not changed.

With the pencil removed and the vacuum advance hose connected, observe the movement of the "frozen" mark as you increase the engine speed. It should advance the timing smoothly. If you alternately connect and disconnect the vacuum hose while the engine is running, the mark should move quickly back and forth—if not, the vacuum diaphragm has a leak and should be replaced. Never "power time" the engine on the road, especially if yours is one of the majority of engines with emission control devices.

EMISSION CONTROL SYSTEM

Not mentioning emission control devices here would be parallel to compiling a history of ship disasters without including the Lusitania. In some form or another, your car has emission control equipment which is required by law, helps make the air cleaner, and tends to lower your gas mileage. In addition, the presence of these devices makes it even more critical that you pay close attention to routine maintenance and adjustments—if a tuned emission-controlled car can run poorly, one that is out of tune may be lucky to run at all. However, emission controls are a fact of life which must be accepted even if you are interested in getting the most miles from your gallon.

Your car may depend primarily on engine modifications to lower emissions. If so, its ignition timing is slightly retarded, the spark advance curve a little slow, the compression ratio lowered, and the carburetor adjusted about as lean as it will go. Don't be tempted to arbitrarily advance the timing. Besides putting your engine emissions beyond legal limits, you can end up with too much advance at high speed and damage your engine. Keep the engine adjusted as specified in

your owner's manual or on the label beneath the hood.

If your engine is equipped with an exhaust gas recirculation (EGR) system, part of the exhaust gas is sent back through the intake manifold to help lower the output of carbon monoxide, nitrogen oxides and hydrocarbons. While performing this social function, the EGR's less potent air-fuel mixture also lowers your gas mileage.

Some cars have an air injector pump which is belt-driven and injects air into the exhaust valve ports to help oxidize hydrocarbons and carbon monoxide before they can enter the atmosphere. The main economy checks to make here are that the drive belt is not too tight, that the pump filter is not dirty, and that the pump turns freely.

Fig. 5–34. Removing the air pump centrifugal filter.

Among other systems which your car may employ are the automatic spark retard, to reduce emissions under certain operating conditions, and the thermal reactor, which involves the injection of air into a special chamber in the exhaust system. On some models, distributor vacuum advance is totally eliminated whenever you're operating in the lower forward gears. This transmission-controlled spark retard is controlled by a switch at the transmission and may include a cold-temperature and a hot-temperature override. With this set-up, distributor vacuum advance may be available only in top gear, or with a four-speed, in the top two gears. If you have a car with transmission-controlled spark retard, try extra hard to get into that economical high gear as soon as you can.

The drop in gas mileage due to the various emission control systems and devices is significant, but hard to pinpoint, since cars have become heavier (partly due to crashability and safety requirements) at the same time that they've become emission-controlled. However, one very believable study, using gas mileage data collected by the Environmental Protection Agency, has concluded that a 4000-pound 1971–1973 model traveled 12% fewer miles per gallon than a pre-1968 model of the same weight.[8]

Since there's little that you can legally do to avoid gas mileage loss due to emission controls, make sure that you keep your emission systems maintained as recommended by the manufacturer. If you do this, at least they won't reduce your gas mileage any further than authorities deem necessary for the clean air effort.

Transmission and Drive Line

Rear Axle

Reduce rear axle friction by keeping the differential topped-up with the proper lubricant to the level specified. In general, oil should be added until the level reaches the bottom of the filler plug hole. If you're using a suction gun to add the oil, be sure to let the excess flow out

before you install the filler plug. Limited-slip rear axles don't use the same oil as conventional designs, so be careful to use the proper lubricant. If you're using an ordinary oil pump-can to do your adding, make sure that you don't get it mixed up with a similar can that contains ordinary engine oil.

Automatic Transmission

Incorrect fluid level can cause an automatic transmission to slip and waste gasoline. Before checking the fluid level, warm up the car until the transmission is at its normal operating temperature. With the car on a level surface, shift the transmission through all drive positions and return it to the Park position. With the engine idling, locate the dipstick and clean all dirt and grease from the cap. Remove and wipe off the dipstick, then return it to the filler tube until it is fully seated. Withdraw the dipstick and observe the oil level. Add enough fluid to raise the level to the FULL mark, but don't overfill.

Manual Transmission and Clutch

For efficient operation of the gears, keep the transmission topped up to the level of the bottom of the filler hole. For

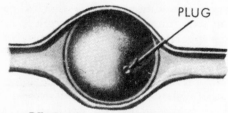

Fig. 5–35. A rear axle filler plug hole.

Fig. 5–36. Clutch pedal free travel.

the smooth shifting that driving for economy demands, lubricate the pivot points of the shifting arms. Be sure that the car is on the level when you're checking the oil level and that you don't overfill. Excess oil could find its way to the clutch lining and reduce your miles per gallon to zero. Before venturing beneath the car, have the transmission in gear and the handbrake firmly set.

When the clutch pedal is lightly depressed by hand, it should move very easily for about an inch and a half, then become more difficult to push. The distance traveled before resistance increases is the free play. If your clutch pedal doesn't have enough free play, the resulting slippage will lower clutch life as well as your gas mileage.

Wheel Bearings and Brakes

Faulty wheel bearings and dragging brakes can make your engine think it's pulling a small trailer. With the car lifted, rotate the wheels to check resistance to turning. Because of their constant pressure against the rotor, disc brakes can be expected to drag slightly. Drum brakes should spin freely. Because of drive train resistance, the driving wheels will not spin as easily as the other two. However, you'll still be able to detect the rumble of a bad bearing or the sound of a dragging brake.

Tires

Pressure

With a little magic from a tire pressure gauge, you can mystify your friends by turning air into gasoline. Under-inflated tires, with their higher rolling resistance, can cost you 1 mile per gallon.[9] In addition, soft tires will wear out faster, run hotter, and involve a higher risk of failure. Figure 5-37 shows the tread wear pattern of a tire that has been under-inflated most of its life. If your tires look like this, give them more air and you'll burn less gas. While an over-inflated tire will roll easily, it will also wear out more quickly than one carrying the cor-

Fig. 5–37. Heavy outside wear indicates under-inflation that is wearing out your tires and lowering your gas mileage. *Source:* Rubber Manufacturers Association.

rect pressure. If you're considering saving gas by pumping your tires to the limit, consider the uneven wear of the tire in figure 5-38.

Check pressures when the tires are cold, never when warm or after driving. Setting a warm tire to the correct cold pressure will result in the tire being too soft. When driving at high speeds or hauling loads, check your owner's manual for the extra pressure needed for these conditions. If you buy a good tire gauge and use it, it'll save you gas money for as long as you own a car with tires. It will also be more accurate than the gas station tower gauges you may otherwise use—a study

Fig. 5–38. An over-inflated tire will increase your gas mileage, but will quickly wear out as shown here. *Source:* Rubber Manufacturers Association.

by the National Bureau of Standards revealed that 45% of the station gauges tested were off by at least 3 psi.[10]

Tread Thickness

A bald tire will give better gas mileage—at least until it goes flat. With less rubber on the tread to squirm, a worn-out tire will have less tread flexing and lower rolling resistance. However, before you consider driving around on bald tires, consider that they are illegal, that they are up to 44 times as likely to go flat, and that, if you drive them in the rain, you'll think that your car's wearing water skis. Replace any tire that has less than $1/16$ inch of tread. If you want your tires to have low rolling resistance, get a good set of radials.

Rotation

The Rubber Manufacturers Association recommends that, for even wear and long tread life, tires be rotated every 6000 to 8000 miles as described in figure 5-39. If you happen to have a mixture of radial and belted bias tires, it's best to leave them where they are. While snow tires should not be rotated, you can equalize wear on your present tires by having the fronts and backs take turns sitting out consecutive winters. Since some manufacturers may not recommend periodic rotation for their tires, check with your dealer before rotating.

Balancing

When do three ounces weigh 36 pounds? When they're rotating on your car's wheel rim at a road speed of 70 miles per hour. A wheel that is out of balance by as little as three ounces can make your car's front wheels act as if they were being hopped on by a 36-pound kangaroo. While such imbalance might not have much effect on your economy today, it could lower gas mileage quite a bit in the future. With a worn-out front end controlling tires which don't know which way to roll, gas mileage won't be good. The faster you drive, the more im-

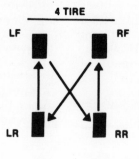

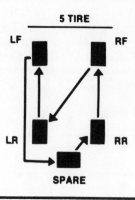

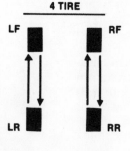

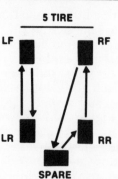

Fig. 5-39. Recommended tire rotation patterns. See text for tire mixing precautions. *Source:* Rubber Manufacturers Association.

portant it is to have your front wheels balanced, both for safety and economy.

Wheel balancing takes two forms—static and dynamic. Static balance is obtained when the weight of the wheel and tire is evenly distributed around the axis of the wheel, and is tested with a so-called bubble balancer. Dynamic balancing checks the distribution of weight about the vertical centerline of the wheel, and is often done with the wheel installed on the car. A small electric motor turns the wheel at high speed while a stroboscopic light winks each time the heaviest point is at the bottom. The result is a "freezing" of the wheel while the serviceman determines which part of the rim needs more weight. Sophisticated off-the-car equipment is also used for dynamic balancing.

While the rear wheels are less sensitive to imbalance problems, you should have the front ones balanced every 6000 miles or so. Although static balancing is better than nothing, dynamic balancing is preferable if you spend most of your driving time at highway speeds.

Front Wheel Alignment

Toe-In

The car in your driveway is pigeon-toed, and the reason for this stance is to ensure that the front wheels end up running parallel when rolling resistance forces them outward at highway speeds. Toe-in is generally expressed as the amount by which the front wheels are closer together at the front than they are at the back. For example, if the toe-in were zero, the wheels would be parallel. Tires with little rolling resistance—those radials again—require almost no toe-in because they are not forced outward as readily as other tires. So if you've installed radial tires on your car, be sure to have the mechanic set the toe-in accordingly. The same advice goes for belted bias tires, except that their higher rolling resistance won't permit quite as much reduction in the amount of toe-in. Even if you have conventional bias tires, you should still have the toe-in set as close to zero as specifications allow. As with so many other adjustments, improper toe-in can lower your gas mileage. It has been estimated that, besides wearing out tires more rapidly, incorrect toe-in can cost you about .3 miles per gallon.[11] Front wheels roll best when they're going in the same direction.

Camber

Camber is simply the angle at which a wheel deviates from the vertical, being positive when the top of the wheel tilts outward, negative when it tilts inward. In automotive terms, a bow-legged person could be described as having positive

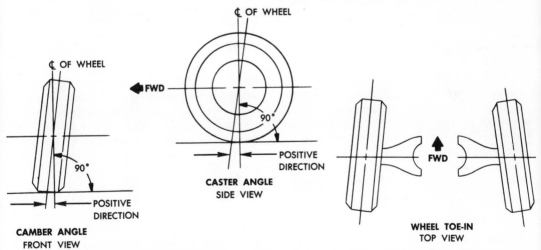

Fig. 5–40. The geometry of toe-in, camber, and caster are shown in these diagrams.

camber. Likewise, an individual with knock-knees would exhibit a negative camber in his stance. Although the front wheels are those most often in need of checking, proper camber in all four wheels is important for the best tire life and gas mileage. Camber helps the front wheels to keep from being forced outward, so a tire that rolls easily shouldn't require as much camber as one with more rolling resistance. Zero camber is best for gas mileage because the different parts of the tire will have the same rolling radius, thus reducing the amount the tire must flex.

Caster

A front-end angle that your mechanic may check when he's looking at the toe-in and camber is the caster angle. Caster makes it possible for you to lift your car (slightly, of course) just by turning the steering wheel. It's similar in function to the rearward tilt of a bicycle's front fork, and helps provide directional stability. It also produces the self-centering behavior of your steering wheel after you've completed a turn. While caster is not as important for gas mileage as the other front-end angles, incorrect caster can cause your car to wander and steer erratically—thus making it more difficult to maintain constant speed and directional momentum when you're driving for economy.

Other Checks

AIR CONDITIONER REFRIGERANT

If you have an air conditioner, you can minimize the amount of time it must be turned on by recharging the system when necessary. With the engine idling and the air conditioning on its coolest setting, inspect the sight glass for foam or bubbles in the passing refrigerant. If they are present, the system's efficiency will be improved by recharging the refrigerant.

WEATHER SEALING

Whether it's the air conditioner in summer or the heater in winter, you don't

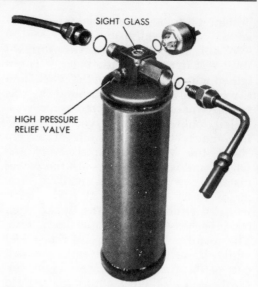

Fig. 5–41. The sight glass of a car air conditioning system.

want to waste the gasoline that helped to make the inside temperature more comfortable. Check the rubber strips around doors and vent windows for flexibility and tightness. If they are, and you'd like to keep them that way, apply some rubber lubricant from time to time.

EXHAUST SYSTEM

Earlier in the chapter, we were primarily concerned with helping your engine inhale. However, engines, like people, have to breathe both ways. Check your car's exhaust system for dents and restrictions. A clogged exhaust system will increase engine resistance and lower your gas mileage.

WAX

If you've ever waxed your car, you may have noticed how easily a rag slides over the waxed surface. Although surface skin friction is something more closely related to ships and airplanes, it applies to anything that's driven through a resisting medium. Besides helping to maintain your car's appearance, a coat of wax wouldn't hurt your gas mileage either. Naturally, don't expect your gas mileage to immediately double. This is one of those tips that skeptics might compare to painting the front of your car white and the rear black. Remember those little rotating vanes that run in a vacuum, are painted white on one side, black on the other, and receive their go-power from the energy contained in light? Because the black side absorbs more energy than the white side, the thing turns as if by magic. This is another item that won't enable you to burn your gasoline credit cards. However, if you do expect to be painting your car soon. . . .

6 · Planning for Economy

Now that you know the forces of nature you're up against, and are buying, driving, and maintaining for economy, it might seem that there's little more chance for improvement. Wrong. With just a bit of preparation and planning, you can increase your miles per gallon still further. In this chapter you'll find that ideas to help you get better gas mileage are supplemented by tips to help you get mileage without using any gas at all. However, since you didn't get this book to have someone tell you to ride the trolley, emphasis will be on more miles per gallon.

Long Trips

STAY OFF THE ROOF

Hauling 60 pounds can hurt your car's gas mileage more than hauling 1000 pounds. Though hard to believe, it's true—if the 60 pounds happens to be a sailboat on your roof and the 1000 pounds is a small camping trailer following behind. When you're cruising on a level highway, the boat is going to steal more gas than a trailer weighing 15 times as much. Naturally, if you've forgotten to take down the sail, the boat will be at an even greater disadvantage. Anything on your roof—be it a sailboat, foot locker or grand piano—is going to increase the effective frontal area of your car, thus increasing the air resistance your engine must overcome. In addition, because of the disruption of air flow around your car, the car-plus-load combination is going to be less streamlined than the car alone, thus affecting the drag coefficient discussed in Chapter Two. Just as a 98-pound weakling could easily trail the Green Bay Packers as they push through a stadium crowd, a low trailer follows in your car's "wake" as the car breaks through the air. The trailer enjoys the same low air-resistance advantage which served the 138 mph bicyclist of Chapter Two.

If you need the extra carrying capacity

and often travel at steady highway speeds, opt for a small luggage trailer as your source of space. You'll get better gas mileage on the interstates, but may have to pay an extra fee on some toll roads. However, since we can travel practically anywhere without riding a toll road, this shouldn't prove to be too important. While the trailer will be an advantage on the open highway, it's not as practical in traffic where its extra weight makes it less economical than a load carried on the roof.

When you're packing for a long trip, eliminate the electric toothbrush and other unnecessary items, then try your creative best to squeeze the survivors into the car, where air resistance won't be able to find them.

KNOW WHERE YOU'RE GOING

Intelligent use of a road map can go a long way toward reducing the frustration and wasted gasoline of trying to find your way around unfamiliar surroundings. When you're stopping every 5 minutes to ask directions, it's hard to maintain the smoothness that economical driving demands. Make your navigational notes before the trip, including approximate mileages between important decision-making points. Things look a lot simpler on the map than they do on the road, especially if you're traveling through a congested area where other drivers are more interested in getting home for supper than in welcoming you to their state. Maps of the areas you intend to visit or travel through will generally be available from gas stations, oil companies, Chambers of Commerce, and state agencies promoting tourism.

Besides knowing where you're going, it's handy to know when you're going to get there and, should gasoline stations be scarce, if you have enough fuel to make it without stopping. If you're calling ahead for motel reservations, it can be a good idea to make the call as soon as you're within cruising distance. Knowing your car, its gas mileage under different driving conditions, how to convert the gas gauge readings into gallons-left, and how far you need to go can all be helpful in avoiding an out-of-gas emergency in the middle of nowhere. If you do run very low on gas, don't speed up so that you'll get to a station sooner. This is a natural tendency which only defeats your purpose. By going slow, you'll have a better chance of being able to stretch your gas until you reach a station.

BEATING THE ELEMENTS

The mailman might be able to get through wind, rain, snow, hail and sleet, but he's not going to get good gas mileage while he's doing it. When faced with wet or snow-covered roads, take it easy for economy as well as safety reasons. Rolling resistance will be higher on these roads, and higher speeds will be even more expensive than they are under normal conditions.

Because higher temperatures favor more efficient combustion and better gas mileage, your miles per gallon will not be as good if you travel at night. In addition, night driving requires more use of the lights and heater, thus raising demands on the alternator and its supplier, the engine. One exception to this rule is late-night driving through heavily populated areas, by which you can avoid the usual daytime delays and traffic jams. Another exception is the driver who absolutely requires air conditioning whenever temperatures rise—for him, the best strategy is to travel from early in the morning until early afternoon in order to minimize use of the air conditioner.

As discussed earlier, remember not to make up time while driving into a headwind. Driving 50 mph into a 20 mph headwind will make your engine think it's going 70, and it will drink gas accordingly. Recall also the resistance effects of various road surfaces. Try to make up time only when the elements are in your favor. If he had known about the lower economy of night travel, Paul Revere might have waited until the next day before making his famous ride.

AVOID THE CROWD

There are two types of crowds that the economy-minded driver should try to avoid. The first type snarls the highways and tourist facilities by flocking to the most popular parts of the country at the most popular times. Two ways of avoiding them are: 1) go to a popular area in the off-season, or 2) go to an unpopular area anytime. Besides saving gas on the way, you'll also find that tourist accommodations are priced at a lower rate. You may not end up deciding to vacation in Maine in the winter or Florida in the summer, but at least consider the possibility of such off-season ventures.

The second type of crowd to stay away from is the breakfast, lunch, and dinner mob at roadside restaurants. By stopping for supper at five o'clock, you'll be doing the following to your gas mileage: First, because your car will be shut off longer, it'll take longer to warm up when you get back on the road. Second, having spent the extra time in the crowded restaurant, you may be tempted to make it up by rushing at uneconomical speeds for the rest of your trip. By stopping for meals either a half-hour before or after the peak periods, you'll be doing both your stomach and your gas mileage a favor.

TAKING THE LONG WAY

Sometimes the long way can be the short way, especially if your measuring stick is how many gallons of gas each alternative will take. A limited-access highway, even though part of a longer route, may actually save you gas compared to a shorter route to the same destination. With the more steady speeds it allows, the limited-access road will provide you with more miles per gallon, even though it does involve more miles. For example, you're better off traveling 15 miles at 25 miles per gallon than in traveling 10 miles at only 12 miles per gallon. Many stop-and-go routes which look short on the map are costly in terms of both time and gasoline. When you're considering alternative routes, measure distances in gallons, not just miles.

Short Trips

ATTACKING THOSE ERRANDS

One of the best ways to save gasoline on short local trips is to combine as many of them as possible into a single effort. Not only will you travel fewer miles, but you'll get more miles per gallon while you're at it. Figure 6-1 shows what happens to a car's gas mileage as the length of an urban trip increases in a low (10°F.) outside temperature.[1] Although the car could achieve 12.8 miles per gallon when warmed up, it got only 8 mpg on a 4-mile trip, and only 5 mpg when trip length was reduced to 2 miles. While it might take a little advance planning to schedule your errands so they can be handled in fewer trips, it will pay off in gasoline savings.

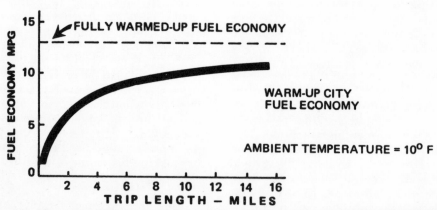

Fig. 6–1. The uneconomical warm-up period hurts your gas mileage on short trips. *Source:* Charles E. Scheffler and George W. Niepoth, *Customer Fuel Economy Estimated from Engineering Tests,* SAE Rept. No. 650861, Report to the National Fuel and Lubricants Meeting, Society of Automotive Engineers, Tulsa, Okla., Nov. 2–4, 1965 (New York: Society of Automotive Engineers, 1965).

Once you've combined a number of errands into a single trip, you can save further by deciding on the best order in which to make these stops. In the world of business, this has a counterpart called the "traveling salesman problem," in which the idea is to figure out the order in which the salesman should make his calls in order to minimize the total distance traveled. Depending on the number of places the salesman has to stop, the problem can become very complex in a hurry. While you may not want to apply the various mathematical solutions of the traveling salesman problem to your own situation, at least compare a few of the alternatives that you think deserve consideration. With one-way streets, no-left-turns and other obstacles, it might help if you made a little sketch of the possible routes you could take—if you have more than four places to visit, taking them in the best order can mean savings of both time and gasoline.

USE YOUR GARAGE

If you have a garage, use it. A car that's been sitting out all night is going to require a longer time to warm up. If you're driving only a few miles, it won't get warmed up at all. Even if you're using multiple-viscosity oil in the crankcase, every moving part of the car—from wheel bearings to universal joints—is going to require more horsepower than if the car had been in the warm garage.

SHORTCUTS

If you frequently travel the same roads, you may sometimes tend to follow them even when you shouldn't. For example, if there were a breakdown delaying your morning traffic, would you have an escape route to avoid the tie-up and still get to work on time? Having commuted with a shortcut-conscious friend one day, I was so impressed with his contingency planning that I rode with him again the next day and took notes on each alley, side street and back yard he used as he made his way into the city. If you don't happen to know someone with a Master of Shortcuts degree, do the next best thing and refer to a good map.

PARKING

When you're about to park your car, think beyond just looking for an open space. For example, consider the case of a jammed parking lot near a major university. Some hopefuls circle the lot a dozen times while waiting for a space to become available. Others stake out a claim to an aisle, then idle their engines until someone happens to leave. Both strategies waste time and gas. In the meantime, there may be abundant parking just across a bridge 200 yards away. Don't be afraid to park a short walk from where you're going—after you've walked to your destination, the parking lot cruisers will still be going around in circles or tapping on their steering wheels.

When parking, look ahead to the conditions you'll face when you're going to leave. Pulling forward into a parking stall may seem harmless at the time, but when the ball game's over and everybody comes out at once, you're going to be at a gas-wasting disadvantage trying to back out into the rush. Avoid having to cross bumper-to-bumper lanes—favor parking lots from which you'll want to turn right when you leave. This is especially true at events where crowd members all head for their cars at the same time.

Any Trips

DRESS FOR ECONOMY

Be aware that your fashion boots or steel-toed work shoes are going to affect the operation of that (hopefully, by now)

Illus. 6–1. It's OK to save gas by making your car lighter, but be sure that your rear brakes aren't dragging.

sensitive right foot that feeds gas to your engine. Besides increasing the weight of your foot on the gas, awkward shoes will make it more difficult for you to smoothly move the throttle in order to keep the carburetor accelerator pump from squirting raw gas into your engine.

Avoid making unnecessary work for your air conditioner and heater. It's not efficient for you to wear your business suit while you drive, then expect the air conditioner to cool you off because you're hot—if possible, put your coat on a hanger and take a load off your air conditioner as well as your shoulders. Likewise, wearing light clothes while driving in the winter is not going to make your heater's job any easier. Both the air conditioner and heater use up energy that the engine must work to provide.

LOSE SOME WEIGHT

For every 100 pounds added to your car's weight, your gas mileage will drop by between .1 and .4 miles per gallon.[2] The lighter your car and the more stop-and-go driving you do, the more that extra weight will hold you back. Take a bumper-to-bumper inventory of your car and the extra weight it may be hauling around. Check your trunk for bowling balls, unnecessary tools, patio bricks, empty beer cases, snow tires or chains, vacation left-overs, and anything at all that isn't necessary for the safe operation of the car. Unless you want to chance being stuck with a highway flat, don't plan on losing weight by removing your jack and spare tire. While economy run drivers have been known to remove back seats, bumpers, hub caps, spare tires, jacks, tools, sun visors, ash trays, glove compartment lids, and window washer fluid, don't go to this extreme.

Gasoline weighs 6 pounds per gallon. By carrying only a quarter of a tank on local trips, you can lighten your car by 40 to 120 pounds. If you have a trailer hitch, remove the coupling ball during the off-season—you'll keep the ball brighter and your car lighter. If the hitch is easily bolted on and off, you may even consider removing it when it won't be used for awhile. In the winter, remove accumulated snow from your roof, trunk

and engine lids, and fender wells—wet snow can easily add 100 pounds to the weight you're hauling. If you have a removable luggage rack, take it off and save on both weight and air resistance. While you needn't trade your Saint Bernard for a toy poodle, remember that extra weight uses extra gas.

SNOW TIRES

Snow tires, with their higher rolling resistance, require more gasoline than conventional tires. If you live in an area where you must have snow tires installed much of the year, consider radials instead of the normal variety. While radial snows will still have a thick tread, their tire body construction will facilitate easier rolling and the belts will minimize tread squirming on dry roads. Driving on snow tires, especially the studded type, can be a real waste of tires and gas in high-speed summer driving. In addition, it can be dangerous. The thick tread squirming

Illus. 6–2. This is the most economical place for your snow tires.

against a hot road, combined with flexing of the heavy tire body, can raise tire temperatures above the critical 250°F. level.

If you don't mind a few tire changes during the winter, have your snow tires mounted on their own wheels and put them on yourself only when they're needed. By investing a couple of hours each winter into changing wheels, you can get better gas mileage as well as snow tire life far beyond the normal two years.

OH SAY, CAN YOU SEE?

Driving for economy requires anticipation of what lies ahead and awareness of what is happening around you. If your visibility is poor, you'll tend to be more hesitant, jerky and less economical in your driving. Keep a rag handy for cleaning the headlights, mirrors, and windows. Maintain your windshield washer fluid at the proper level, including anti-freeze in the cold months. If your windshield washer nozzles wash the roof instead of the windshield, use a straight pin to aim them in the right direction. Crack open a side window in the snow or rain to help prevent the windows from frosting up. Don't be one of those lazy drivers who only scrapes snow off the left side of his rear window.

THE RUSH HOUR

If you're forced to drive in rush hour traffic, follow the advice given in Chapter Four. Avoid rush hour traffic by short-cutting, leaving your home or office at off-peak times, or by riding public transportation. Try to work out an arrangement with your boss to allow you to start early and quit early or to start late and quit late. If he doesn't go for that, climb the corporate ladder more quickly by offering to start early and quit late.

No Trips

NON-VACATIONS

Depending on how badly you want to travel, you can save gas by vacationing at home and avoiding confusion, crowds, hucksters, and food poisoning. In addition, you can use the travel money you save in order to buy something you can enjoy all year round. For example, a fireplace, pool table, pinball machine, bowling alley, or dart board, could be purchased depending on the cost of the vacation you don't take.

USING THE PHONE AND MAIL

Many local trips can be handled by using the telephone and mail facilities available in your own home. Checks can be sent to the bank, catalog orders can be placed from the "wish book," you can mail Aunt Emily the hiking socks you knitted for her, and you don't have to be there to pound on the desk when you complain about your electric bill. While you can't use Railway Express to bring Johnny home from his tuba lesson, consider the dial-a-gallon possibility whenever you reach for the car keys.

LEAVE THE DRIVING TO THEM

Public transportation and car pools are other ways to save gasoline, though they each involve costs of their own. Mass transit, when it fits your schedule and your location, can be both practical and desirable. Car pools, like public transportation, require that you depend on others and abandon some of your freedom of movement. However, with increasing governmental pressures—such as penalizing lone commuters with higher toll and parking fees—abandoning some freedom of movement may become preferable to abandoning sizable amounts of your money.

BURNING CALORIES INSTEAD OF GAS

Depending on where you live, walking or cycling may be able to replace many of those 5 mpg short trips in which your car travels only a couple of miles. Bicycles may be equipped with luggage racks and baskets, and the three-wheeled bicycle (tricycle?) for adults comes equipped with a carrying basket larger than the trunks of some sports cars. In addition, the physical fitness and ecology movements are leading the way to commuter bicycle lanes and other means of helping to make bicycles even more practical as a method of local transportation.

That Sunday Drive

When you're Sunday-driving for family or personal relaxation, you may have a difficult time deciding which direction to turn when you reach the highway. The reason is simple—as long as the road is smooth and the scenery enjoyable, you probably don't really care which way you go. If so, here's another tip: go with the wind. By starting the day in the direction the wind's blowing, you'll cut air resistance and do your gas mileage yet another favor. On the way back home, the wind will tend to be more calm, as it normally is in the late afternoon and early evening hours, and you'll have gained some free energy in the process.

In the next chapter, you'll read of an unusual Sunday drive taken by a family of five and their large dog. The family used gas-saving ideas from this and preceding chapters, plus a few that do not lend themselves to everyday use. Besides not stopping for milkshakes, the family broke with tradition in one other way—they got 55 miles per gallon of gas.

7·55 MPG
on a Sunday Drive

"Hey, Pierre; there's a station wagon over there with two people, three kids, and a police dog. Do you think they want to enter the economy run?" "I don't know, Tim. But if they do, we'd better let them—that dog must weigh 100 pounds." So went the opening commentary as the Weiers family prepared for their local sports car club's annual economy run.

Economy Runs

In case you've never heard of an economy run, it's a driving contest in which the fastest driver never wins. The idea is to travel as many miles as you can for each gallon of gas that you use. After you've filled up (and had your gas cap sealed) at the starting point, you drive as economically as possible over a prescribed route, then return to the starting point for a refill. When your car is refueled, the amount of gas is carefully measured, then your performance is converted into miles per gallon. (There's no "I can drive for two weeks on a tankfull" in this league.)

In order to allow all cars, large and small, to compete on an equal footing, economy run planners either group the contestants into classes or award trophies based on ton-miles per gallon. This is simply your miles per gallon multiplied by the number of tons your car weighs. Thus, if you can squeeze 25 miles per gallon from your 4000-pound car, that's 50 ton-miles per gallon—enough to make you a trophy contender.

The rules for an economy run depend on the sponsor, but always require that contestants obey traffic rules which apply to all drivers, economy-runners included. As a further control, competitors are faced with either actual or possible check points to ensure that they are following the prescribed course and staying within the law. Disqualification can be for a number of reasons: 1) if your odometer reading indicates that you didn't travel far enough to complete the required

89

route, 2) if your average speed is less than that required to get you back to the starting point on time, 3) if you tamper with the seal on your gas cap, 4) if you get out of your car for anything except an emergency, or 5) if you receive a traffic citation for any moving violation. Some economy runs even require the presence of an impartial observer to ensure that the driver complies with all the rules of the event and the state in which he is driving.

The economy run we entered used ton-miles per gallon as the method of evaluating the performance of all competitors, included all of the rules just described, and had an initial odometer check to discover if our odometer registered 10 miles after we had covered the first 10 miles.

PREPARATION

Our preparation for the economy run did not deviate much from the advice of the previous chapters. We had already bought for economy: Our car was a Volkswagen Squareback station wagon weighing about 2200 pounds, equipped with Michelin-X steel-belted radials and four-speed manual transmission. The car had always been pampered with the combination of proper-octane gasoline and frequent changes of top-quality engine oil. Just to help ensure that engine resistance was absolutely minimized, a can of anti-friction additive, normally a stranger to the car, joined the brand-new oil in the crankcase.

Normal maintenance operations were carried out slightly ahead of schedule to provide every possible edge for the economy run. On the morning of the event, the following operations were performed: new spark plugs and ignition points were installed; ignition dwell and timing were set. The front end was greased and the rear drum brakes were adjusted to eliminate even a hint of drag. Idle speed was lowered to the minimum required to keep the engine from stalling. Tires were inflated to their maximum allowable pressures as indicated on the sidewall. The car was washed with plain cold water in order to avoid removing that slippery wax. The air cleaner was rinsed out and topped up with fresh oil. Oil was

changed (SAE 10W-40) and the oil strainer cleaned.

BEFORE THE START

During the pre-start registration activities, most competitors stand around and converse while their cars stand around and get cold. The result is a car that has to warm up a little during the first part of the route—not desirable for economy. Until a few minutes before our scheduled starting time, we kept the car's moving parts heated up by driving in the vicinity of the filling station.

In fairness to the service station operator who is providing the facilities for the economy run, it's proper etiquette to show up at the event with a tank that needs some gas. To this end, our 10.6 gallon tank arrived at the pump with barely a half-gallon left. However, our purpose was not entirely altruistic. The day was unseasonably warm—70+ degrees in early March isn't normal in Pennsylvania—and cold gasoline from the underground tank tends to expand as it is heated. As a matter of fact, ten gallons of gasoline will expand by about eight-tenths of a quart when the temperature goes up by 30° F. This is why your tank overflows when you fill up and park on a hot day, and is also the reason for our near-empty tank.

With our full tank of cold (about 40° F.) gasoline expanding by nearly a quart during the afternoon, the fill-up at the end would require that much less, hence increasing our miles per gallon. Had the outside temperature been colder than that of the underground gasoline, our empty-tank strategy would have backfired, leading to shrinking gasoline which would have required a bigger fill-up at the end. If you're thinking about entering an economy run and applying this idea yourself, keep in mind that a quantity of gasoline will expand by seven-tenths of one percent for every 10° F. increase in temperature. Thus, if the temperature of 20 gallons of gasoline were to increase by 10° F., the resulting volume of gasoline would be 20×1.007, or 20.14 gallons, an increase of .14 gallons—not much by everyday standards, but quite significant in a hotly-contested economy run.

Christopher Columbus would have appreciated our happiness at knowing the route in advance. Besides providing an opportunity to take a practice run, this made it less likely for us to get lost. In two of the preceding three years we had become hopelessly lost and either finished too late or had to drive uneconomically in order to return to the start on time. As it was, with a map and full set of instructions, I still managed to go off course twice during my solo practice trip.

Just before leaving the station, we double-checked the route instructions, then had our tank filled to the brim. During the filling process, the car was shaken from side to side in order to avoid the formation of costly air pockets in the tank. (You can't travel many miles on a gallon of trapped air.) Before starting our engine to leave the station, we waited until passing traffic was clear—this enabled us to move directly onto the road without losing momentum.

ON THE ROAD

As we turned right and headed up the hill, we accelerated at a rate that wouldn't have snapped a giraffe's neck. Taking advantage of the low speed, we lowered the radio antenna and folded back the side mirrors in order to lower air resistance—making these modifications back at the station would have been embarrassing. After all, who in his right mind would take three kids and a dog on an economy run, then lower the antenna to save gas? The flow-through ventilation vents were opened wide on both sides of the dash. It was taken for granted that we would minimize air resistance by keeping the side windows up whenever the car was moving.

Having reached 4th gear and 35 miles per hour, we merged onto the four-lane section of the run—along this route, the minimum speed was posted as 40 mph. Except for the times when gravity made us go faster, the speedometer was glued to 40 mph for the next half-hour. The best speed control device going is a steady right foot—minus shoe, of course, for a better "feel" of the gas pedal.

Finally leaving the four-lane road, we encountered gradually rolling hills and a string of traffic signals. The engine was always shut off whenever a signal didn't go our way, then restarted as we slowly accelerated back to our desirable cruising speed of about 35 mph. Whenever possible, the car was driven 25–30 mph in 4th gear. This is difficult for many small cars, but the combination of electronic fuel injection for engine smoothness and radial tires for low rolling resistance made it seem that we were moving almost without effort. However, since we had to average about 32 miles per hour in order to make it back to the starting point on time, speeds below 30 were a luxury we couldn't afford to enjoy for too long.

Continuing along the curvy back roads, it was possible to cruise smoothly without braking and to climb most hills without gearing down. Naturally, the brake was avoided as though it were a land mine. Having had the chance to make a practice run the week before, we were aware of the terrain and the various obstacles to our maintaining a slow and constant speed. For example, knowing in advance that a stop sign would be around the next curve made it possible to begin slowing down earlier and use less gas until we got there. In addition, knowledge of the conditions ahead made it easier to keep to 30–35 mph in 4th and to make gradual increases as we knew they would be necessary.

From time to time, our low but legal rate of speed would attract followers. Whenever possible, we pulled to the right to allow them to pass. Whenever impossible, we maintained speed while I pretended that my right foot was paralyzed. At these times, the presence of the dog in the back window helped to entertain the people behind and sustain their patience. (The kids' puppet show probably helped, too.) When pressured from behind, the temptation to speed up and waste gas becomes very strong—feeling as though we had to do something about it, we sometimes pretended to be looking for a turn-off or house number as we continued along at a constant speed.

At times, we would come up behind other Sunday drivers who were either trying for super-economy or were in no hurry to reach their destination. But then, that's what Sunday driving is all about. We passed them as soon and as gently as we could. Although economy-run competitors were assigned to leave the starting point at three-minute intervals, we were passed by two or three who roared by as if they were less interested in winning than in the free gas provided by the sponsor at the end of the run.

About three-fourths of the way through the 96 mile route, we were directed to enter a weighing station in order to find out how many tons our car weighed. This was to be used in the ton-miles-per-gallon calculation to be made at the finish. Our station wagon, including driver and assorted occupants, weighed in at 3010 pounds. While stopped on the scale, we relaxed and opened the side windows for some air. Because of our very constant speeds and the ability of the engine to pull smoothly, our extra weight (which included a 40-pound trailer hitch) seemed to be doing very little damage to our economy.

Throughout the trip, the family portion of the family drive was up to par, with the kids playing, eating, and looking for various farm animals along the way. Canine companion Schultzie was also interested in the farm animals, and would sometimes disrupt driving-for-economy with her loud challenges to them from the safety of her (slowly) moving car. Besides providing directions, the navigator planned different treats and games for the various legs of the course. The most popular diversion was the "it's my turn to get in back with the dog" game. The second most popular diversion was the "it's your turn to get in back with the dog" game.

AT THE FINISH

We had just driven 96 miles at the most economical speeds possible and had used every trick in this book to maximize our miles per gallon. Like many other Sunday drivers, we had covered a scenic route at a more relaxed pace—however, our arrival back home was probably a bit more tense than that of other families on the road that day. Back at the station, contestants were already beginning to cluster around the gas pumps to peek at the number of gallons required by their fellow competitors. Over the protests of drivers who claimed their tanks were already full, event officials squeezed in ever more gas in order to reach the generous pre-run tank level for each car.

Poke-alongs that we were, ours was one of the last cars to return. Stopping at the pump, we watched and took our turn objecting as officials unsealed the gas cap and filled the tank to its initial level. After an economy run, every drop spilled looks like a gallon. Considering the distance covered, nobody was surprised when the pump reading passed the one-gallon mark—after all this was a station wagon, not a motorcycle. What was surprising to onlookers and rewarding to us was that the tank satisfied its thirst after only 1.75 gallons, a quantity which indicated that we had obtained 54.7 miles per gallon.

When combined with our weight of 3010 pounds (1.5 tons), our performance was calculated as 82.2 ton-miles per gallon—enough to put us in first place. The runner-up's aerodynamic Opel GT had actually delivered 2.5 more mpg, but its lighter (by 520 pounds) weight meant less bulk hauled around the course, leaving him with 71.1 ton-miles per gallon. The first-place trophy was accepted with thanks and apologies for not having done better—we probably could have gotten another 5 miles per gallon if only the dog's harness hadn't broken just as we were clearing the top of a hill.

8 · Trucks, Recreational and Other Vehicles

Air, rolling, acceleration, gravity, and engine resistance are universal forces which really don't care what type of vehicle is trying to fight them. For this reason, many of the buying, driving, maintaining, and planning guidelines offered earlier in the book will apply to the 50 ton over-the-road truck as well as to the 500 pound motorcycle and rider combination.

Long Haul Trucks

Considering their loads, long-distance trucks are already economical. For example, if a truck with a 50 ton gross weight achieves just 4 miles per gallon, it has delivered 200 ton-miles per gallon—two and a half times the performance of the author's economy-run-winning car in its 82 ton-miles per gallon effort. However, despite its efficiency at hauling loads, the long-haul truck can be made to do even better.

ENGINE

Three-fourths of the nation's long distance trucks are already diesel powered, with the proportion likely to increase in the future, so the Chapter 9 commentary on the diesel engine will apply to these vehicles as well as to passenger cars.

Fig. A1–1. A typical diesel truck engine.

Fig. A1-2.

Engine Tuning

While the diesel engine doesn't require the periodic attention that a gasoline engine needs, there are two important checks which can help to maintain the truck diesel's efficiency—the air intake check and the overhead (valves and injectors) adjustment. The intake air restriction should be checked against restriction limits specified by the engine manufacturer. A dirty air cleaner or other blockage of the intake system can reduce fuel economy just as effectively as in a passenger car. In addition to checking the valves and injectors at recommended intervals, be sure that fuel pressure and governor settings haven't changed slightly over the miles. According to the Cummins Engine Company, a 10% in-

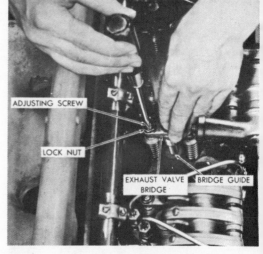

Fig. A1-3. Adjusting the valves on a diesel truck engine.

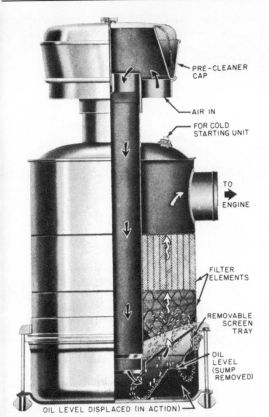

Fig. A1-4. Regularly checking air intake is very important for truck economy. Shown is a typical diesel air cleaner—much more complex than the one in a car.

Fig. A1-5. The temperature controlled fan on a diesel truck engine.

crease in power caused by a too-high fuel pressure or governor setting can result in the consumption of 15% more fuel.[1]

Temperature Controlled Fan

As in a passenger car, the engine fan consumes a significant amount of horsepower even when it's not needed. At 60 miles per hour, it requires about 5% of the engine's rated horsepower just to turn the radiator fan.[2] Driving a 28 inch cooling fan at 2300 RPM drains 14 horsepower away from the output of the engine.[3] Depending on the vehicle, engine, and gearing, the installation of a temperature-controlled fan can reduce fuel costs by 3 to 6%.[4]

Derate the Engine

If the engine already has power to spare for the job it's doing, fuel savings can be achieved by derating the engine to a lower horsepower. However, the engine should not be derated to the point where it will not be able to maintain a cruising speed in top gear. As an example of the fuel saving possible with the derating of an engine, the Cummins Engine Company found that fuel savings were 2.3% when a 290 horsepower engine was derated to 255 horsepower.[5] While derating the engine will usually increase fuel economy, it will also tend to increase the time required to make a given trip. However, when derating is combined with other measures designed to reduce engine, air and rolling resistance, the same level of performance can be maintained.

Reduce Engine RPM

Because the engine is more efficient at lower speeds (down to 1800 rpm), fuel economy will increase significantly provided that the truck has enough power to maintain cruising speed at the new RPM setting. However, the 8–10% fuel saving possible for some vehicle-engine-gearing combinations may be offset by 5–6% increase in time required for a given trip.[6]

Turbocharge the Engine

Besides raising engine performance, a turbocharging kit can reduce exhaust smoke, engine noise, and fuel consumption. The turbocharger pumps more air

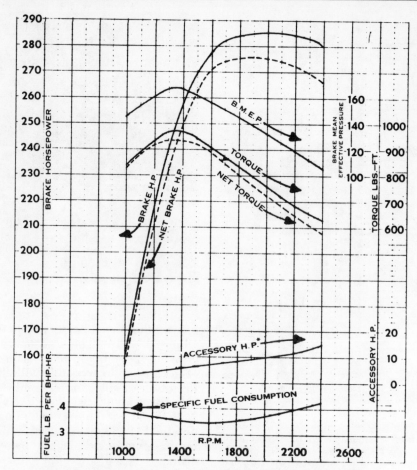

*NOTE: ACCESSORY HORSEPOWER CURVE SHOWN WITH THERMO-STATICALLY CONTROLLED FAN OPERATING AT MINIMUM POWER

Fig. A1–6. This chart shows the exact effect of derating a diesel engine from 325 hp. to 385 hp. Both torque and horsepower are slightly reduced, but derated engines run more economically, longer, and cleaner than engines rated at full power. *Source:* Mack Trucks, Inc.

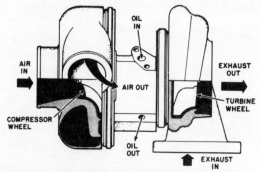

Fig. A1–7. How an exhaust driven turbocharger works.

into the cylinder in order to allow a larger quantity of fuel to be burned in the combustion chamber. The energy of the exhaust gases are used to drive the tur-

bocharger blower. As an example of the efficiency gained by this modification, Cummins found that installation of their turbocharger on one truck increased its miles per gallon by 4.2% and reduced trip time by .4%.[7]

DRIVING

Slow Down

Driving more slowly is helpful only when efficient use can be made of top gear. When engine speed drops too low, it will be necessary to gear down and cruise uneconomically at high engine RPM. On trucks presently in operation, longer trip times are necessary in order to save fuel by cruising below the truck's maximum speed. The following table represents Cummins findings on the effect of reduced speed on a 65,000 pound GCW, 13.5-foot van tractor/semi-trailer combination: [8]

Engine	Geared Speed at 2100 rpm	Cruise Speed Limit	Engine rpm at Cruise	Avg. Speed (mph)	Fuel Econ. (mpg)
Super-250	59 mph	none	2100	54.9	4.51
		55 mph	1950	50.9	4.86
		50 mph	1780	47.1	5.10
NTC-290	64 mph	none	2100	59.5	4.26
		60 mph	1970	56.9	4.60
		55 mph	1800	52.0	4.93
NTC-350	70 mph	none	2100	64.7	3.85
		65 mph	1950	60.4	4.35
		60 mph	1800	56.9	4.60

Minimize Idling

As with passenger cars, excessive idling will waste truck fuel. In addition to the loss of fuel, idling times in excess of five minutes may foul the injectors and cause the engine to be less efficient when returning to highway speeds.[9]

Maintain Momentum and Make Gradual Speed Changes

Because of a truck's great mass of weight, it becomes more important to maintain steady speeds, to anticipate stops and slow-downs, and to accelerate as gradually as possible. As with passenger cars, over-revving in the lower gears hurts fuel mileage more than it helps acceleration.

LOWERING RESISTANCES

Lower Air Resistance

A truck's large frontal area causes a proportionate increase in air resistance at highway speeds compared with an automobile. Truck trailers with over 100 square feet of frontal area are not unusual. In addition to the normal resistance of frontal area, the sudden change in shape between the cab and trailer and the gap between the cab and trailer both contribute to total air resistance. One de-

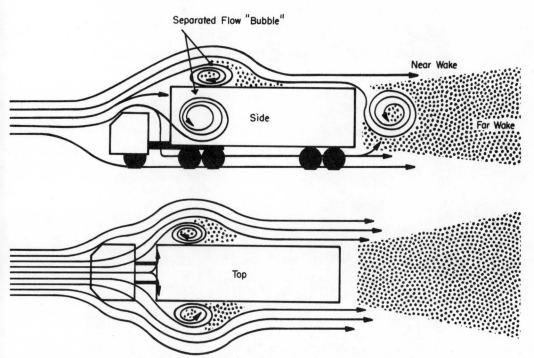

Fig. A1–8. These drawings show a truck's path through air. Note in both drawings that even though air flows smoothly over the windshield area, it then strikes the large frontal area of the trailer.

vice which can lower air resistance on present trucks is a wind deflector mounted on the roof of the cab, with the purpose of re-directing air toward the top of the trailer instead of allowing it to hit the trailer's box-shaped front. Another streamlining device is the "vortex stabilizer" designed to smooth the passage of air past the gap between the cab and trailer. With both devices added to a typical tractor-van combination, air resistance can be lowered by 20%, and fuel consumption reduced by about 5%.[10]

Since air resistance is proportionate to a truck's frontal area, reducing the height of the trailer hauled will increase fuel economy accordingly. This is especially promising when the trailer being used is rarely loaded to the top—a lower trailer can be used in these cases. In one study, lowering trailer height from 13.5 feet to 11.0 feet resulted in 4.7% lower fuel consumption.[11]

Lower Rolling Resistance

As with passengers cars, the use of radial tires will decrease truck rolling resistance by about 30% when compared to conventional bias-ply tires. The lower rolling resistance of radial truck tires can deliver 8–10% more miles per gallon.[12] Proper vehicle wheel alignment and the use of wide-base single tires instead of duals are other paths to lower rolling resistance and better economy.

Other Economies

Another means of reducing truck fuel consumption is to use single drive axles whenever horsepower and traction requirements permit. Each drive axle will absorb about 5% of the total power being transmitted to the road, thus making possible fuel savings of about 3% when a single axle is chosen instead of tandems.[13] These savings become even

Fig. A1–9. In this photograph a wind deflector is mounted on the cab roof and a vortex stabilizer is mounted on the front of the trailer.

more significant when frequent curves and sharp turns are encountered.

When a truck is purchased, attention to the proper combination of engine transmission, and axle ratio can ensure the best possible fuel economy for the driving conditions to be encountered. As a general rule, it's better to operate a larger engine at lower RPM than to run a smaller engine at full RPM in order to maintain the same cruising speed. Unlike conventional passenger car engines, truck diesels become more efficient at lower engine speeds. In order to cruise efficiently at 60 mph, a truck might be geared and powered so that it is able to cruise at 70. This gives top gear enough power reserve to enable it to maintain economical cruising speed on slight grades without frequent downshifting.

A strategy for using less fuel rather than just increasing miles per gallon is to increase a truck's payload and make fewer trips. This is where payload ton-miles per gallon becomes important. (In the economy run of Chapter Seven, I would have needed over 500 miles per gallon in order to match the payload ton-mile per gallon capability of a long-haul truck moving 50,000 pounds at 5 miles per gallon. That would be a real challenge.)

As an example of the effect of increased payload on fuel required, consider the example of a truck required to shuffle 12,600,000 pounds of freight over a 200 mile route.[14] (See above.)

Payload Pounds per Trip	Number of Trips Needed	Miles per Gallon	Gallons per Ton of Freight Hauled
25,000	504	4.64	3.46
30,000	420	4.55	2.93
35,000	360	4.45	2.56
40,000	315	4.36	2.30
45,000	280	4.28	2.08

As these figures indicate, the fuel savings from increasing payload are greater than those generated by other methods. Although miles per gallon performance decreases, the number of gallons used goes down a great deal faster.

Combined Measures

As an example of the possible effects of a combination of fuel saving steps applied in stages to a typical vehicle, the Cummins Engine Company has determined the effects of the modifications shown below.[15]

This last modification needs further clarification. Several manufacturers have come out with diesels designed to produce constant horsepower over a wide range of engine rpm. Because higher turbulence in the combustion chambers permits efficient operation at a lower rpm, these engines can operate well below the normal speed range and save fuel ordinarily burned up in engine friction.

Baseline Truck	TRIP TIME SAVED		FUEL SAVED	
	Change	Total Change	Change	Total Change
6 x 4 Tractor/13.5 ft. van. 70,000 lb, geared for 63 mph (4.11 axle, 10.00 x 22 tires), NTC-290	BASE		BASE	
Add steel-belted radial tires	+2.5% = 2.5%		+8.1% = 8.1%	
Add wind deflector/vortex stabilizer	+1.1% = 3.6%		+6.8% = 14.9%	
Add temperature modulated fan	+1.0% = 4.6%		+6.2% = 21.1%	
Derate to 270 hp @ 2100 rpm	−2.6% = 2.0%		+5.3% = 26.4%	
Derate to 1950 rpm, use 3.70 axle	+1.0% = 3.0%		+4.1% = 30.5%	
Use NTC-350, 3.55 axle, Impose 64 mph max. speed	−3.0% = 0%		+5.5% = 36.0%	

Gasoline Powered Trucks

Smaller trucks, generally powered by gasoline engines, can also benefit from the air and rolling resistance measures described in the preceding section. In addition, their gasoline engines require the more frequent checks and adjustments described for passenger car engines in Chapter Five. As with any heavy vehicle, gasoline powered trucks must be driven at steady speeds and with gradual acceleration if they are to deliver their best economy. The large frontal area of any truck causes sharply reduced mileage at higher speeds, during which the usual lack of streamlining becomes a greater consumer of horsepower.

The prospective buyer of a gasoline powered truck would do well to consider the purchase of a truck powered by a diesel engine. Depending on the type of application used, the diesel can be a real fuel saver. The amount saved will depend on a number of factors, including loads, speeds, and amount of time spent idling. For example, a typical gasoline engine will idle for about 50 minutes on a gallon of fuel, whereas a diesel engine of the same horsepower will idle for up to four hours on the same amount.[16] The more time spent in stop-and-go operation and idling, the more fuel will be saved with the diesel engine. In tests conducted by the U. S. Post Office Department, under postal operation conditions, a 5-ton diesel truck had double the fuel mileage, and half-ton and 1-ton diesel trucks had 50% greater fuel mileage than gasoline trucks of the same size.[17] Further discussion of the diesel engine is included in Chapter 9.

Fig. A1–10. When buying a motor home, look for one that at least makes an attempt at streamlining. While not a sports car, this model will have relatively low air resistance because of its sloped front section.

Recreational Vehicles and Trailers

MOTOR HOMES

The motor home buyer, when making his choice, should especially consider vehicles which make some attempt at streamlining, and which have a small frontal area relative to their inside space. The weight of most motor homes necessitates a heavy chassis and the use of truck tires. For this reason, the addition of radial truck tires can add about 10% to the miles per gallon of a motor home. The sheer weight of a motor home makes it desirable to travel at steady speeds for the purpose of minimizing acceleration resistance. For this reason, a larger engine may actually provide better economy by allowing the driver to maintain his speed on slight grades. Since most motor homes are equipped with an automatic transmission, which "locks up" and becomes more efficient at higher speeds, the momentum-saving ability of the

Fig. A1–11.

larger engine becomes even more desirable. Like his truck driving counterparts, the motor home driver can profit from most of the driving, maintaining, and planning strategies discussed earlier in the book. In addition, the driver of a motor home may especially benefit from the installation of a miles per gallon gauge such as that described in Chapter Three.

TRAILERS

Like motor homes, trailers come in assorted shapes and sizes. The most economical trailers to pull are those which collapse for less air resistance on the road—these are the so-called tent-trailers which, depending on the manufacturer and price, may or may not consist of an actual tent. Many are cranked up into position at the campground while others require a bit of do-it-yourself in order to raise the roof. If you're thinking of buying a non-collapsible trailer, avoid showroom fever and buy one just large enough for your needs, preferably a unit with small frontal area and at least token streamlining.

When pulling any trailer, remember that anticipation of stops, gradual acceleration, and steady speeds are even more important than when driving in the car alone. During a trip across the Midwest, our economy-run car pulled a collapsible tent trailer at steady 65 mph speeds and delivered 27 miles per gallon in the pro-

cess. During acceleration and hill climbing, the 4000 pound weight of the car-trailer combination would have pulled gas mileage down to the teens or low twenties, but steady speed on a level road was very economically maintained. For safety as well as low rolling resistance, keep the trailer tires inflated to the proper pressure. Since gas station tower gauges are notoriously inaccurate, carry your own pressure gauge in order to avoid improper inflation pressures that could damage either your tires or your fuel bill.

Motorcycles

Motorcycles already travel great distances on a gallon of gas, but can still benefit from proper maintenance, gentle riding, and reasonable planning. For prospective car buyers, a good question might be: "Can you make do with a motorcycle?" According to the Motorcycle Industry Council, a cycle in the under 100 cc engine displacement category can get 90 miles per gallon without much effort, a 100–200 cc bike about 65 mpg, a 200–300 cc around 50 mpg, and 300 cc and up approximately 40 mpg, depending on the conditions under which it is used.[18] Since the preceding figures include some off-road riding, even greater

Fig. A1–12. A touring type motorcycle with windshield and fairing attached. Besides streamlining, such devices add to driver comfort on the road.

economy could be expected in smooth road, commuting operation.

With the possible exception of installing a windshield, there is little that the motorcycle rider can do to reduce his already low air resistance. Rolling resistance may be higher for knobby tires than for the relatively smooth street tires, thus making the trail bike a little less economical than the street model. In addition, trail bikes usually have larger rear sprockets and are geared for higher engine speeds in any gear at a given road speed. For more miles per gallon from a vehicle that is already very good, get a street bike, then drive and maintain it for economy.

The Motorcycle Industry Council has estimated the cost of operating a motorcycle as approximately $420 per year, compared to the nearly $1190 yearly cost of operating a car—both figures include depreciation, repairs, gasoline, and all other costs of ownership.[19]

Other Motorized Vehicles

Other vehicles—e.g., golf carts, snowmobiles, go-carts, riding mowers, tractors, and farm machinery—should be purchased with the intention of getting the smallest and lightest vehicle that will do the job required. Driving or riding any of these vehicles involves little air resistance, but may include relatively great rolling, engine, or gravity resistance. Minimum acceptable engine speed settings should always be used and speed and acceleration kept to a moderate level. As with any motor-powered vehicle, miles per gallon, snowdrifts per gallon, or lawns per gallon will depend largely on the quality and frequency of the maintenance provided.

9 · Alternate Power Sources

Most of today's cars are powered by the conventional internal combustion engine that has been around for more than 80 years. During this time, it has provided dependable service and reached a very high state of development. However, increasingly tight emission control requirements, combined with the constraints of technology, weight, economy, and driveability, have caused it to face increased competition from other actual and potential sources of automotive power. Some of the alternative engines described are in actual use. Others are in the experimental stage, but have some degree of promise for future use.

Some of the alternatives are based on the four-cycle principle of the conventional engine, a principle that is illustrated in figure A2-1. During the intake stroke, the intake valve opens and the moving piston draws an air-fuel mixture into the cylinder. As the crankshaft continues to rotate, the intake valve closes and the piston moves upward to compress the air-fuel mixture for improved burning. The power stroke occurs after the mixture explodes, forcing the piston downward. Finally, the exhaust valve opens and the piston moves upward to push the exhaust gases from the cylinder.

Wankel Rotary Engine

The Wankel rotary engine, named after its inventor, is an internal combustion engine which operates on the same four cycles as the conventional engine just described. However, instead of using pistons which travel back and forth in their cylinders, the Wankel engine has a triangular rotor with sections removed in order to form three combustion chambers. The corners of the rotor are in constant contact with the walls of the egg-shaped housing in which it turns. The rotor is connected to the crankshaft by means of internal gears, and when rotating inside the housing, resembles a triangular flying saucer trying to escape from a hockey rink. As the rotor turns, its three

103

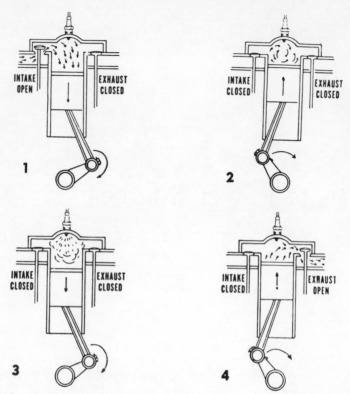

Fig. A2–1. Although you won't find this T-head engine in your car, it presents a clear view of the intake, compression, power and exhaust strokes of the conventional piston engine. *Source:* Champion Spark Plug Company.

sealing corners form three separate combustion chambers which are constantly changing in size in order to bring about the four cycles of intake, compression, power, and exhaust. As a combustion chamber passes the intake port, it picks up an air-fuel mixture. As it continues its journey, it reduces in size and compresses the mixture it is carrying. A little further along, the spark plug ignites the mixture and causes it to push the rotor around still further until the exhaust gases can escape through a fixed exhaust port. The combustion chambers continuously chase each other around the egg-shaped housing and result in three power strokes during each rotation of the crankshaft—power delivery is so smooth as to be almost continuous. Some Wankel engines have more than one rotor and provide an even smoother power flow along with their higher output.

The Wankel engine enjoys a number of advantages over its conventional piston counterpart. With only two major parts, the rotor and the crankshaft, its construction is simple and its mass production likely to be inexpensive. For a given horsepower output, it is much smaller and lighter. In addition, it will burn fuel of a much lower octane rating than can be tolerated in today's conventional engines. These advantages enable designers to construct smaller, lighter, roomier, lower, more powerful and better handling cars than would be possible with a conventional engine.

However, the Wankel is not without its problems. One drawback is its thirst for fuel—according to the Environmental Protection Agency, the fuel economy of a Wankel engine is about 35% worse than a conventionally powered vehicle of the same weight.[1] However, this is slightly misleading, since any given car with a transplanted Wankel engine would have equal or better performance and be lighter than the same car with a conventional engine. A problem in past Wankels has been the rotor seals which prevent

How the Rotary Engine Works

1. Intake.

Fuel/air mixture is drawn into combustion chamber by revolving rotor through intake port (upper left). No valves or valve-operating mechanism needed.

2. Compression.

As rotor continues revolving, it reduces space in chamber containing fuel and air. This compresses mixture.

3. Ignition.

Fuel/air mixture now fully compressed. Leading sparkplug fires. A split-second later, following plug fires to assure complete combustion.

4. Exhaust.

Exploding mixture drives rotor, providing power. Rotor then expels gases through exhaust port.

Mazda s rotary engine licensed by NSU-WANKEL.

Fig. A2–2.

gases from traveling from one combustion chamber to the next. However, rotor seals are an engineering matter which should be under control by now; and improved economy via two-stage combustion (similar to that of stratified charge piston engines), could mean the beginning of a Wankel revolution.

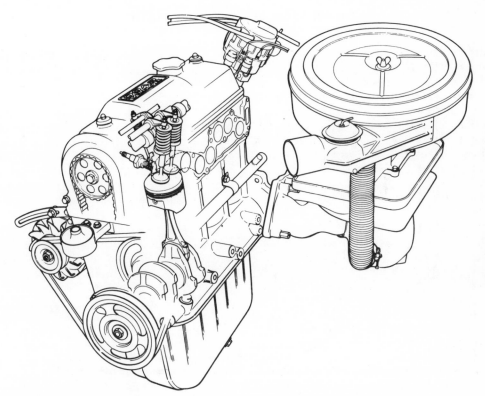

Fig. A2–3. Key components of the Honda CVCC stratified charge engine. *Source:* American Honda Motor Company.

Stratified Charge Engine

With one difference, the stratified charge engine is exactly the same as the conventional piston engine. However, the difference is an important one, as are its effects. In an emission-controlled conventional engine, a lean mixture is desired in order to reduce the output of carbon monoxide and hydrocarbons. On the other hand, a relatively rich mixture is desirable in order to reduce emissions of nitrogen oxides. Since a conventional engine can't have a rich mixture and a lean mixture at the same time, the result is the multitude of hang-on emission control pumps, hoses, and other gadgets you see in your engine compartment.

The stratified charge engine does the one thing that a conventional engine can't do—have a rich mixture and a lean mixture at the same time. One such stratified charge engine is the CVCC (Com-

pound Vortex Controlled Combustion) engine developed by Honda and illustrated in figure A2-3.[2] As the sketch shows, it is similar in construction to the conventional engine on which it is based. The big difference, however, is in the cylinder head—besides having two intake valves instead of one, it also contains a small pre-chamber beside the spark plug.

The idea of a stratified-charge engine is to ignite a small amount of rich mixture which then spreads the flame to a large amount of lean mixture. The result is a simultaneous lowering of hydrocarbons, carbon monoxide, and nitrogen oxide emissions at the same time—something that the conventional engine is unable to do without the hang-on devices. Figure A2-4 shows the extent to which the Honda CVCC is able to lower total emissions compared to a conventional engine.

The operation of the CVCC engine is shown in figure A2-5. During the intake stroke, the small intake valve introduces

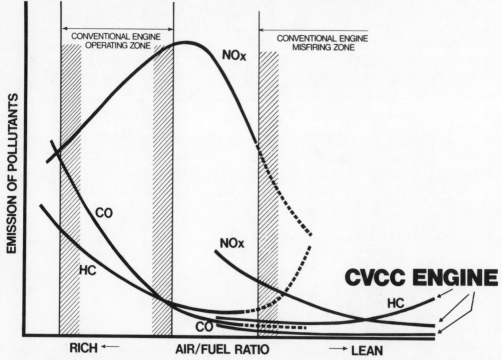

Emission Characteristics vs. Air-Fuel Ratio

Fig. A2–4. Honda CVCC engine reflects advantages of stratified charge design, which include low emissions and good driveability. *Source:* American Honda Motor Company.

a small amount of rich mixture near the spark plug, while the normal intake valve brings in a large quantity of lean mixture. The compression stroke then keeps the rich mixture near the spark plug and forces a little mixing between the rich and lean sections, thus providing three mixture strengths—rich at the top, moderate in the middle, and lean at the bottom. The spark plug easily ignites the rich mixture, which gradually passes the flame along to the leaner sections below and provides the power stroke. During this period, the lean mixture continues to burn slowly and the temperature of the burning gas is held at a high level over a relatively long time. The result is an engine which operates happily on a very lean overall mixture—something that the conventional engine can't do without severe driveability problems.

Another type of stratified charge engine is the open chamber design (e.g.,

Ford's PROCO engine), in which the idea is the same, but the pre-chamber is not used. Either engine produces good economy and driveability with low emissions and little need for further pollution devices to control hydrocarbons, nitrogen oxides, and carbon monoxide. According to the Environmental Protection Agency, the pre-chamber stratified charge engine will deliver fuel economy at least equivalent to conventional engines, while the open chamber stratified charge design is expected to provide a 12% improvement.[3]

Diesel Engine

While the conventional engine relies on ignition spark to ignite the fuel-air mixture in the cylinder, the diesel engine

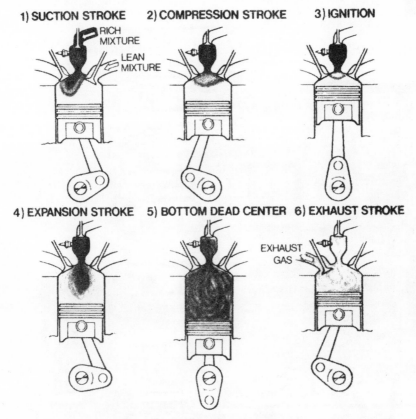

Fig. A2–5. Operating cycle of the stratified charge engine depends on igniting a small amount of rich mixture, which then proceeds to ignite a large amount of lean mixture. *Source:* American Honda Motor Company.

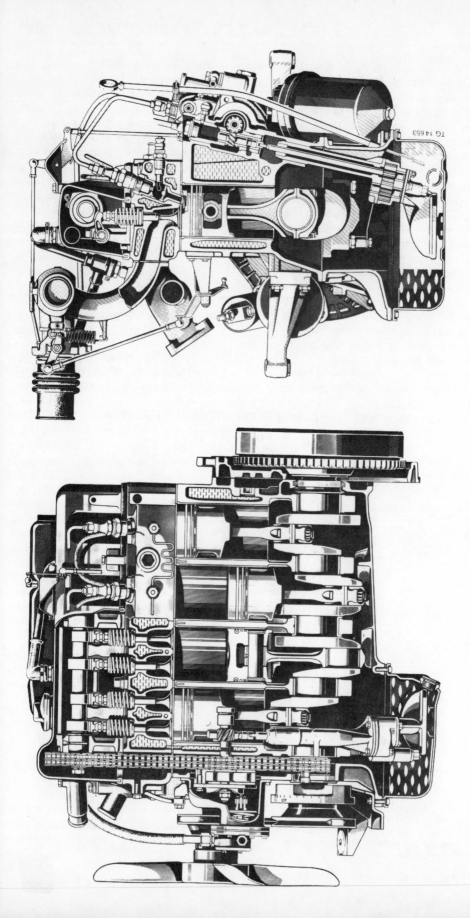

Fig. A2–6. Inside view of the economical Mercedes-Benz 240D diesel engine. *Source:* Mercedes-Benz of North America.

uses a very high compression ratio (often over 20:1) to squeeze the intake air until it can ignite fuel from its own heat. Although the engine is otherwise similar in construction to a gasoline engine, its parts must be more rugged in order to withstand the greater loads and rougher combustion imposed by the high compression pressures. Since the diesel engine has no carburetor to pre-mix air and fuel, air comes in through a normal intake manifold and the fuel enters by way of an injector in the cylinder head. This allows fuel entry to be carefully timed, thus preventing pre-ignition. A typical injector sprays fuel into the combustion chamber or pre-combustion chamber just as the piston is nearing its uppermost position during the compression stroke.

The biggest advantage of the diesel engine is its economy. According to the Environmental Protection Agency, a diesel will obtain from 40–70% better fuel mileage than a gasoline engine.[4] Since the diesel has a much higher compression ratio, it will burn fuel more completely and convert more of the available fuel energy into horsepower. An additional advantage is that a gallon of diesel fuel contains more energy than a gallon of gasoline—an average of 137,750 BTU per gallon compared to only 123,500 for gasoline.[5] The Cummins Engine Company has estimated the diesel vs. gasoline "savings ratio" for various types of truck operation. Either the number of no-load to full-load cycles per day or the per cent of time spent idling can determine the fuel savings of a diesel compared to a gasoline engine as estimated by the following table: [6]

Thus, if a diesel truck were to completely start and stop 150 times a day, it would get between three and four times the fuel mileage of a gasoline powered truck operated under the same conditions. Low speed operation makes the diesel's advantage even greater. For example, in steady speed tests at 30 mph, the Mercedes-Benz 220D sedan achieved 51 miles per gallon versus the gasoline-powered U. S. 220 sedan's 23 miles per gallon, an improvement of over 100%.[7]

Because the diesel has neither ignition system nor a carburetor, there are no spark plugs, contact points, condensers, coils, or ignition wires to replace or maintain. The fuel injection system which replaces the carburetor is, like the rest of the engine, relatively maintenance-free. Other diesel advantages are improved durability and driveability. With emission controls making other engines balky and uneven-running, the diesel's high compression design and controlled distribution of fuel enables it to meet emission standards with ease.

Disadvantages of the diesel engine for passenger cars include low horsepower per weight and displacement, slow acceleration, occasional hard-starting in sub-zero temperatures, a more crucial demand on oil quality (diesel fuel often contains sulphur), an inherently noisy combustion process, exhaust smoke under certain operating conditions, and a slightly higher (about $200 more for the Mercedes) initial cost than for a gasoline engine. However, as gasoline engines become more complicated and expensive, this cost differential is almost sure to decrease.

Diesel fuel Saving Ratio	No load-full load cycles per day	(or)	% Time spent Idling
1.5	0–50		Less than 20%
1.5–2.0	50–100		20%
2.0–2.5	100–125		40%
2.5–3.0	125–150		60%
3.0–4.0	over 150		80%

Other Possible Power Sources

While the conventional, Wankel, stratified-charge, and diesel engines are the most likely to be used in automobiles of the near future, there are other, more long-term possibilities. These include the gas turbine, battery, fuel cell, various

Source: The *VW Autoist*, official publication of the Volkswagen Club of America.

hybrid engines combining two or more different sources of power, Stirling, Rankine, and steam engines. Each has its proponents and opponents as well as possible application in cars a decade away. However, we aren't likely to be driving cars powered by them in the very near future.

Regarding sources of fuel, an interesting possibility is the ultrasonic emulsification of fuel with up to 25% water just prior to combustion. The technique has been used to reduce fuel consumption in boilers by 20%, and may have application to home furnaces and automobiles.[8] It's believed that the improved combustion results from the vaporizing water droplets aiding the vaporization of adjacent oil droplets. Similar research is now being conducted on some U.S. Post Office Department trucks to determine if water-emulsified fuel can improve gas mileage and reduce exhaust emissions.[9] Instead of stepping on the gas in our car of the future, maybe we'll have to bang on the radiator pipes.

10 · 125 Ways to Improve Your Gas Mileage

1. Buy a lighter car.
2. Consider buying a subcompact station wagon.
3. Choose a car with small frontal area.
4. Choose a streamlined car.
5. Get the standard engine.
6. Buy a diesel powered car.
7. Get a car with a manual transmission.
8. Order an economy rear axle ratio.
9. Specify an overdrive transmission if available.
10. Avoid power steering, power brakes, and other power accessories.
11. Don't order air conditioning.
12. Be your own automatic speed control.
13. Avoid trailer towing packages which include a numerically higher axle ratio.
14. Avoid the permanent roof rack.
15. Buy radial tires.
16. Use proper octane gas—but don't overbuy.
17. Don't fill 'er up all the way.
18. Use good engine oil of proper viscosity.
19. If you can't afford radials, get belted bias ply tires.
20. Avoid wide-tread tires.
21. Rustproofing adds weight, Rust subtracts weight; take your choice.
22. Add anti-friction compound to the engine oil.
23. Buy an electronic ignition system if you don't intend to tune your car regularly.
24. Replace a worn out exhaust system with a free-flow type.
25. Install a temperature controlled or variable pitch radiator fan.
26. Install a vacuum gauge or miles per gallon meter.
27. Drive slowly.
28. Maintain steady speeds.
29. Don't brake when travelling uphill.
30. Accelerate gradually.
31. Brake sparingly on level roads and downhill.
32. Pass and merge smoothly.
33. Hold the steering wheel steady.
34. Make a lane change to retract the disc brake pads slightly.

35. Don't pump the gas pedal.

36. Don't activate the secondary carburetor barrel(s).

37. Practice moving the gas pedal until you know what it takes to avoid activating the accelerator pump.

38. Keep the windows up when moving.

39. Turn the heater fan off when travelling over 50 mph.

40. Use the air conditioner sparingly.

41. Avoid the breakfast table warm-up.

42. Turn the engine off at long red lights and delays.

43. Avoid unnecessary use of any electrical accessories.

44. On crowded two lane roads, turn left to reverse direction.

45. Make that difficult left turn by turning right.

46. Use the brakes, not Reverse, to stop before backing.

47. Use the brakes, not 1st or Drive, to stop after backing.

48. With a manual transmission, skip a gear during downhill starts.

49. Drift for a few feet before applying gas during downhill starts.

50. Don't accelerate uphill except in emergencies.

51. With an automatic transmission, attack hills briskly, gradually press the gas to maintain momentum.

52. When climbing a hill in a light car, allow the speed to drop off and regain momentum on the way down.

53. Read signs and terrain to anticipate conditions ahead.

54. "Read" the timing of stop lights ahead and anticipate the change from red to green.

55. Change lanes smoothly with the traffic flow.

56. Minimize distance by taking the inside track on curves—but stay in your lane.

57. Don't tailgate.

58. Use the rear view mirrors—don't get boxed in.

59. In traffic, watch at least two cars ahead for advance start and stop cues.

60. In a tunnel, watch the walls and ceiling for signals from brake lights ahead.

61. Don't make up time into a headwind.

62. Get into high gear as soon as possible, especially if you have a transmission-controlled spark retard.

63. Try driving with your right shoe off.

64. Pretend that gas costs $5 a gallon.

65. Relax and think economy when stuck in a traffic "pipeline."

66. Check the accuracy of your speedometer.

67. Tie a helium balloon to your right foot.

68. Drive slowly for the first few miles after a cold start.

69. Check for a too tight drive belt adjustment.

70. Make sure that your exhaust manifold heat control valve isn't stuck.

71. Check for a faulty thermostat that's keeping the engine too cold or slowing down the warm-up.

72. When the heater isn't needed, keep the temperature control turned to off or cool.

73. Check the sealing of the radiator cap—a pressurized system runs easier.

74. Be sure your automatic choke isn't sticking.

75. Adjust the automatic choke for the leanest setting which will provide fast starts.

76. Check the fuel system for leaks.

77. Replace dirty fuel and air filters.

78. Check for too high fuel pump pressure.

79. Change the engine oil at intervals not exceeding 3 months or 3,000 miles.

80. Change the oil filter at recommended intervals.

81. Reduce the carburetor idle speed to the minimum necessary for proper operation of the car.

82. Check the accelerator pump stroke for improper adjustment.

83. Check and/or replace the PCV valve.

84. Check at night for electrical leakage or crossfire from high tension ignition wires.

85. Keep the spark plugs and ignition points clean, gapped, and replaced at proper intervals.

86. "Read" your spark plugs for information about your engine and gas mileage.

87. Set the spark plug gap as wide as specifications allow.

88. After tracking down the cause, consider the use of hotter plugs if fouling continues to occur.

89. Keep the ignition timing adjusted to specifications.

90. Check the distributor rotor for erosion on the tip.

91. Check the distributor cap for corroded connections, wear of carbon bearings, and tracking.

92. Keep the transmission, engine, and rear axle topped up with the proper lubricant.

93. Spin the wheels to check for faulty wheel bearings and dragging brakes.

94. Keep the tires properly inflated—use your own gauge.

95. Set the toe-in and camber as close to zero as specifications allow.

96. Check the air conditioner for efficiency—recharge the system if bubbles appear in the refrigerant.

97. Check the weatherstripping for loss of insulation.

98. Wax the car to lower surface air resistance.

99. Avoid roof racks—stuff luggage inside or use a low trailer on trips.

100. Know in advance where you're going and how to get there.

101. Drive during daytime whenever possible.

102. Avoid high speeds on rain or snow covered roads.

103. Travel off season and stop for meals at off peak hours.

104. Measure distances in gallons, not miles (the long way can be the short way).

105. Combine errands whenever possible.

106. Make errand stops in the most efficient order.

107. Use your garage for overnight parking.

108. Know contingency shortcuts to use if traffic is tied up ahead.

109. Park and walk—don't circle and look.

110. Before parking, think about driving conditions you will face when you come back.

111. Don't wear awkward or heavy footwear when you drive.

112. Minimize heater use by dressing warmly in winter.

113. Minimize air conditioner use by dressing coolly in summer.

114. Check your car for excess weight carried in the trunk, under seats, etc.

115. Remove the trailer hitch ball in the off season.

116. Don't carry a full gas tank on local trips.

117. Don't keep snow tires mounted for any longer than necessary.

118. Clean accumulated snow from the trunk, hood, and roof before driving in winter.

119. Remove thick snow and slush deposits from the fender wells.

120. Ask your boss if you can start late and/or quit early to avoid low mpg commuter traffic.

121. Use the phone and mail as replacements for some short trips.

122. Go with the wind when starting a Sunday drive.

123. Have correct change at toll booths, especially if mechanical collectors are available for use.

124. Test your skill by entering an economy run.

125. Drive as if you've entered an economy run.

11· The Basics of Engine Operation

Cross section of a typical V8 engine (© Ford Motor Co)

The modern automobile engine is certainly the most complex and highly stressed of all household machines. Its parts are subjected to higher temperatures, greater pressures and vibration, and more extreme frictional loads and changes in velocity than those of other common machines. It has also been developed and refined to a greater extent than most machines. As a result, while the basic operating principles are fairly simple, the specifics are quite complex, and even the smallest deviation from the norm in the dimensions or the condition of a part, or in the setting of an individual adjustment can result in an obvious operating defect.

This first section is designed to relate engine operating principles to the most

114

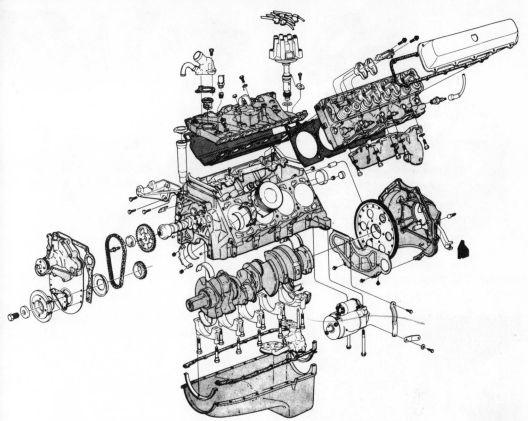

An exploded view of a typical water-cooled V8 engine (© G.M. Corp)

common malfunctions so that the trouble-shooter may visualize the physical relationship between the two. While it will be a review for many, it should help to provide the type of understanding that will enable the reader to replace time-consuming guesswork with quick, efficient troubleshooting.

The engine is a metal block containing a series of chambers. The volume of these chambers varies in relation to the position of a rotating shaft. There is a port for each chamber which provides for the admission of combustible material and another port for the expulsion of burned gases. The combustion chambers' volumes must be variable in order for the engine to be able to make use of the expansion of the burning gases. This ability also enables the chamber to compress the gases before combustion, and to purge itself of burned material and refill itself with a combustible charge after combustion has taken place. (A description of how these four functions are accomplished follows the material on basic engine construction.)

The upper engine block is usually an iron or aluminum alloy casting, consisting of outer walls which form hollow water jackets around the four, six, or eight cylinder walls. The lower block provides an appropriate number of rigid mounting points for the bearings which hold the crankshaft in place, and is known as the crankcase. The hollow jackets of the upper block add to the rigidity of the structure and contain the liquid coolant which carries the heat away from the cylinders and other parts of

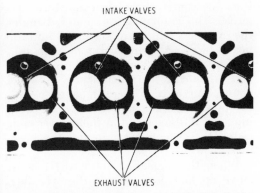

INTAKE VALVES

EXHAUST VALVES

The combustion chamber in a typical V8 cylinder head (© G.M. Corp)

A typical V8 cylinder block, bottom view (© G.M. Corp)

TIMING MARKS

THRUST PLATE SCREWS

The block provides mounting points for the engine's camshaft and its drive mechanism (© G.M. Corp)

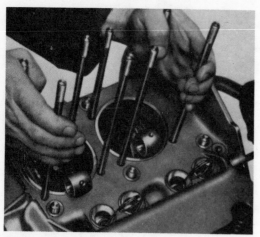

The crankcase of an air cooled engine (© Volkswagon of America, Inc)

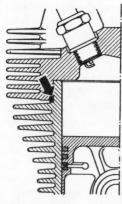

Cross-section of an air-cooled cylinder showing the cooling fins on the cylinder (© Volkswagon of America, Inc)

the block. The block of an air-cooled engine consists of a crankcase which provides for the rigid mounting of the crankshaft and for the studs which hold the cylinders rigidly in place. The cylinders are usually individual, single-wall castings, and are finned for cooling.

The block (both air-cooled and water-cooled) also provides rigid mounts for the engine's camshaft and its drive gears or drive chain. In water-cooled engines, studs are installed in the top of the block to provide for the rigid mounting of the cylinder heads on to the top of the block. The water and oil pumps are usually mounted directly to the block.

The crankshaft is a long iron alloy or steel fabrication which consists of bearing points or journals, which turn on their own axes, and counterweighted crank throws or crankpins which are located several inches from the center of the shaft and turn in a circle. The crankpins are centered under the cylinders which are machined into the upper block. Aluminum pistons with iron sealing rings are located in the cylinders and are linked to the crankpins via steel connecting rods. The rods connect with the pistons at their upper ends via piston pins and bushings, and at their lower ends fasten to the crankpins around the bearings.

When the crankshaft turns, the pistons move up and down within the cylinders, and the connecting rods convert their reciprocating motion into the rotary motion of the crankshaft. A flywheel at the rear of

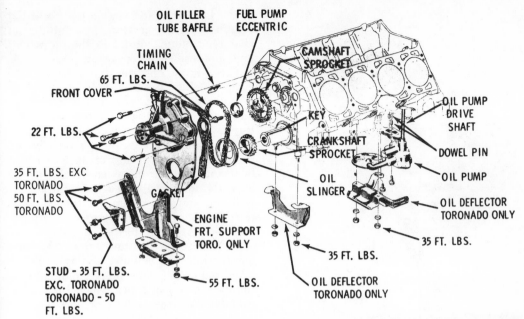

The water and oil pumps are usually mounted directly to the block (© G.M. Corp)

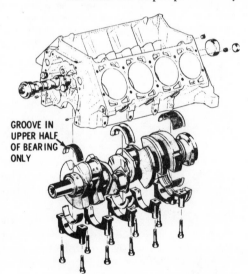

The crankshaft (© G.M. Corp)

the crankshaft provides a large, stable mass for smoothing out the rotation.

The cylinder heads form tight covers for the tops of the cylinders, and contain machined chambers into which the contents of the cylinders are forced as the pistons reach the upper limit of their travel. Two poppet valves in each cylinder are opened and closed by the action of the camshaft and valve train. The camshaft is driven at one-half crankshaft speed and operates the valves remotely through pushrods and rocker levers via its eccentric lobes or cams. Each combustion chamber contains one intake valve and one exhaust valve.

A typical piston and rod assembly (© G.M. Corp)

The cylinder heads also provide mounting threads for spark plugs which screw right through the heads so their lower tips protrude into the combustion chambers.

Lubricating oil, which is stored in a pan

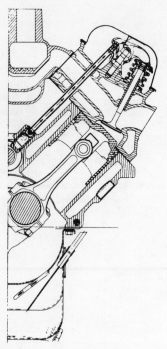

at the bottom of the engine and force-fed to almost all the parts of the engine by a gear type pump, lubricates the entire engine and also seals the piston rings.

The engine operates on a four-stroke cycle which is described below.

1. *Intake Stroke:* The intake stroke begins with the piston near the top of its travel, the exhaust valve nearly closed, and the intake valve opening rapidly. As the piston nears the top of its travel and begins its descent, the exhaust valve closes fully, the intake valve reaches a fully open position, and the volume of the combustion chamber begins to increase, creating a vacuum. As the piston descends, an air/fuel mixture is drawn from the carburetor into the cylinder through the intake manifold. (The intake manifold is simply a series of tubes which links each cylinder with the carburetor and the car-

The camshaft operates the valves through push-rods and rocker levers (© G.M. Corp)

1. Oil pick-up
2. Lifter feed
3. Rocker arm valve tip feed
4. Splash lube to timing chain, fuel pump cam & dist. & oil pump drive
5. Left main gallery feed
6. Cam bearing feed
7. Main bearing feed
8. Rod bearing feed

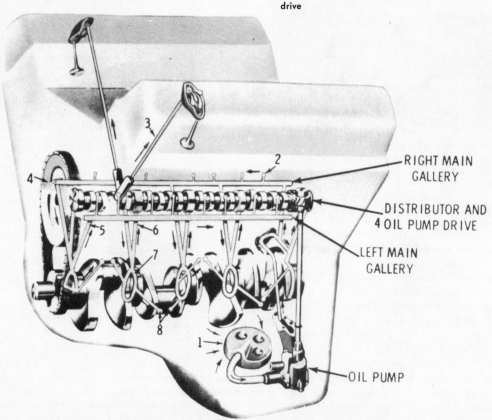

The lubrication system of a large V8 engine (© G.M. Corp)

buretor is a device for using the motion of air moving into the engine to mix just the right amount of fuel into the air stream.) The intake stroke ends with the piston having passed the bottom of its travel. The intake valve reaches a closed position just after the piston has begun its upstroke. The cylinder is now filled with the fuel/air mixture.

2. *Compression Stroke:* As the piston ascends, the fuel/air mixture is forced into the small chamber machined into the cylinder head. This compresses the mixture until it occupies 1/8th to 1/11th of the volume that it did at the time the piston began its ascent. This compression raises the temperature of the mixture and increases its pressure, vastly increasing the force generated by the expansion of gases during the power stroke.

3. *Power Stroke:* The fuel/air mixture is ignited by the spark plug just before the piston reaches the top of its stroke so that a very large portion of the fuel will have burned by the time the piston begins descending again. The heat produced by combustion increases the pressure in the cylinder, forcing the piston down with great force.

4. *Exhaust Stroke:* As the piston approaches the bottom of its stroke, the exhaust valve begins opening and the pressure in the cylinder begins to force the gases out around the valve. The ascent of the piston then forces nearly all the rest of the unburned gases from the cylinder. The cycle begins again as the exhaust valve closes, the intake valve opens and the piston begins descending and bringing a fresh charge of fuel and air into the combustion chamber.

Several cars that have been imported into the United States use two-stroke cycle engines. These operate with only a compression stroke and a power stroke. Intake of fuel and air mixture and purging of exhaust gases takes place between the power and compression strokes while the piston is near the bottom of its travel. Ports in the cylinder walls replace poppet valves located in the cylinder heads on four-stroke cycle engines. The crankcase is kept dry of oil, and the entire engine is lubricated by mixing the oil with the fuel so

The appearance of the combustion chamber at the beginning of the compression stroke (© G.M. Corp)

Troubleshooting When the Engine Won't Start

Check:

1. **The Starting System**

2. **The Ignition System**

3. **The Fuel System**

4. **Compression**

that a fine mist of oil covers all moving parts. The ports are designed so the fuel and air are trapped in the engine's crankcase during most of the downstroke of the piston, thus making the crankcase a compression chamber that force-feeds the combustion chambers after the ports are uncovered. The pistons serve as the valves, covering the ports whenever they should be closed.

This should provide a basic understanding of what is going on inside the engine. The ignition, fuel, and engine auxiliary systems will be described later, each in its own troubleshooting section.

12 · The Starting System

How It Works

The battery is the first link in the chain of mechanisms which work together to provide cranking of the automobile engine. In most modern cars, the battery is a lead-acid electrochemical device consisting of six two-volt (2 V) subsections connected in series so the unit is capable of producing approximately 12 V of electrical pres-

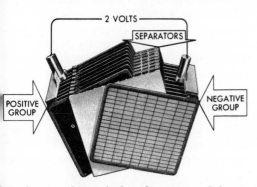

The battery plates which make up one of the six cells (© G.M. Corp)

sure. Each subsection, or cell, consists of a series of positive and negative plates held a short distance apart in a solution of sulfuric acid and water. The two types of plates are of dissimilar metals. This causes

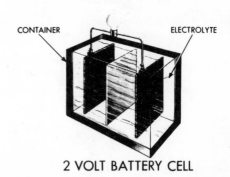

2 VOLT BATTERY CELL

Simplified drawing of a battery cell (Courtesy, Delco-Remy) (© G.M. Corp)

a chemical reaction to be set up, and it is this reaction which produces current flow from the battery when its positive and negative terminals are connected to an electrical appliance such as a lamp or motor. The continued transfer of electrons would eventually convert the sulfuric acid in the electrolyte to water, and make the two plates identical in chemical composition. As electrical energy is removed from the battery, its voltage output tends to drop. Thus, measuring battery voltage and battery electrolyte composition are two ways of checking the ability of the unit to supply power. During the starting of the engine, electrical energy is removed from the battery. However, if the charging circuit is in good condition and the operating

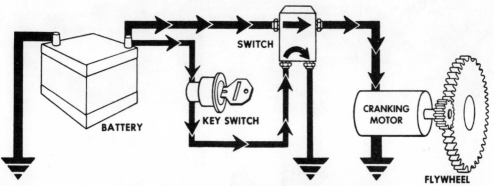

The chain of mechanisms that crank the engine (© G.M. Corp)

conditions are normal, the power removed from the battery will be replaced by the generator (or alternator) which will force electrons back through the battery, reversing the normal flow, and restoring the battery to its original chemical state.

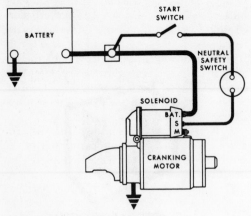

The starting circuit (© G.M. Corp)

The battery and starting motor are linked by very heavy electrical cables designed to minimize resistance to the flow of current. Generally, the major power supply cable that leaves the battery goes directly to the starter, while other electrical system needs are supplied by a smaller cable. During starter operation, power flows from the battery to the starter and is grounded through the car's frame and the battery's negative ground strap.

The starting motor is a specially designed, direct current electric motor capable of producing a very great amount of power for its size. One thing that allows the motor to produce a great deal of power is its tremendous rotating speed. It drives the engine through a tiny pinion gear (attached to the starter's armature), which drives the very large flywheel ring gear at a greatly reduced speed. Another factor allowing it to produce so much power is that only intermittent operation is required of it. Thus, little allowance for air circulation is required, and the windings can be built into a very small space.

The starter solenoid is a magnetic device which employs the small current supplied by the starting switch circuit of the ignition switch. This magnetic action moves a plunger which mechanically engages the starter and electrically closes the heavy switch which connects it to the battery. The starting switch circuit consists of the starting switch contained within the ignition switch, a transmission neutral safety switch or clutch pedal switch, and the wiring necessary to connect these in series with the starter solenoid or relay.

A pinion, which is a small gear, is mounted to a one-way drive clutch. This clutch is splined to the starter armature shaft. When the ignition switch is moved to the "start" position, the solenoid plunger slides the pinion toward the flywheel ring

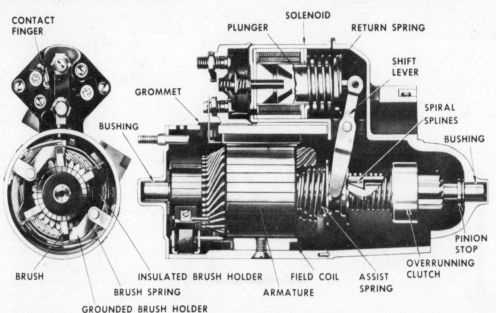

A typical starting motor (© G.M. Corp)

gear via a collar and spring. If the teeth on the pinion and flywheel match properly, the pinion will engage the flywheel immediately. If the gear teeth butt one another, the spring will be compressed and will force the gears to mesh as soon as the starter turns far enough to allow them to do so. As the solenoid plunger reaches the end of its travel, it closes the contacts that connect the battery and starter and then the engine is cranked.

As soon as the engine starts, the flywheel ring gear begins turning fast enough to drive the pinion at an extremely high rate of speed. At this point, the one-way clutch begins allowing the pinion to spin faster than the starter shaft so that the starter will not operate at excessive speed. When the ignition switch is released from the starter position, the solenoid is de-energized, and a spring contained within the solenoid assembly pulls the gear out of mesh and interrupts the current flow to the starter.

Some starters employ a separate relay, mounted away from the starter, to switch the motor and solenoid current on and off. The relay thus replaces the solenoid electrical switch, but does not eliminate the need for a solenoid mounted on the starter used to mechanically engage the starter drive gears. The relay is used to reduce the amount of current the starting switch must carry.

Quick Reference Guide For Starting System Troubleshooting

A. *Inspect the system:* Crank the engine and evaluate the condition of the cranking system by analyzing the response. See the chart of symptoms. If this does not reveal the source of trouble, proceed with the quick checks below. If there is no response but the accessories work, see J.

B. *Make quick checks:* Check the battery terminals and the condition and tension of the fan belt, and evaluate recent operating conditions. If these checks do not reveal the location of the problem, proceed with the more detailed checks below.

C. *Test amperage and voltage:* Check the starter amperage draw in conjunction with battery voltage during cranking. Evaluate the results with the voltage amperage chart.

D. *Check specific gravity of battery cells:* Check the specific gravity of each battery cell and evaluate the battery condition. Charge and replace as necessary.

E. *Check for engine mechanical problems:* Check the viscosity of the engine oil, and check for noises during cranking. Replace the oil if it is of the wrong viscosity. Service the cooling system if the problem exists only when the engine is hot.

F. *Check mechanical condition of the starter and drive:* Remove the starter assembly and check for a stuck pinion gear or other mechanical problems.

G. *Check condition of wiring between battery and starter:* Check the wiring, connections, and switches for high resistance.

H. *Check starter ground circuit:* Check the connections and cable for high resistance.

J. *Check starter switch circuit:* Check the wiring and connections for high resistance. Check switches for continuity and proper linkage operation.

Starting System Troubleshooting

A. Inspect the System:

1. Turn off all accessories. Place manual transmissions in Neutral; automatic transmissions in Park. Depress the clutch pedal all the way on cars with manual transmissions.

2. Turn the ignition switch firmly to the start position. If the engine cranks, hold it there for 15 seconds.

3. If you are familiar with the vehicle, listen for normal starting sounds. If they are unfamiliar, cranking may be checked by looking at the vibration damper on the front of the engine. It should turn steadily at about 1/3 normal idle speed. Turn on the headlights and check brightness during cranking.

Generally a problem falls into one of the following categories:

a. Starter drive mechanical problems: The starter turns, possibly with a gear clashing noise, but the engine does not turn. The trouble is in the starter pinion or its engagement mechanism, or possibly in the flywheel ring gear. The starter must be removed and the faulty parts repaired or replaced.

b. Engine mechanical problems: The starter turns the engine briefly and then stops very suddenly, or hums but does not turn the engine at all. The engine is hydrostatically locked or has some other severe mechanical defects. Attempt to turn the engine over using an 18 in. flex drive and socket on the crankshaft pulley mounting nut. Inability to turn the engine using this technique confirms the existence of mechanical engine problems. If the engine can be turned but the symptoms above apply, remove the starter and check for starter drive mechanical problems.

c. Malfunction in solenoid switch: The solenoid clicks loudly and the headlights remain bright, but there is no action or noise from the starter motor. The problem is in the solenoid switch and its wiring. Remove the starter and repair the switch.

d. Starter switch circuit: There is no click or other response from starter, but the headlights work normally. Check the starter switch circuit as in section J. If that is not the problem, check G and then H.

e. Bad solenoid: The starter clicks repeatedly, but the lights burn brightly. Check H and I. If no fault is found, replace the solenoid.

f. Bad battery, wiring, or starter: If cranking is sluggish and the lights are dim or the solenoid clicks and the lights are dim, or there is no response at all, follow checks B through J in alphabetical order.

B. Make Quick Checks:

1. Check both battery terminal connections for corrosion. Turn on the headlight switch and watch the headlights while twisting a screwdriver between the cable clamps and terminals, as a further test. If this causes the headlights to brighten, or if the clamps show corrosion, service them as follows: disconnect both clamps, remove corrosion from conducting surfaces, reinstall them securely, and then coat them with petroleum jelly or grease. Avoid the use of force in every way possible. If clamps are bolted together, loosen the nuts

and force the terminals open before removing them. Clamps which are not bolted should be forced on with gentle strokes of a soft mallet. If the starter now cranks properly, return the vehicle to service.

2. Check the tension and condition of the belt(s) which drive the alternator or generator. If there is inadequate tension and belt surfaces are heavily glazed—indicating slippage—replace the belts, tighten them to specifications, recharge the battery, and return the vehicle to service.

3. Evaluate recent operating conditions. If your accessory load has been unusually heavy and the vehicle has been operated at moderate speeds with frequent stops, recharge the battery, and return the vehicle to service. If this is a recurrent problem, the electrical system should be checked for proper generator and regulator performance. In some cases, the regulator can be readjusted to reduce the severity of this problem.

NOTE: *During the tests below, the coil-to-distributor low-tension lead should be disconnected and securely grounded to prevent the vehicle from starting and to protect the ignition system from damage.*

C. Test Amperage and Voltage:

Checking starter amperage draw in conjunction with voltage during cranking will give excellent clues to the nature of the problem.

1. Connect a voltmeter between the positive post of the battery and a good ground.

2. If an induction type starter amperage indicator is available, place the yoke of the meter around a straight section of the cable between the battery and starter. Otherwise, disconnect the battery end of the lead that runs to the starter and securely connect an ammeter of 300 ampere capacity between the battery post and the lead.

A carbon pile rheostat can also be used. Measure voltage during cranking and then connect it in series with the ammeter across the battery terminals. Turn the rheostat until voltage is the same as during cranking. The reading on the ammeter will then show starter draw.

3. Crank the engine for 20 seconds and note the average readings. If you are using

an induction type meter and it reads down-scale, reverse the position of the yoke.

4. Evaluate the readings according to the chart below. On 12 V systems, voltage should be 9.6 or more; on 6 V, 4.8 or more. On 12 V systems, amperage should be 100–200, depending on the size of the engine and its compression ratio. Double the amperages for 6 V systems.

Condition	Voltage	Amperage	Check Section
1	low	normal or low	D
2	near normal	high	E, F*
3	near normal	normal or low	G, H

* NOTE: If sections E and F do not reveal the problem, remove the starter for repair of ground or short circuit.

D. Check Specific Gravity of Battery Cells:

1. Test the specific gravity of each of the battery cells with a battery hydrometer. Do so before attempting to charge the battery. If the battery has been recently charged, or if the electrolyte level is below the level of the plates and requires replenishment, special procedures must be followed to ensure an accurate test. See the section on testing the electrical system for these procedures. Take your measurements carefully, filling and emptying the hydrometer several times to ensure adequate removal of material left in the hydrometer and allowing time for the temperature to come to an accurate reading. Read the gravity scale from the liquid level at the center of the column, not from around the edges where it seeks an abnormally high level. Correct the readings according to the temperature scale on the hydrometer. If a hydrometer and battery thermometer must be used independently, this means subtracting 0.004 for each 10° below 80° F, and adding 0.004 for every 10° above that temperature. Readings not corrected according to temperature are meaningless.

2. Evaluate the readings. A fully

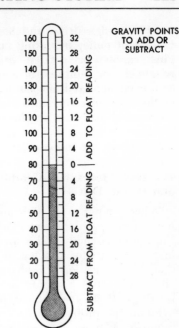

Hydrometer correction chart (Courtesy, Chysler Corp)

charged battery will read between 1.260 and 1.280. Readings must be over 1.220 for the battery to be capable of cranking the engine. If any are below 1.220, or if the readings are far apart, see the section on testing the electrical system for information on evaluating the need for battery replacement or recharging dead batteries. If the battery requires replacement on recharging, be sure to test the charging system before placing the vehicle back in service.

E. Check for Engine Mechanical Problems:

Where amperage is high, a problem may exist in the engine itself or in the starter drive mechanism. If ambient temperature is below freezing, the engine oil should be a multigrade or light straight grade approved for winter use. Normal-weight oil can cause improper cranking in cold weather without any mechanical or electrical malfunction.

1. If improper lubrication is suspected, change the oil (and filter) and refill with the proper grade for the weather conditions. Return the vehicle to service if this permits good cranking.

2. If cranking is accompanied by a mechanical grinding or scraping noise and is very rough and unsteady (not merely sluggish), attempt to rotate the engine using

an 18 in. flex drive and socket on the crankshaft pulley mounting nut. If the engine cannot be rotated or if extreme roughness, or tightness in a sporadic pattern is encountered, mechanical damage is evident. Remove the starter and check for mechanical problems in the starter drive. If none are found, major engine mechanical problems are indicated.

F. Check Mechanical Condition of Starter and Drive:

Where amperage is high and no engine mechanical problems are evident, remove the starter assembly and inspect the pinion and ring gears for sticking or severe wear due to lubrication problems, etc. Also check the starter motor armature shaft bearings. If no mechanical problems are evident, the problem is caused by starter motor or solenoid electrical problems.

G. Check Condition of Wiring Between Battery and Starter:

Normal voltage with low amperage indicates a poor connection somewhere in the starter circuit. The circuit between the battery and starter may be checked as below.

1. Connect the positive lead of a voltmeter (reverse the leads for a negative ground system) to the positive battery terminal. Connect the negative lead to the connector which carries power from the solenoid switch to the starting motor. Crank the engine and take note of the voltmeter reading. The reading should be 0.3 V or less. If the reading is acceptable, proceed to H. Otherwise proceed to step 2.

2. Isolate the faulty component by repeating the test with the voltmeter negative lead connected to each of the following:

a. The starter motor terminal of the solenoid;

b. The battery terminal of the solenoid;

c. Starter terminal of starter relay (if your vehicle has one);

d. Battery terminal of starter relay.

(If the vehicle has a starter relay, it will usually be mounted on one of the fender wells.) The voltage reading should drop slightly as each component is eliminated from the portion of the circuit being tested. If the voltage drops more than 0.1 V when eliminating the solenoid switch or

the relay, the unit is faulty. (Check for burned contacts inside; this is the most common problem.) The resistance of the battery cable should not exceed 0.2 V. Individual connections may be tested for high resistance by placing the probe of the negative lead first on the stud to which the connection is made, and then on the connector on the end of the cable leading to the connection. A measurable difference in the voltage drop indicates a bad connection which must be disassembled and cleaned. Usually bad connections will also be corroded or oil-covered. Be sure, when cleaning, to remove all the oxidized material and to reassemble the connection snugly. A wire brush or sandpaper will help.

H. Check Starter Ground Circuit:

1. Connect the negative lead of the voltmeter to the negative post of the battery (reverse hook-ups for positive ground systems) and the positive lead to a clean, unpainted spot on the starter housing. Crank the engine and note the voltmeter reading. If the reading is higher than 0.2 V, the system may be at fault, and step 2 should be followed. If no defects in the engine, battery, or wiring have been found, the starter should be removed for repair of its electrical circuitry.

2. Repeat the test outlined in step 1 with the positive voltmeter probe connected to:

a. The ground cable to engine or frame connection;

b. The battery negative cable to engine or frame connection;

Individual connections should be tested as in G. The ground cables should have resistances that cause the reading to change less than 0.2 V. Resistance of connections should be negligible.

J. Check Starter Switch Circuit:

1. If the system has a separate starter relay, locate the wire from the starter switch circuit to the relay and disconnect it. If the system uses only a solenoid, locate the wire from the starter switch circuit to the solenoid and disconnect it.

2. If the vehicle has an automatic transmission, make sure it is fully in Neutral or Park. If the vehicle has a manual transmission, the clutch pedal will have to be fully depressed during testing.

3. Connect the positive lead of the voltmeter to the end of the disconnected cable. Have someone turn the ignition switch to the start position and test for voltage. If about 12 V are present, the solenoid or relay is at fault, in most cases. Also check the ground for the relay, or the solenoid-to-starter connection and starter motor ground circuit in systems using a solenoid only.

4. If there is low or no voltage, the problem is in the starter switch circuit. Check for voltage at either side of the neutral safety or clutch pedal safety switch, and for voltage at the ignition switch connection that feeds the starter relay or solenoid. (If the warning lights work, current is getting to the ignition switch.)

When working from the ignition switch toward the starter, the faulty component or connection is between the last point where voltage is detected and the first point which is dead. If the neutral safety switch is a combination type with four prongs, use a jumper cable to find the two prongs which operate the back-up lights, and then test the other prongs only. If the faulty component proves to be the neutral safety switch or clutch switch, remember to check the linkage for proper operation before condemning it. The linkage may be disconnected and moved through the full travel of the switch mechanism while checking for voltage to find out whether or not the fault is in the linkage.

13 · The Ignition System

How It Works

The coil is the heart of the ignition system. It consists of two coils of wire wound about an iron core. These coils are insulated from each other and the whole assembly is enclosed in an oil-filled case. The primary coil is connected to the two primary terminals located on top of the coil and consists of relatively few turns of a heavier wire. The secondary coil circuit consists of many turns of fine wire and is connected to the high tension connection (the wire going into the top of the distributor), on the top of the coil. Energizing the coil primary with battery voltage produces current flow through the primary winding; this in turn produces a very large, intense magnetic field. Interrupting the flow of primary current causes the field to collapse. Just as current moving through a wire pro-

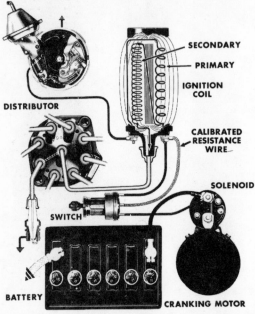

A typical conventional ignition system (© G.M. Corp)

duces a magnetic field, moving a field across a wire will produce a current. As the magnetic field collapses, its lines of force cross the secondary winding, inducing a current in that winding. The force of the induced current is concentrated because of the relative shortness of the secondary coil of wire.

The distributor is the controlling element of the system, switching the primary current on and off and distributing the current to the proper spark plug each time a spark is produced. It is basically a stationary housing surrounding a rotating shaft. The shaft is driven at one-half engine speed by the engine's camshaft through the distributor drive gears. A cam which is situated near the top of the shaft has one lobe for each cylinder of the engine. The cam operates the ignition contact points, which are mounted on a plate located on bearings within the distributor housing. A rotor is attached to the top of the distributor shaft. When the bakelite distributor cap is in place, on top of the unit's metal housing, a spring-loaded contact connects the portion of the rotor directly above the center of the shaft to the center connection on top of the distributor. The outer end of the rotor passes very close to the contacts connected to the four, six, or eight high-tension connections around the outside of the distributor cap.

Under normal operating conditions, power from the battery is fed through a resistor or resistance wire to the primary circuit of the coil and is then grounded through the ignition points in the distributor. During cranking, the full voltage of the battery is supplied through an auxiliary circuit routed through the solenoid switch. In an eight-cylinder engine, the distributor cam will allow the points to close about 60 crankshaft degrees before the firing of the spark plug. Current will begin flowing through the primary wiring to the positive connection on the coil,

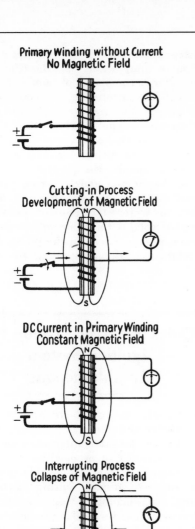

**Primary Winding without Current
No Magnetic Field**

**Cutting-in Process
Development of Magnetic Field**

**DC Current in Primary Winding
Constant Magnetic Field**

**Interrupting Process
Collapse of Magnetic Field**

Ignition coil operation (© G.M. Corp)

magnetic field. The condenser consists of several layers of aluminum foil separated by insulation. These layers of foil, upon an increase in voltage, are capable of storing electricity, making the condenser a sort of electrical surge tank. Voltages just after the points open may reach 250 V because of the vast amount of energy stored in the primary windings and their magnetic field. A condenser which is defective or improperly grounded will not absorb the shock from the fast-moving stream of electrons when the points open and these èlectrons will force their way across the point gap, causing burning and pitting.

The very high voltage induced in the secondary windings will cause a surge of current to flow from the coil tower to the center of the distributor, where it will travel along the connecting strip along the top of the rotor. The surge will arc its way across the short gap between the contact on the outer end of the rotor and the connection in the cap for the high-tension lead of the cylinder to be fired. After passing along the high-tension lead, it will travel down the center electrode of the spark plug, which is surrounded by ce-

through the primary winding of the coil, through the ground wire between the negative connection on the coil and the distributor, and to ground through the contact points. Shortly after the engine is ready to fire, the current flow through the coil primary will have reached a near maximum value, and an intense magnetic field will have formed around the primary windings. The distributor cam will separate the contact points at the proper time for ignition and the primary field will collapse, causing current to flow in the secondary circuit. A capacitor, known as the "condenser," is installed in the circuit in parallel with the contact points in order to absorb some of the force of the electrical surge that occurs during collapse of the

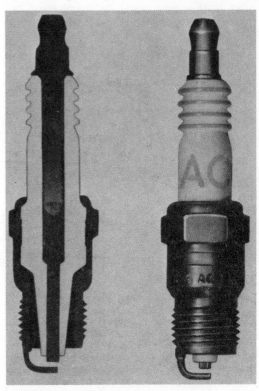

Cross-section of a spark plug. The white portion is the insulator. (© G.M. Corp)

ramic insulation, and arc its way over to the side electrode, which is grounded through threads which hold the plug in the cylinder head. The heat generated by the passage of the spark will ignite the contents of the cylinder.

Most distributors employ both centrifugal and vacuum advance mechanisms to advance the point at which ignition occurs for optimum performance and economy. Spark generally occurs a few degrees before the piston reaches top dead center (TDC) in order that very high pressures will exist in the cylinder as soon as the piston is capable of using the energy—just a few degrees after TDC. Centrifugal advance mechanisms employ hinged flyweights working in opposition to springs to turn the top portion of the distributor shaft, including the cam and rotor, ahead of the lower shaft. This advances the point at which the cam causes the points to open. A more advanced spark is required at higher engine speeds because the speed of combustion does not increase in direct proportion to increases in engine speed, but tends to lag behind at high revolutions. If peak cylinder pressures are to exist at the same point, advance must be used to start combustion earlier.

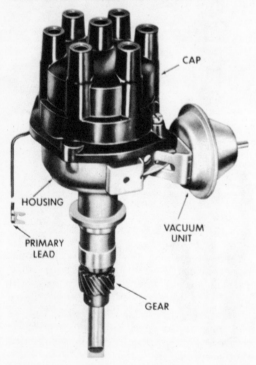

The location of the vacuum advance unit (© G.M. Corp)

Vacuum advance is used to accomplish the same thing when part-throttle operation reduces the speed of combustion because of less turbulence and compression, and poorer scavenging of exhaust gases. Carburetor vacuum below the throttle plate is channeled to a vacuum diaphragm mounted on the distributor. The higher the manifold vacuum, the greater the motion of the diaphragm against spring pressure. A rod between the diaphragm and the plate on which the contact points are mounted rotates the plate on its bearings causing the cam to open the points earlier in relation to the position of the crankshaft.

Quick Reference Guide For Ignition System Troubleshooting

A. *Check for normal cranking.* Correct any deficiencies.

B. *Check for an adequate spark.* If spark is acceptable, proceed to O.

C. *Inspect system for visible deficiencies.* Inspect: primary wiring, secondary wiring, cap, and rotor. Make sure that the distributor shaft turns and the points open and close. If the points are severely burned or do not have the proper gap, remove them, clean with a point file, and reinstall them with the proper gap.

NOTE: *In D through J, the ignition switch should be turned on and the points should be open—unless otherwise indicated.*

D. *Test for voltage at points (with points open).* There should be voltage between the movable breaker arm and ground when the points are open. If there is voltage, proceed to J.

E. *Test for voltage to coil.* If there is no voltage with the ignition switch on, check for voltage during cranking. Voltage only during cranking indicates a bad resistance wire or resistor, in most cases, but the ignition switch should also be suspected.

F. *Test for a ground.* Test for a ground in the coil or another component by disconnecting the lead to the coil positive terminal and checking for amperage between the disconnected lead and the positive terminal with the points open. If there is no amperage, reconnect the wire and proceed to H.

G. *Find the ground.* Reconnect the coil positive wires. Check for amperage between the coil-to-distributor wire (disconnected) and the coil negative terminal. If there is no amperage, replace the coil. If there is amperage, continue to test until the faulty component is isolated.

H. *Test for voltage.* If there is no voltage to the ignition points and no ground exists, test for voltage to find the open circuit. Test at each connection in the circuit. The faulty component will be between a hot connection and a dead connection. If there is no voltage to the coil positive terminal, the problem is between there and the battery.

J. *Check coil polarity.* The polarity of the coil should be the same as the polarity of the battery. If necessary, use a voltmeter and check for negative voltage at the coil tower.

K. *Check coil primary resistance.* Resistance should be 1.0 ohms with external resistor, 4.0 ohms with internal resistor. Replace coil if resistance is not approximately correct.

L. *Check coil secondary resistance.* Resistance should be 4,000–10,000 ohms for a normal-duty coil. Replace if the resistance is outside the acceptable range.

M. *Inspect rotor and cap.* Replace any unserviceable parts and clean as necessary.

N. *Inspect secondary wiring and check its resistance.* Resistance should be about 8,000 ohms per foot.

O. *Clean and gap plugs.* Inspect and replace the plugs if they are defective.

P. *Adjust timing and dwell.* Use a dwell tach, if possible, for the dwell adjustment. Use a stroboscopic timing light, if possible, for the adjustment of ignition timing.

Ignition System Troubleshooting

A. Check for Normal Cranking.

Turn the ignition switch to the "start" position and check for normal cranking. If cranking is not normal, repair any problems in the starting system before inspect-ing the ignition system. Low voltage, whether caused by excessive battery drain or poor battery performance, and/or other starter system malfunctions, can affect the performance of the ignition system.

B. Check for an Adequate Spark.

Pull off a spark plug lead and hold it about $3/16$ in. from a good ground. If possible, pull back the rubber boot covering the end of the lead so bare metal is exposed. A good fat spark should appear at regular intervals. Try at least two leads so you can be sure the problem is not just a bad individual cable. If the spark is good, proceed to O. Otherwise, proceed with the checks below.

C. Inspect the System for Visible Deficiencies.

1. Inspect the primary wiring, cap, rotor, and secondary wiring. Look for bad connections, frayed insulation, and grounds in the primary wiring. Look for brittleness, cracks, and carbon tracking in the secondary circuit. Make sure all secondary connections are fully pressed in.

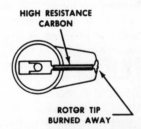

Distributor rotor malfunctions (© G.M. Corp)

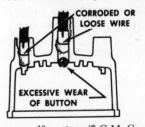

Distributor cap malfunctions (© G.M. Corp)

Correct any deficiencies. Bad wiring must be replaced. A distributor cap or rotor with no cracks and contacts that are still intact may be cleaned in soap and water to remove carbon tracks. Wiring that is wet may be dried with a clean, dry rag or treated with a spray made especially for that purpose.

2. Crank the engine with the distributor cap removed and the high-tension lead to

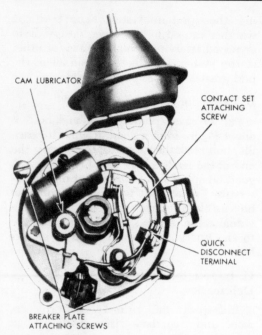

CAM LUBRICATOR

CONTACT SET
ATTACHING
SCREW

QUICK
DISCONNECT
TERMINAL

BREAKER PLATE
ATTACHING SCREWS

The appearance of the ignition points and condenser. The condenser is the cylindrical component. (© G.M. Corp)

the distributor grounded. Check to see that the distributor turns and the points open and close. If the distributor shaft does not turn, the problem is in the drive gear at the lower end of the shaft, and the entire distributor assembly will have to be removed and repaired or replaced.

If the points are severely burned and pitted or they do not have an adequate gap (they should open visibly), remove them, clean them with a point file, and reinstall them. If they are in extremely bad shape, replace them. Repeated excessive burning in less than approximately 12,000 miles points to a faulty condenser or use of the wrong type of condenser. Replace the condenser, if necessary. It may be checked for a short by removing it, and connecting an ohmmeter's leads at the pigtail lead and to the body of the condenser, if malfunction is suspected. The resistance reading will be infinite if the condenser is usable. Points can also burn if the gap (or dwell) is improper, or if an oily gauge has been used to adjust them.

Check the fiber block on the contact points assembly for excessive wear. Excess wear is indicated if it is difficult to adjust the points for a proper gap upon reinstallation, as described below. Make sure the fiber block and cam have a light coating of

clean, high-temperature grease. If they do not, clean and lubricate them carefully. If the fiber block is worn excessively in spite of proper lubrication, or if there is evidence that excessive wear is a problem (timing and dwell go out of adjustment, and the car goes out of tune rapidly), suspect distributor mechanical troubles. Carefully check the cam for roughness or scoring after wiping it clean if this type of problem is suspected. The shaft and bushing wear should also be tested by checking the play in the shaft with a dial indicator. Mechanical problems may also be detected on an electronic distributor tester.

Reinstall the ignition points in their proper position. Using a clean feeler gauge, adjust the position of the stationary contact with the fiber block on the high part of the distributor cam to the specified gap. Unless you are adjusting new points, it will be necessary to avoid contact with built-up material on one of the contact surfaces. A wire gauge may be of help but, in any case, the proper gap must be measured between two parallel surfaces that are neither pitted nor built up with transferred material.

D. Test for Voltage at Points with Points Open.

When the distributor cam is in a position which will hold the points open, the ignition switch is on, and the electrical system is functioning normally in all other respects, there will be approximately 12 V all the way from the battery to the movable contact point. This may be checked by placing the positive probe of a voltmeter on the movable breaker arm and grounding the negative probe. Reverse the polarity for positive ground systems. A test lamp may also be connected between these two spots to make this check. If voltage is good at this point (there should be nearly 12 V if you are using a voltmeter) the primary circuit is in acceptable shape to produce a spark, in most cases, provided the ignition points are not too badly burned. If rotating the distributor until the points close causes the voltage to drop to zero, the points are in functional condition.

If the system passes these two tests, proceed to J. Otherwise, it will be necessary to perform the tests in E. through H. to track down the problem in the primary circuit.

E. Test for Voltage to Coil.

Connect a voltmeter between the positive terminal of the coil and ground following the polarity of the battery. Make sure the ignition switch is turned on. If there is no voltage, jiggle the key, leaving the switch in the "on" position. If voltage appears only when the key is jiggled, the ignition switch is faulty. If jiggling the key has no effect, turn the key to the start position. If this produces voltage at the coil, the problem is most likely the resistor wire that carries current to the coil only when the switch is in the normal running position. If the oil and generator lights do not come on, the problem is most likely in the ignition switch or in the connections on the switch. The switch should be removed and checked for continuity with the internal mechanism set for the "on" position. A wiring diagram will indicate which terminal of the switch receives voltage from the battery and which terminals receive voltage when the switch is on. The connections and the wiring from the battery will have to be checked if the switch has continuity between the proper terminals.

F. Test for a Ground.

Test for a ground in the coil or another component by disconnecting the lead or leads to the coil positive terminal. Test for voltage between each lead and ground. If neither lead is hot, the problem is in the wiring, resistor, or ignition switch, and you should go on to H.

The voltage test in the paragraph above was performed to locate the lead which supplies voltage to the coil while the ignition switch is in the normal running position. Connect an ammeter between that lead and the coil positive terminal. If there is no amperage, proceed to H. If there is amperage, go on to G.

G. Find the Ground.

Reconnect the wires to the coil positive terminal. Disconnect the wire from the coil negative terminal and check for amperage between the terminal and disconnected lead. If there is no amperage, the coil is faulty because of an internal ground and should be replaced.

If there is amperage flowing from the coil to the rest of the system, then there is a ground in the coil-to-distributor wire, or in the points, the condenser or their wiring. Inspect the wires that lead to the points and condenser from the connection inside the distributor. Grounds frequently occur in these wires because they are twisted whenever the vacuum advance diaphragm changes the position of the mounting plate. Grounds will be evidenced by frayed and burned insulation at a spot where the wire contacts the body of the distributor.

If this test reveals no ground, check the condenser for a ground by removing its lead wire and checking for amperage between the connection on the end of the lead and the terminal on the inside of the distributor. If there is any amperage, the condenser is faulty and should be replaced.

If these tests have not located the ground, it is probably in the wire from the coil to the distributor at a spot where it touches metal; in the rubber grommet which carries the primary circuit through the wall of the distributor, in the insulated terminal on the contact points assembly, or in the hinge on the contact points. In most cases, close examination for burning should reveal the location of the problem. If not, testing for amperage as described below may help locate the ground.

Remove the lead from the coil where it connects to the contact point assembly. Test for amperage between the lead's connection and the terminal on the contact assembly. If there is no amperage, the ground must be in the grommet where the primary circuit passes through the distributor, or in the coil-to-distributor wire. Replacing these two parts, which are generally supplied as an assembly, should rectify the problem.

H. Test for Voltage.

The tests above will have revealed whether or not there is voltage to the coil, and will have eliminated the possibility of a ground existing in the circuit. If there is voltage to the positive terminal of the coil, there is an open circuit between there and the ignition points. Otherwise, the problem must be between the ignition coil's positive terminal and the battery.

Proceed in the appropriate direction

from the coil positive terminal, checking for voltage at each connection. The faulty component is between a hot connection and a dead one. For example, if voltage exists at the coil positive terminal, but not at the negative terminal of the coil, the coil must be faulty. Before replacing a component, it might be wise to check it for continuity with an ohmmeter. This will eliminate the chance of mistaking a bad connection for a faulty component. Wiring should have very low resistance (but not zero), and the coil should behave as in K. Keep a sharp eye open for bad connections. Any connection which is dirty, corroded, loose, or burned should be cleaned and tightened.

J. Check Coil Polarity.

While a coil that is connected backward will still produce a spark, weakened ignition system performance will result from improper polarity. If the top of the coil indicates positive and negative terminals, the polarity can be checked visually. The wire coming from the ignition switch should be the same polarity (positive or negative) as the wire going from the battery to the starter, while the coil-to-distributor wire should be the same polarity as the battery ground. If the coil is unmarked, remove the high-tension lead from the coil tower, contact the metal portion of the coil tower with the positive lead of a voltmeter, and ground the voltmeter's negative lead. Crank the engine until a spark is produced. The spark should move the voltmeter's needle downscale. Otherwise, reverse the leads to the coil.

K. Check Coil Primary Resistance.

A weak spark or no spark at all can occur because of an open circuit or ground in either circuit of the coil. The coil can have a very small short or ground which might not show up in general primary system testing but which would have a significant effect on primary circuit resistance.

Disconnect wiring to both primary terminals of the coil. Connect an ohmmeter to the primary circuit—one lead to each primary terminal. The resistance of the coil will depend on whether or not it uses an external ballast resistor. Most coils are externally resisted to permit full battery voltage to be used during cranking. If there are two wires to the positive ter-

minal of the coil, this is a sure sign that the coil is externally resisted. A small component wired in series with the coil in the wire to the positive terminal is another sure sign.

Coils that are externally resisted should have a resistance of approximately 1.0 ohms. Coils that have no external resistor should have about 4.0 ohms resistance. If the resistance is greatly above this figure, or zero (infinite) resistance is indicated, the coil must be replaced.

L. Check Coil Secondary Resistance.

Even if the primary circuit checks out as in K, the coil could be faulty. With the primary leads disconnected, attach an ohmmeter across the secondary circuit of the coil to check for a short or open secondary winding. One probe should go to the metal connector inside the coil tower, while the other *must* go to the positive terminal of the primary circuit. The negative side cannot be used because the secondary is not connected to that side of the primary winding. The resistance should be between approximately 4,000 and 10,000 ohms. These figures are typical of normal-duty coils, but do not apply to heavy-duty equipment. If the resistance is much higher or lower than this, or if it reads zero, replace the coil.

The coil tower should also be checked very carefully for evidence of cracked or burned plastic, or burned metal in the connector inside the tower. Evidence of damage here indicates that the coil should be replaced. If the only burned spot is on the metal conductor, it may be sanded and the coil may be reused, provided the metal is not burned through and a smooth surface can be created.

In cases of coil tower damage, the coil-to-distributor high-tension lead must either be replaced or very carefully checked for burned connectors. If the surface can be smoothed by sanding, the lead may be reused. Use of a bad lead with a new coil can cause recurrence of the burning problem.

M. Inspect Rotor and Cap.

The cap must be gone over with a fine tooth comb to properly check its condition. First, if there is any evidence of carbon, clean the cap carefully in a mild detergent and water solution. After a thorough drying, inspect it very carefully, looking for the following:

1. Looseness of any of the terminals.
2. Excessive burning of any of the terminals.
3. Hairline cracks due to breakage or prolonged arcing.
4. Failure of the spring to push a button type center contact firmly downward.

If the cap is serviceable, sand away any roughness on any of the contacts before reusing it.

Inspect the rotor for any signs of burning, cracking, or breakage. If it uses a spring type of pick-up to contact the carbon button in the center of the cap, make sure there is sufficient tension in the spring for firm contact, bending the pick-up slightly, if necessary. Make sure the contact at the outer end of the rotor is in good condition and will come within about $\frac{3}{16}$ in. of the inner surfaces of the terminals in the cap. If the contact surface cannot be smoothed by sanding, replace the rotor.

N. Inspect Secondary Wiring and Check its Resistance.

Inspect all wiring for badly burned connectors, brittleness, or cracks, and replace if any such wear is found. Remove slight burning or roughness with sandpaper.

Connect the probes of an ammeter to either end of each wire to check resistance. It should be approximately 8,000 ohms per foot. Replace high-resistance wire. This, of course, includes wire that shows zero resistance, indicating a completely open circuit.

O. Clean and Gap the Spark Plugs.

Badly burned spark plugs can cause misfiring, poor gas mileage, and difficult starting. Clean any carbon and lead deposits off both electrodes so a good inspection can be made. A relatively soft wire brush is the best tool for this job and is available as a part of many combination feeler gauge and spark plug tools.

The side electrode should be square and uniform in shape along its entire length and should extend well over the center of the center electrode. Burning will shorten this electrode and round it off near the free end. The center electrode should be uniform in diameter (not burned thinner near the top) and should form a relatively

flat surface under the side electrode. A very round top surface, or only slight extension above the insulator, indicates extreme burning. The insulator should be smooth and round, entirely free of cracks, and tightly molded in place. If shaking the plug up and down causes the insulator to move up and down, it is severely damaged. Replace plugs which show any evidence of burning or damaged insulators.

The outer insulator should also be inspected for cracks after a thorough cleaning. Any evidence of cracking or arcing here means the plug is defective.

If the plugs are severely burned, the problem is usually one of the four below:

1. Improper torquing in the head, meaning poor cooling.
2. Use of a plug of too high a heat range.
3. Advance ignition timing, or lean carburetion.
4. Extremely prolonged use.

See the section on correcting poor engine operation for additional information.

If the plugs are in good condition, they may be reused if they are thoroughly cleaned and properly gapped to the manufacturer's specifications. A wire feeler gauge must be used to set the gap. The gap is correct when a slight pull is required to free the gauge from between the two electrodes. Bend the side electrode

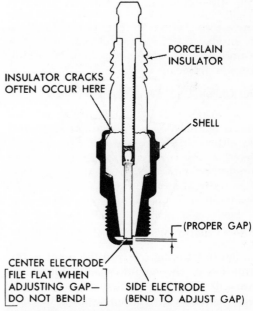

Cross-section of a spark plug showing where gap is to be measured (© G.M. Corp)

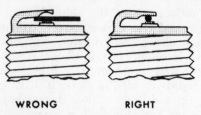

WRONG   **RIGHT**

Proper gapping of spark plugs (© G.M. Corp)

only when closing or opening the gap, using a spark plug tool. The gap should be set according to the manufacturer's specifications, which can be found on the sticker under the hood on post-1967 cars. Full-size American engines usually use a 0.035 in. gap. Smaller gaps are used with most smaller engines. Reinstall the plugs, using new gaskets, and torque to approximately 14 ft lbs for 10 mm plugs, or 30 ft lbs for 14 mm plugs. Use 3 ft lbs less, in either case, for engines with aluminum heads.

P. Adjust Timing and Dwell.

The dwell angle is the amount of time, measured in degrees of distributor shaft rotation, that the contact points remain closed. Dwell angle is an indirect measurement of point gap. Increasing the point gap will decrease the dwell angle, as the cam will then separate the points earlier and allow them to close later. Decreasing the point gap will increase the dwell angle as the points will then be in contact with the distributor cam for a shorter period of time.

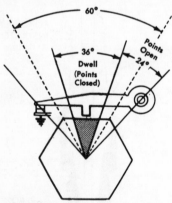

Dwell angle (© G.M. Corp)

Ignition timing refers to the point in the rotation of the engine when ignition occurs. It is measured in degrees of crankshaft rotation in relation to TDC in number one cylinder when the cylinder is on the compression stroke. Timing is gener-

ally set at an engine speed which requires no centrifugal or vacuum advance, although in some cases vacuum retarding action is in effect.

The dwell angle *must* be set before the timing is adjusted and must *never* be disturbed unless timing is reset immediately thereafter. While ignition timing has no effect on dwell angle, a dwell change will affect timing because the distributor cam will separate the points at a different point in the rotation of the distributor shaft after the dwell adjustment.

Adjust timing and dwell as follows:

1. Connect a dwell-tach to the ignition system with the engine off. The negative or black clip goes to a good ground, while the positive or red clip should be attached to the negative (distributor) terminal of the coil primary circuit.

2. Make sure the wires are away from the fan and other engine auxiliaries. Start the engine and place it in or out of gear, as the manufacturer recommends on the engine compartment sticker or in a manual. If setting the timing requires disconnecting the vacuum lines, etc., perform these operations before setting the dwell. Switch the dwell tach to the tachometer function and to the proper setting for the number of cylinders in the engine. Making sure you are reading the right scale, check to see if the idle speed is as specified for setting the timing. Dwell should be set at this speed because some distributors on late-model cars change their dwell settings as rpm changes. Adjust the idle speed if it is not as specified.

3. Switch the dwell-tach over to the dwell function and read the dwell angle. If

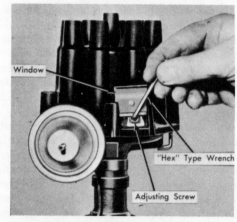

Adjusting the dwell angle (© G.M. Corp)

the dwell is outside the range specified by the manufacturer, adjust it.

4. Readjust the dwell, increasing the point gap if the dwell angle is too large, and decreasing it if the angle is too small. On some distributors, this may be done with an allen wrench through a window in the side of the distributor while the engine is running.

5. Turn off the engine and locate number one (no. 1) cylinder. Most engine blocks (or intake manifolds) are marked. Number one cylinder is usually the front one on inline engines, or the right front one on V8 engines. The timing light is usually connected by inserting a high-tension connection between the no. 1 plug and its wire and then connecting two 12 V leads to the battery—red to positive; black to negative. Making sure that no wires are near the fan, start the engine and, if necessary, put the transmission in gear.

The timing mark and scale (© G.M. Corp)

6. Aim the timing light at the pulley on the front of the engine. The timing mark, which is usually a groove in the outer flange of the pulley, should be visible each time the timing light flashes. It may be necessary to stop the engine and mark the groove with chalk if visibility is poor.

7. Line up the timing mark with the scale, pointer, or mark on the engine. If necessary, loosen the distributor locking bolt and turn it until the pulley mark aligns with the proper mark on the engine. (Check the manufacturer's specifications.) Tighten the locking bolt and recheck the timing before shutting off the engine.

Electronic Ignition Systems

Electronic ignition systems are a product of the age of automotive emissions. While they have been available from the early sixties, their proliferation occurred in the seventies with the advent of controls limiting automotive exhaust emissions. Two of the main advantages of electronic ignition systems are their greater voltage-delivering capacity and their lack of scheduled maintenance. The ability to deliver a greater voltage to the spark plugs enables the engine to burn a leaner mixture efficently, a lean mixture is necessary in order to lower emissions. Electronic ignition has, for the most part, either replaced or changed the function of the points and condenser of the conventional ignition system. With these parts changed, a major portion of tune-up maintenance is eliminated. Since the plugs are being fired with a higher secondary voltage, the result is that they will remain cleaner longer as the deposits which would foul a plug in a conventional system are burned off by the electronic system. Therefore, replacement intervals for spark plugs have been extended anywhere from 20,000 to 35,000 miles.

As for how it works, first go back and read the explanation of the conventional system so you have a thorough understanding of the system. The reason for this is that both systems work similarly. Basically it's like this: inside the distributor a pick-up unit senses the change in the magnetic field which occurs when the distributor shaft

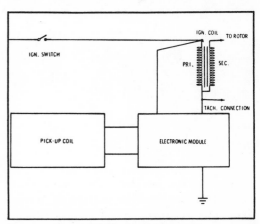

Fig. A: A simplified electronic ignition system schematic (Courtesy Chevrolet Motor Div.)

(cam-reluctor) passes in and out of alignment with a pick-up unit. This triggers a voltage in the pick-up unit to be sent to the 'black box' or electronic brain. The voltage sent by the pick-up unit is read by the brain to either build up or collapse the primary circuit. When the signal is to collapse the primary circuit, a high voltage is induced in the secondary circuit which fires the plug. Since the system is being instantaneously trigger fed by the module rather than through a point set, no voltage is lost arcing across the points; full battery voltage can be delivered to the ignition coil. The condenser which would absorb the excess voltage passing through the points in a conventional system, in an electronic system merely filters any excess amount of current which would interfere with radio reception.

TROUBLESHOOTING

In order to properly troubleshoot an electronic ignition system, you must have a good set of instructions in front of you which apply specifically to the system you are working on. These can be found in *Chilton's Auto Repair Manual, Chilton's Import Automotive Repair Manual* or one of *Chilton's Repair and Tune-Up Guides* for a particular car. We'll outline here a few simple things which could affect any electronic ignition system.

First of all, no system is totally maintenance free. The parts may not wear out as often as in the old systems, but they are still affected by use. At least once a year, you should take a look at the components of the system and check for visible damage, that is, cracks in the distributor cap, worn insulation around the spark plugs, wires, loose wire boots and anything else you can see by just poking around under the hood.

When you suspect a problem, do not immediately jump on the ignition system for being at fault. Make certain it is not in another system such as the fuel or emission control system. Start by eliminating the obvious and working down to other possibilities. Something as simple as a tankful of low grade gas can cause symptoms which act and feel like ignition problems. When you think you've got the problem narrowed to the ignition system, don't immediately think overhaul. Look around, check the wires for tightness, cracks, and broken insulation, pull out a spark plug and check it.

When you are ready to start working on the system, take your time and make sure you read the instructions. Also do not skip any steps that do not seem important at the time, go through the system step by step until you finally locate and solve the problem.

14 · The Fuel System

How It Works

The fuel burned in a gasoline engine is a mixture of hydrocarbon liquids—all with different boiling points. The purpose of the fuel system is to mix the proper amount of fuel with the air that the engine demands, effectively evaporate most of the fuel, and conduct the air/fuel mixture to the engine cylinders. The fuel system also regulates the flow of mixture to the engine for control of power output.

The fuel is stored in a tank which generally serves to allow for settling of water and other foreign material by picking up the fuel several inches off the bottom of the tank. A strainer is frequently used in the pick-up inside the tank.

Most engines employ a mechanical fuel pump which is driven by an eccentric on the camshaft. The pump is a flexible diaphragm mounted inside a housing. The eccentric on the camshaft forces the diaphragm down for intake of fuel and a spring forces the diaphragm back up. When fuel is not required by the carburetor, the spring remains compressed and the diaphragm remains motionless during what would normally be a discharge

A typical carburetor (© G.M. Corp)

stroke for the pump. A line connects the fuel pick-up in the tank with the pump so the suction created by the pump can pull fuel from the tank to the pump inlet. A similar line connects the pump outlet to the carburetor. Some vehicles use electrically driven pumps that operate much as the engine-driven pump, but use solenoids to move the pump diaphragm up and down. A few vehicles employ in-tank centrifugal, electrical pumps.

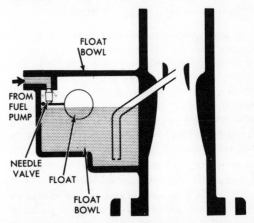

The carburetor float system (© G.M. Corp)

The carburetor stores the fuel in a vented tank known as the "float bowl." A float-operated valve maintains the level of fuel in the bowl within a narrow range. As the fuel level rises, the float will rise and close off the valve, thus causing the movement of the fuel pump diaphragm to be reduced because of reduced discharge of fuel.

The carburetor handles all the air which the engine receives and regulates its flow through the action of a throttle. The air passes through a slight restriction in the carburetor, known as a "venturi." The venturi causes some of the atmospheric pressure that is pushing the air to be lost as the air speeds up in passing through the restriction. The pressure in the venturi

139

drops as the air flow increases. In order to improve the accuracy of the metering at low speeds, a booster venturi is frequently used. It is a much smaller venturi, mounted above the regular one, in the center of the carburetor bore.

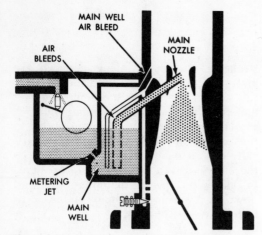

The carburetor main circuit (© G.M. Corp)

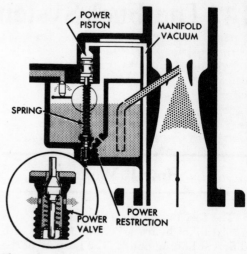

The carburetor power system (© G.M. Corp)

A main metering system, consisting of a nozzle and a discharge tube which carries the fuel to a spot inside the venturi in the throttle bore, conducts the fuel to the airstream during most driving conditions. Since vacuum in the venturi is proportional to the amount of air passing through it, the air/fuel ratio is fairly accurately governed by the amount of vacuum available to lift fuel from the bowl to the discharge. If the carburetor uses a booster venturi, fuel is discharged at the center of the booster to provide the best possible metering at low speeds. The arm which carries fuel to the booster venturi and supports it is usually integral with several other carburetor parts, such as idle or accelerator pump passages. The assembly is known as the "venturi cluster" and can be separated from the main body of the carburetor during disassembly. In some carburetors, a metering rod, which is positioned by the throttle linkage, throttles the flow of fuel through the main discharge nozzle for increased metering accuracy.

The flow of fuel through the main nozzle is supplemented at very high throttle openings by a power enrichment system that provides sufficient fuel to ensure fullest use of the air inducted by the engine at full power conditions. This system consists of an auxiliary fuel passage and metering valve on carburetors which do not employ

metering rods, and an auxiliary metering rod positioning mechanism on those which do. In either case, a piston is kept in an inactive position by high manifold vacuum. When manifold vacuum becomes very low, as at full throttle, the piston either opens the valve in the auxiliary fuel passage, or, in the case of units using metering rods, moves the rod slightly further out of the main metering nozzle, or "jet." A spring generally forces the system to operate when manifold vacuum drops off.

The carburetor also employs an idle passage which conducts fuel from the float bowl to a spot below the throttle. When the throttle is nearly shut, the vacuum created in the venturi is negligible, but manifold vacuum under the throttle is very high, and pulls the fuel required at idle through this small auxiliary system. Flow of fuel through this system is adjustable by a mixture screw accessible from outside the carburetor.

The carburetor also employs a pump that is operated by the throttle linkage to discharge a spray of fuel into the airstream during sudden increases in throttle opening. This pump provides instant response to sudden changes in conditions.

Many carburetors use two or four venturis to provide better distribution of fuel to the engine or to permit progressive use of two sets of venturis for more accurate metering of fuel over a wider range of air flow conditions.

The fuel is conducted by a series of tubes from the carburetor to the intake ports of the engine block. These tubes are known as the "intake manifold" and branch away from the carburetor base. Small tubes are used all the way from the carburetor to each cylinder to avoid the restriction to mixture flow that would result if large ducts were suddenly narrowed down to the size of the intake valves. The high velocity in the intake manifold also helps the fuel to be more completely evaporated by the time it reaches the combustion chambers.

Evaporation is also aided by designing the carburetor to thoroughly atomize the fuel and by heating the manifold slightly with exhaust manifold heat. Some exhaust manifold heating systems employ a thermostatic valve to channel the flow of hot gases either toward or away from the intake manifold walls depending on temperature conditions.

During cold-engine operating conditions, evaporation of fuel is very poor. The carburetor uses a choke to permit smooth cold-engine operation. The choke is constructed much like the throttle, but is located above the venturi so that closing it will produce a vacuum that will increase the amount of fuel flowing from the carburetor jets into the air stream. This very rich mixture will contain sufficient fuel to provide a combustible mixture, even though the cold temperatures will retard the evaporation process.

The choke is operated by a thermostatic spring, the tension of which is relaxed by heat from the exhaust manifold as the engine warms up. Intake manifold vacuum also affects the position of the choke, which is mounted off center in the carburetor bore. Increased flow of air will thus tend to open the choke and maintain a fairly even vacuum at the fuel metering jets. A vacuum-operated diaphragm may also be used to prevent cold operation from being excessively rich. The diaphragm is linked to the choke through a lever arm and opens the choke slightly as soon as there is a vacuum in the manifold.

An air cleaner is mounted on top of the carburetor to remove dust and dirt from the air and to avoid excessive wear of engine parts. Most recent air filters are made of a sufficiently porous paper to permit a relatively unrestricted flow of air while catching dust particles.

DETONATION

Detonation, or "knock" or "ping," is a severely damaging form of explosive combustion. During normal engine operation, combustion is only partly complete as the piston passes TDC at the beginning of the power stroke. The full energy of the fuel is released gradually as the piston descends and is converted to mechanical energy almost as fast as heat is created by combustion. Detonation occurs as a result of extreme temperatures and pressures in the cylinders. Cylinder temperatures become so high that the pressure increase caused by combustion near the spark plug raises a great portion of the total charge to a temperature above its ignition point, causing simultaneous combustion at many points in the chamber rather than the normal gradual spreading of the flame. The result is a violent shock to the piston and cylinder walls and searing heat.

Gasoline octane rating refers to the ability of the fuel to resist rapid combustion of the type that damages the engine. Detonation may be caused by use of the wrong spark plug, an incorrect fuel mixture, improper ignition timing, or overheating. However, by far the most common cause, assuming the engine is reasonably well maintained, is use of a fuel of too low an octane rating. Use a reputable brand of

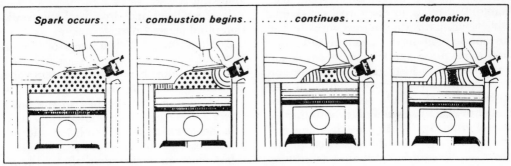

Detonation

gasoline of regular or premium grade, depending on the manufacturer's recommendations for the particular engine. In some cases, this will still result in slight detonation because of variations in individual engines. A fuel with sufficient anti-knock quality should be used to avoid audible detonation.

VAPOR LOCK AND PERCOLATION

Vapor lock is the evaporation of fuel into vapor due to heat conducted to the fuel pump. This vapor paralyzes the pump. The pump has only limited ability to handle gaseous material. The vapor simply expands and contracts as the diaphragm operates, rather than flowing in and out. Some air-conditioned cars have a return line designed to allow fuel vapor to be shunted back to the fuel tank.

Percolation is a related phenomenon, but occurs in the carburetor. Fuel vapor formed by heat increases the pressure in the float bowl, causing it to overflow into the throttle bores. Flooding problems result when the engine is hot.

Quick Reference Guide For Fuel System Troubleshooting

A. *Inspect the system.* Make sure there is fuel in the tank. Remove the air cleaner and check it for clogging. Clean or replace it as necessary. Check the choke for freedom of operation and proper response to temperature conditions. See subsection F. if the choke appears to be malfunctioning. Check the throttle bores for the presence of excess fuel. Check for fuel in the carburetor by operating the throttle linkage and looking for accelerator pump discharge. If there is no discharge, check further by cranking the engine with one of the spark plug leads disconnected, and then removing a spark plug to check for the presence of fuel. Tap the carburetor bowl sharply several times, then crank the engine with the high-tension lead connected to check for relief of the flooding or no-fuel condition. If this permits the engine to start, go directly to subsection G. Check all accessible carburetor mounting nuts and screws for tightness.

B. *Check the fuel supply system.* Disconnect the fuel line at the carburetor. Crank the engine and collect fuel in a clean glass container. If the fuel volume appears to be adequate and the fuel is clean, see subsection C. and then skip D. and E. if pump pressure is adequate. If the fuel contains water, drain the tank and refill it with clean fuel. If fuel volume is minimal and there are bubbles, see D.

C. *Check pump output pressure.* Pressure should be approximately 3–7 lbs. If pressure and volume are all right, go to subsection F.

D. *Check pump suction.* Check for loose connections at the pump inlet and fuel tank. Check the pump's ability to pull vacuum. It should pull about 15 in. If vacuum is inadequate, the pump must be replaced. If vacuum is adequate but pressure and volume problems are evident, check the strainers and lines as in E. Replace the pump only if these checks do not improve performance.

E. *Check strainers and lines.* Check the condition of the fuel tank strainer and clean it if necessary. Blow out the tank-to-pump and pump-to-carburetor lines. Check all lines for cracks or bad fittings. Check and clean the carburetor strainer if necessary. If the fuel pump has a strainer, check it and, if necessary, clean it.

F. *Check the choke and throttle linkages.* Make sure the throttle linkage works freely and permits the throttle to open fully. Check the choke for freedom of operation and proper response. Correct any binding and check all adjustments.

G. *Check for carburetor internal problems.* If sticking of the float was noted in A., it would be wise to attempt treating the carburetor with a solvent first to avoid unnecessary disassembly. Remove the carburetor and disassemble it. Make the following checks:

1. Float level and drop, and the condition of all related parts.

2. Mounting and cleanliness of venturi cluster.

3. Metering valve or power system valve adjustment, and the condition of parts.

4. Appearance of the fuel in the bowl. Check for leakage in the bowl.

5. Accelerator pump condition and adjustments.

6. Condition of throttle shafts and bores and cleanliness of jets.

H. Check for miscellaneous fuel system problems, which cause bad idle, vapor lock, stalling, or running on. Check manifold bolts, idle speed, idle mixture, and solenoid or dashpot operation. Check for leaks in the intake system, and check the function of the PCV system. Check the operation of the manifold heat control valve. Check for proper routing of the fuel lines.

Fuel System Troubleshooting

A. Inspect the System.

Make sure there is fuel in the tank. Turn on the ignition switch and look at the gauge. If the gauge responds normally and reads anywhere but at the extremes, there is probably fuel in the tank. Unless you're sure that there is fuel in the tank, gently push a clean, slender object down the tank filler to check. If fuel level cannot be clearly determined in this way, the best procedure is to put a gallon or two of fuel in to ensure the pick-up is covered.

Remove the air cleaner to check its condition. It should be possible to see a bright light through a paper element. If the element is dirty, blow the dirt off from the inside with air pressure. If this will not do an adequate cleaning job, the filter element should be replaced.

An oil bath unit will rarely clog enough to severely restrict air flow but it would be wise to clean a very dirty unit by dipping it in a solvent and moving it back and forth until the dirt has been effectively removed. Drain the oil from the base, remove the residue with solvent, and refill the base to the mark with clean engine oil. Do not reinstall the air cleaner until the fuel system problem has been found.

Open the throttle slightly to allow the automatic choke to set itself, and then check its position. If the engine is dead cold, and the outside temperature is as low as 70° F, the choke will generally close fully. The choke should be wide open at operating temperature. At temperatures in between these extremes, the choke should seek a middle position. After observing the position of the choke, move the flap very gently back and forth holding the throttle part-way open. If the choke does not come

to an appropriate position, or if it does not move freely, see F.

Check for flooding next. Inspect the throttle bores for the presence of liquid fuel. If there is an obvious smell of raw fuel and the bores are lined with liquid, the engine is flooded. Flooding may be caused by improper starting technique—primarily, pumping of the throttle. If this is not suspected, tap the carburetor bowl firmly with a light but solid object, and then crank the engine for 20–30 seconds with the throttle held firmly to the floor. If this procedure allows the car to start, the problem is a stuck float. If the carburetor was flooded, see subsection C. on checking fuel pump pressure, and then go to subsection G.

To test for the presence of fuel in the carburetor, move the throttle from idle position to full throttle while watching for accelerator pump discharge. If there is no discharge, check further before assuming there is no fuel in the carburetor. Disconnect one of the spark plug leads. Crank the engine for 15–20 seconds with the throttle slightly open. Immediately pull the spark plug where the lead was disconnected. Check the electrodes for the presence of fuel. If the electrodes are dry, either the carburetor is malfunctioning or there is no fuel getting to it. Tap the carburetor bowl several times with a light but solid object, and then replace the spark plug and repeat the test. If this puts noticeable amounts of fuel on the plug's electrodes or enables the engine to start, the problem is a stuck float and subsection G. should be consulted without going through the others. Go to G. also, if the accelerator pump discharges fuel.

B. Check the Fuel Supply System.

Disconnect the fuel line at the carburetor. Ground the distributor high-tension lead. Crank the engine for about 15 seconds with a clean glass container held under the open end of the fuel line. Fuel should be discharged regularly and forcefully, and it should not contain bubbles. If the discharge is minimal, see D. and E. to find out whether the problem is in the pump or lines. If there are bubbles, see E.

The fuel collected in the glass should be carefully inspected for the presence of water and dirt. If very small water bubbles are present, the fuel in the tank may be treated with any of several products designed to make the water mix with the gas and thus be eliminated from the system. If a layer of water is formed on the bottom of the glass, the fuel system must be thoroughly cleaned as follows:

1. Drain the gas tank. Drains are provided on many tanks for removal of the water and dirt which tend to accumulate there. If no drain is provided, the fuel line will have to be disconnected, and the tank will have to be dismounted so the water and dirt can be drained out the filler pipe. The tank should be flushed with clean fuel before replacing the fittings and restoring it to service.

2. Check the condition of the fuel tank strainer, generally located in the pick-up and fuel gauge assembly, and replace it if it is damaged.

3. Blow out the tank-to-pump line and the pump-to-carburetor line with compressed air.

C. Check Pump Output Pressure.

The pressure may be checked by removing the pump discharge line and connecting a pressure gauge to the pump outlet. There are many gauges on the market for testing fuel pump pressure, manifold vacuum, etc. These employ a connector of standard size which will fit into most fuel pump discharge openings.

A check of pump output pressure will determine the ability of the pump to force fuel to the carburetor, and also check its ability to draw fuel from the tank, and the ability of the tank-to-pump lines to supply it, provided a good discharge volume was noted in B. Most fuel pumps are rated at engine idle speed. If the engine will run, it is best to connect all fuel and ignition lines, start the engine, and allow it to run to fill the carburetor float bowl. Disconnect the fuel line at the pump, hook up the test gauge, and restart the engine, running it at slow idle on the fuel in the float bowl. If the engine will not run, pump operation at cranking speeds will give an indication of whether or not the pump will function well enough to permit the engine to start.

Fuel pump pressures generally range from three to seven pounds. Three pounds will at least supply the carburetor with adequate fuel for starting the engine. At idle speed, however, the pump pressure should be within the range specified by the manufacturer; either low or high pressures can cause operating problems.

If the fuel pump pressure is all right, be sure to check the pump-to-carburetor fuel line and carburetor strainer for clogging. Then go to F.

D. Check Pump Suction.

A check of fuel pump suction will reveal whether or not the pump is faulty. Low output pressure can also result from a restriction or leak in the suction lines.

Disconnect *both* the pump discharge and inlet lines. The discharge is disconnected so there is no chance that a restriction in the line or carburetor strainer, or a normally functioning carburetor float, could restrict pump discharge and prevent the pump from developing its full suction power.

Connect a vacuum gauge to the pump, using an appropriate piece of rubber hose. Crank the engine until the gauge reaches a stable reading. It should be 15 in. or over. If not, the pump is faulty, and should be replaced.

A pump that will pull 15 in. of vacuum *can* be faulty. If checking and cleaning the strainers and lines as in E. does not result in good fuel pump performance, replace the pump.

E. Check Strainers and Lines.

If the fuel pump output pressure is inadequate, but the pump is capable of pulling a good vacuum, the fuel lines are most likely clogged or kinked, or the fuel system fittings are loose or cracked. A careful visual inspection of all accessible parts of the system should be made before the difficult-to-reach parts are checked out. The fitting at the fuel pump suction side should be very carefully inspected for cracks or deterioration. If a flexible hose is used here, the hose should be crack-free and firm in order to resist collapsing, and it must be equipped with good clamps. Replace any doubtful parts. The entire length of the fuel lines along the frame to the fuel tank should be checked for the presence of kinks or dents that might have come from improper installation or road damage. The fuel line should then be removed from the tank and blown out with compressed air or replaced, as necessary. The fuel tank strainer should be inspected to ensure that it is clean and properly installed.

The fuel pump-to-carburetor line should also be checked for kinks, cracks, or bad fittings, and blown out with compressed air. The fuel strainer in the carburetor should be checked for cleanliness and cleaned or replaced as necessary. If the vehicle employs an inline fuel filter or strainer, be sure to check its condition and connections.

F. Check the Choke and Throttle Linkages.

An inoperative throttle linkage could prevent starting by keeping the choke from closing during cranking or failing to supply adequate fuel/air mixture. Also, inadequate performance can frequently be traced to a linkage which does not open the throttle all the way. Have someone depress the accelerator pedal to the floor while you watch the throttle blade. It should reach a perfectly vertical position as the accelerator pedal reaches the floor. Adjustable linkages usually employ some sort of clamp or turnbuckle arrangement which is easily adjusted. Nonadjustable types that do not provide proper throttle operation usually perform improperly because of a bent bracket or a stretched cable.

Some four-barrel carburetors employ special air valves at the tops of their bores for controlling the metering of fuel. Check to see that the shafts which bear these valve flaps turn freely in their bores. Disassemble them and clean the shaft and the shaft bores if there is binding.

If a four-barrel carburetor uses vacuum diaphragm actuation of the secondary bores, the throttles must be observed with the engine running and air cleaner removed. At full-throttle position and high rpm, the secondary throttles should open fully. If they do not operate properly, check for binding or a leaky vacuum diaphragm.

An improperly functioning automatic choke is one of the most frequent causes of difficult starting. Because it operates through a delicate balance of carburetor air and thermostatic spring pressures, its tolerance to the accumulation of dirt is very low. Its delicate mechanism is also easily damaged.

An excellent indication of choke condition is its position when the engine is cold. Remove the air cleaner, open the throttle wide to release the choke mechanism from the fast idle cam, and observe what the choke does. It should close all the way if the engine is cold and the outside temperature is 70° or below. Under higher temperature conditions, the choke will generally be part-way closed until the engine thermostat opens (hot water is present in both radiator hoses). If the choke does not respond properly, it should be cleaned very carefully with solvent, and inspected for bent or broken linkage parts. The most effective procedure is to remove the screws that hold the choke flap to the choke (being *very* careful not to drop them down the carburetor throat), unfasten and remove the various parts of the linkage, usually simple metal clips, and pull the shaft and flap out of the carburetor throat. The shaft should be checked for bending, a very common cause of choke binding, and the shaft and the shaft bores in the carburetor very thoroughly cleaned of dirt and carbon deposits. If the choke uses a choke piston, located within the body of the carburetor, particular attention should be paid to determining that the piston and bore are clean, as this is another place binding can occur as a result of accumulated dirt.

During reassembly, all parts of the mechanism should be thoroughly checked to make sure no binding will occur due to bent parts. For example, if a U-shaped link is used in the mechanism, the center portion of the link should be straight, and the two ends should be parallel. There is a secondary air valve lockout, on four-barrel carburetors, which rides along a pin located on the choke flap, parallel to the shaft. This can be bent during air cleaner installation and can cause binding of the choke. In either of these cases, the choke will malfunction even though all parts may be perfectly clean. The watchword is thoroughness. No part of the choke linkage should be above suspicion, and all parts should be carefully removed and inspected.

The same kind of care pays off in the cleaning process. Disassemble the linkage wherever one part turns on another. Treat the unit with solvent and wipe with a clean rag or paper towel to remove any grime loosened by the solvent.

After the mechanism is reassembled, several checks of choke operation should

GUM AND VARNISH DEPOSITS

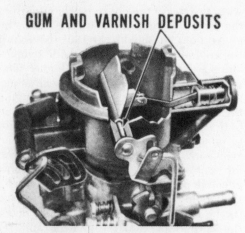

Spots where gum and varnish form on carburetors using choke pistons (Courtesy, Chrysler Corp)

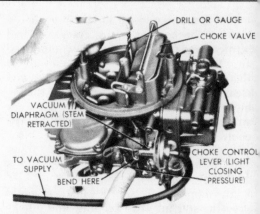

A typical factory manual illustration giving instructions on choke vacuum break adjustment (Courtesy, Chrysler Corp)

be made. These are best made with a factory manual or *Chilton's Auto Repair Manual*. These manuals contain specific instructions on the proper method of adjusting the various linkages and the proper specifications. Some cursory checks and adjustments can be made, however.

1. Choke coil operation. It would be wise to remove and inspect the choke coil. If the coil is housed in a circular chamber which is rotated to make the basic choke adjustment, mark the position of the chamber so it can be replaced in its original position. Remove the choke thermostatic coil housing and inspect the coil to make sure it is intact and clean. If there is evidence of corrosion, replace the choke heat tube or heat well so exhaust gases cannot continue to enter the coil housing. If the engine is hot, a rough check of choke coil adjustments can be made by placing the coil and housing in a cool spot until they have reached room temperature, and then quickly putting them in place on the carburetor, opening the throttle, and watching the choke. If the choke does not close fully, a slight twisting of an adjustable housing or a slight bend of the choke actuating rod, if the housing is not adjustable, will usually correct the problem. Move the choke flap to the wide open position to make sure the adjustment will not keep the choke from opening fully.

2. Choke vacuum break operation. The choke vacuum break is operated by the intake manifold vacuum created when the engine starts, and is placed on the carburetor to eliminate overly rich operation just after the engine has been started from

cold. If the vehicle starts properly, but tends to run richly and smoke for the first few minutes of driving, the choke vacuum break may be at fault. The function of the vacuum diaphragm may be checked by starting the engine and allowing it to idle. Under these conditions, the vacuum diaphragm should recede into the housing and seat firmly. Check to see that this motion will pull the choke part-way open by forcing it toward the closed position until all the play in the linkage is removed and the diaphragm is keeping the choke from moving farther. To check this adjustment precisely, refer to a manual for instructions. These instructions will usually specify that the choke flap must be a certain distance from the front wall of the throttle bore with all the play in the linkage removed and the vacuum diaphragm firmly seated. The wire link between the vacuum diaphragm and the choke linkage is usually bent at the bottom of a U-shaped section to adjust the linkage. The vacuum diaphragm may be seated by running the engine, employing a vacuum pump on the end of the vacuum diaphragm hose, or by gently holding the diaphragm in the withdrawn position by hand. Using vacuum is preferable to handling the delicate mechanism, and guarantees that the diaphragm will be fully seated, if at least 15 in. of vacuum is employed.

If the vacuum diaphragm does not function, check for a cracked or loose hose, a plugged carburetor port, or binding in the linkage. If no problems are uncovered in these areas, replace the vacuum unit. Its diaphragm is probably ruptured.

3. Choke unloader operation. The choke

unloader is operated by the throttle and is placed on the choke to permit the driver to relieve a flooding condition by cranking the engine with the throttle held to the floor. The choke unloader mechanism forces the choke part-way open mechanically, to provide a leaner mixture than is usually required when the engine is cold.

The mechanism usually consists of a tang which is mounted on the end of the throttle shaft near the fast idle cam. When the throttle is opened wide, the tang bears against one side of the fast idle cam. The fast idle cam is mounted on a shaft which protrudes from the side of the carburetor body. A linkage connects the cam and a lever mounted on the end of the choke shaft. The effect is that the unloader tang turns the cam slightly, which in turn, through its linkage, forces the choke valve part-way open regardless of the pressure of the thermostatic spring.

The tang is usually bent to adjust the opening of the unloader. A drill of specified size is inserted between the edge of the choke flap and the carburetor throttle bore wall, the choke is forced gently closed, and the throttle is held wide open. The adjustment is correct when the tang is bent so the unloader mechanism just allows the choke flap to be closed until it contacts the drill. If specific instructions and specifications are not available, an ineffective unloader mechanism can be made more effective by gently bending the tang so the choke will be opened somewhat more.

4. Fast idle adjustment. The fast idle mechanism uses the choke linkage to position a cam, which, under cold conditions, moves under the engine idle adjustment screw or an auxiliary screw provided for fast cold idle. Either cold stalling or racing of the engine can usually be cured by bringing the fast idle adjustment to specifications. Fast idle is generally adjusted with the engine warm in order to standardize the conditions within the manifold and combustion chambers. The fast idle cam is manually turned to place the fast idle screw on the specified spot of the cam, for example, the highest point on the second step of the cam and the screw adjusted until the engine speed meets specifications (as measured by a tachometer).

Of course, adjustments can be made to cure either racing or cold stalling without the use of a tachometer and factory specs. However, such adjustments are frequently inadequate to cure the problem or else cause another problem, perhaps the opposite of the original. Specs and a tachometer allow a much more satisfactory adjustment.

G. Check for Carburetor Internal Problems.

NOTE: *A carburetor is an extremely delicate, precision instrument. Carburetor disassembly and work should be attempted only by someone familiar with carburetion, or at least experienced with general mechanics. If possible, a Chilton Auto Repair Manual or factory manual should be consulted so that disassembly can be accomplished without damage. Also, it is recommended, for safety's sake, that gasoline not be used as a solvent because of its flammability. Other solvents are available at auto parts stores.*

In all cases, a carburetor gasket kit should be purchased before disassembly to permit replacement of all the gaskets that are disturbed in the process of disassembly. Gaskets, in general, *cannot* be expected to survive such an operation intact.

If the problem is a stuck float or other, relatively minor, malfunction, treat the carburetor with a carburetor cleaning solvent. If the only cause of malfunction is dirt accumulation, the problem can frequently be solved by such a treatment, thus saving the time and trouble of disassembly. Persistent problems are probably the result of mechanical wear and disassembly will, therefore, be required.

Disassembly is usually accomplished as follows:

1. Remove the carburetor linkages and fuel line, and then remove the nuts which hold the unit to the manifold. Place the unit on a clean bench.

2. Remove all external linkages.

3. Remove the float bowl cover which is generally held on to the top of the carburetor with screws. The condition of the float, needle, and seat can usually be checked without further disassembly.

4. Remove the choke and float parts. Remove the power piston.

5. Remove the main jets, venturi cluster, and the throttle body from the bowl.

6. Disassemble the throttle body. Do

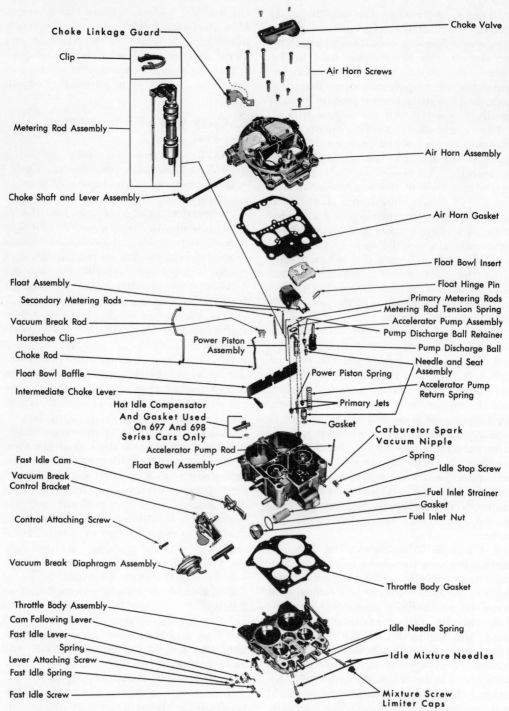

Choke Linkage Guard

Clip

Metering Rod Assembly

Choke Shaft and Lever Assembly

Choke Valve

Air Horn Screws

Air Horn Assembly

Air Horn Gasket

Float Bowl Insert

Float Hinge Pin

Float Assembly
Secondary Metering Rods
Vacuum Break Rod
Horseshoe Clip
Choke Rod
Float Bowl Baffle
Intermediate Choke Lever

Power Piston
Assembly

Primary Metering Rods
Metering Rod Tension Spring
Accelerator Pump Assembly
Pump Discharge Ball Retainer
Pump Discharge Ball
Needle and Seat
Assembly
Accelerator Pump
Return Spring

Power Piston Spring

Primary Jets

Hot Idle Compensator
And Gasket Used
On 697 And 698
Series Cars Only

Gasket

Carburetor Spark
Vacuum Nipple

Accelerator Pump Rod
Float Bowl Assembly

Fast Idle Cam
Vacuum Break
Control Bracket

Spring

Idle Stop Screw

Fuel Inlet Strainer
Gasket
Fuel Inlet Nut

Control Attaching Screw

Vacuum Break Diaphragm Assembly

Throttle Body Gasket

Throttle Body Assembly
Cam Following Lever
Fast Idle Lever
Spring
Lever Attaching Screw
Fast Idle Spring
Fast Idle Screw

Idle Needle Spring

Idle Mixture Needles

Mixture Screw
Limiter Caps

Exploded view of a carburetor (Courtesy, G.M. Corp)

not remove the idle mixture adjustment screws on late-model cars unless damage is evident.

Check the carburetor as outlined below:

a. Shake the float to make sure it is dry inside. If there is any evidence of fuel in-side, replace the float. Inspect the needle and seat for wear. If there is evidence of a groove in the needle, replace the needle and seat. Upon reassembling the float mechanism, make sure the float is aligned properly (so its edge is parallel to the edge of the float bowl cover). Bend the float arm slightly if an adjustment is necessary. Adjust the float level and drop according to the manufacturer's specifications. Ensuring proper float, needle, and seat operation will cure many problems of rough running, hard starting, flooding, and poor fuel mileage.

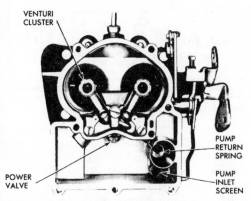

The venturi cluster (© G.M. Corp)

b. Mounting of venturi cluster. If your carburetor is not dirty or badly worn, and full disassembly is not necessary, make sure that all of the venturi cluster mounting screws are snug. A leaky venturi cluster can cause rough idle, flat acceleration, and generally rough running.

c. Metering rod or power system valve adjustment and condition of parts. The metering valves and power system valves cannot be visually inspected. If the vehicle has been run for a long distance without a carburetor overhaul, replace the metering rod or power valve rods and jets, especially if high-speed performance is a problem. Make sure the power piston or metering rod vacuum piston and its bore are smooth and in good condition. Replace scored pistons. Inspect any springs, and replace them if they are distorted or broken. Adjustments should be made during reassembly. Specific procedures must be consulted. Curing power system and metering rod problems will help to eliminate many problems of poor fuel economy and sluggish performance.

d. The appearance of the fuel in the float bowl will indicate whether or not clean fuel is being supplied to the carburetor. If evidence of dirt or water in the bowl exists, clean the fuel system or clean or replace filters and strainers as necessary. The float bowl should be carefully

checked for leakage while it is separated from the rest of the carburetor. This will be evidenced by a rapid drop in the level of fuel in the bowl.

e. Accelerator pump condition. Inspect all points in the mechanical linkages where wear may occur (e.g., shafts, bores, holes in shaft arms, etc.), and replace if necessary. Inspect all shaft arms for tightness on their shafts and replace any loose assemblies. Inspect any leather washers or diaphragms for cracks, turned edges, or damage, and replace as necessary. Inspect check balls for corrosion or other roughness, and replace a rough check ball or distorted retainer or spring. If the pump uses a check needle, replace it if it is bent or grooved. Blow through the pump jets to ensure cleanliness. Curing accelerator pump problems will aid throttle response and, in some cases, improve gas mileage and cure other performance complaints.

f. Inspect the condition of the throttle shafts and bores. About 0.005 in. clearance is normal. Excessively worn parts will cause air leakage and resultant dilution of the mixture. Throttle flaps should be perfectly flat and should have smooth edges. Replace excessively worn parts. Make sure the main jets (if not already checked under item c.) are clean. Use solvent and compressed air for cleaning, as forcing a thin gauge wire or other object through the jets will *invariably* damage them.

H. Check for Miscellaneous Fuel System Problems.

POOR IDLE

A poor idle is most frequently caused by dirty idle jets or an improper idle mixture adjustment. In cars with emission control systems, though, especially where mixture screws are sealed, other problems should be suspected first. Check out the system as follows:

1. Inspect the manifold bolts, and the carburetor mounting bolts and screws for tightness. Look for cracks in the carburetor body or warping, which would be indicated by unevenness in the seams between the various sections of the carburetor. Manifold leaks can be detected by pouring oil on the joints between the manifold and engine block while the engine is idling. Improvement in idle indicates leaks. Intake manifold bolts should be tightened

A typical engine compartment emission control information sticker (© G.M. Corp)

to specifications using a torque wrench. Consult a manual for the specified torque and tightening pattern.

2. If the vehicle has adjustable mixture screws, adjust them for the fastest possible idle speed. A tachometer or vacuum gauge can be used to indicate highest idle speed or manifold vacuum. Follow the instructions on the engine compartment sticker for idle mixture adjustments if the vehicle was built to meet emission standards. Where idle mixture screws are capped, all other possibilities should be exhausted before removing the caps and adjusting the mixture.

3. Make sure the engine is idling at the specified idle speed. Too slow an idle can cause rough running. Use a tachometer and consult the engine compartment sticker or owner's manual for idle speed specifications.

4. Check the PCV system. Replace the PCV valve if pinching the PCV hose near the valve does not cause idle speed to drop 40–80 rpm. Inspect all hoses for bad connections, cracks, or breaks.

5. Check the thermostatically controlled air cleaner. The air cleaner flap should cut off all engine compartment air and draw all air through the heat stove until the engine and compartment are warm. The flap should then remain closed enough to maintain a temperature of 85° F in the air horn. If the flap does not seem to function properly, the system may be tested by placing a small thermometer in the air horn with the air cleaner assembled and the engine operating. Check all hoses and connections, inspect the linkage between

the diaphragm and flap, and test the flap by applying 9 in. of vacuum directly through the supply hose. Replace the diaphragm or repair the linkage as necessary. If the diaphragm tests out to be all right, replace the heat sensor. Supply air at less than 85° F will cause rough idle in cars using air preheat systems because of the very lean idle mixtures used.

6. Check the condition of the spark plugs, ignition timing and dwell, and look for leaks in the vacuum advance lines and diaphragms if fuel system problems are not uncovered. If the carburetor's idle mixture screws are capped, follow the manufacturer's specific instructions for the vehicle so the adjustment will not adversely affect exhaust emissions.

VAPOR LOCK

1. Check for unusual climatic conditions. If the weather is unusually warm for the time of year, vapor lock may occur because the fuel was formulated for easy starting in cooler weather, and thus contains an excessive amount of volatile hydrocarbons for the conditions.

2. Check the routing of the fuel lines to make sure the lines do not touch or run close to a hot engine part. Relocate the lines as necessary.

3. Check for any source of excess heat such as poor ignition timing and dwell, clogged cooling system, or slipping belts. Check to see that the manifold heat control valve operates freely; free it with solvent if necessary.

4. Check to see that fuel pump output and pressure meet specifications, and that

the float system is in good condition and is properly adjusted.

5. If the problem persists in spite of the vehicle being in good mechanical condition, the manufacturer may provide a replacement fuel pump incorporating a vapor return line. Installation of such a kit will usually alleviate the problem.

STALLING

1. Check fast idle and regular idle adjustments and bring them to specifications.

2. If the engine stalls when cold, check the function and adjustment of the choke mechanism as in subsection F.

3. If the engine stalls when warmed up, check the float level and the condition of the float needle and seat as in G. Check fuel pump pressure to make sure it is not too high. Check for worn or loose gaskets that might cause carburetor air or fuel leaks. If an anti-stall dashpot is used, check it for a faulty vacuum hose, ruptured diaphragm, or bent mounting bracket.

4. If the engine stalls only when very hot, check the hot idle compensator if the carburetor has one. This is a thermostatic valve that provides extra air to the carburetor when the engine is idling at higher-than-normal temperatures. It compensates for the abnormal amount of fuel vapor generated under these conditions. The valve draws its air from inside the air horn. Block off this port with the engine idling hot. If there is no reduction in idle speed, the carburetor will have to be disassembled and the compensator checked according to the manufacturer's instructions. The cooling system and manifold heat control valve should also be checked.

RUNNING ON

1. Bring idle speed to specifications. If necessary, set idle with the idle stop solenoid energized and also with it de-energized.

2. Make sure that the throttle linkage allows the throttle to close fully. If the carburetor uses a solenoid to control idle speed, make sure that when the ignition switch is turned off, the solenoid permits the throttle to close so that the slow idle screw becomes effective. Replace a faulty solenoid.

3. Check for any source of excess heat. Check ignition timing, and the condition of the cooling system and manifold heat control valve, and then correct any defects. Check spark plug heat range.

4. If the problem persists, the combustion chambers are probably severely carboned. In some cases, the carbon can be removed by slowly pouring a solvent manufactured for decarbonizing the engine into the carburetor while the engine is idling.

NOTE: *Do not try to correct the problem by removing or changing the cooling system thermostat to a lower temperature unit as this will accelerate engine wear and increase exhaust emissions. In some systems, the thermostat blocks the radiator bypass during heavy load conditions. In these systems, removal can cause over heating.*

15 · Compression

What Compression Is

In the description of engine operation, it was mentioned that, after the closing of the intake valve, the air/fuel mixture is trapped in the cylinder as the piston rises. The volume of the combustion chamber after the piston reaches TDC is about $1/8$th to $1/11$th of the volume of the whole cylinder. Compressing the mixture in this manner raises the pressures and temperatures in the combustion chambers during the power stroke, thus improving combustion and increasing the amount of power delivered to the piston on the downstroke.

Any leakage in the combustion chamber will reduce the pressure created during the compression stroke. The pressure created in the combustion chamber may be measured with a gauge that remains at the highest reading it measures, through the action of a one-way valve. This gauge is inserted into the spark plug hole. A compression test will uncover many mechanical problems that can cause rough running or poor performance.

Positioning the gauge in the spark plug hole (© G.M. Corp)

Compression Testing and Troubleshooting

A. Prepare the engine for the test as follows:

1. Operate the engine until it reaches operating temperature. The engine is at operating temperature a few minutes after hot water begins circulating through both radiator hoses.

2. Remove the primary lead from the positive terminal on the coil. Remove all high-tension wires from the spark plugs.

3. Clean all dirt and foreign material from around the spark plugs (compressed air works well) and remove all spark plugs.

4. If a remote starter switch is available, hook it up according to its manufacturer's instructions.

5. Remove the air cleaner and block or wire the throttle and choke in the wide open position. The secondary bores may be ignored on four-barrel carburetors.

B. Zero the gauge, place it firmly in one of the spark plug holes, and crank the engine for about five compression strokes. Record the reading and the number or position of the cylinder tested. *Release pressure from the gauge.*

C. Repeat the test for all the other cylinders.

D. Evaluate the results. Consult a manual for the compression pressure rating of the engine. Engines with compression ratios of 8:1–8.5:1 usually produce 140–150 lbs pressure. Higher compression ratios produce up to 175 lbs. The readings should be within 25 percent of each other. (See chart.)

If the test had to be performed on a cold engine because it could not be started, the readings will be considerably lower than normal, even if the engine is in perfect me-

Minimum and Maximum Compression Readings

Max. Press. Lbs. Sq. In.	Min. Press. Lbs. Sq. In.	Max. Press. Lbs. Sq. In.	Min. Press. Lbs. Sq. In.
134	101	188	141
136	102	190	142
138	104	192	144
140	105	194	145
142	107	196	147
146	110	198	148
148	111	200	150
150	113	202	151
152	114	204	153
154	115	206	154
156	117	208	156
158	118	210	157
160	120	212	158
162	121	214	160
164	123	216	162
166	124	218	163
168	126	220	165
170	127	222	166
172	129	224	168
174	131	226	169
176	132	228	171
178	133	230	172
180	135	232	174
182	136	234	175
184	138	236	177
186	140	238	178

chanical condition. A substantial pressure should still be produced, and variations in the readings are still indicative of the condition of the engine. If all readings are acceptable, see F.

E. Perform a "wet" compression test if any or all of the cylinders read low. Pour about one teaspoon of engine oil in each of the cylinders with low compression and repeat the test for each cylinder in turn.

F. Further evaluate the results. One or more of the symptoms below should apply:

1. All cylinders fall within the specified range of pressures. The engine internal parts are in generally good condition.

2. One or more cylinders produced a low reading in D. which was substantially improved by the "wet" compression test. Those cylinders have worn pistons, piston rings, and/or cylinder bores.

3. Two adjacent cylinders (or several pairs whose cylinders are adjacent) have nearly identical low readings, and did not respond to the "wet" compression test. These cylinders share leaks in the head gasket. This may be cross-checked by performing the cooling system pressure tests in the cooling system section, and by looking at the oil on the dipstick to see if coolant bubbles are present.

4. Compression buildup in one or more cylinders is erratic—it climbs less on some strokes than on others. Normally, the pressure rises steadily and then levels off. This indicates sticking valves. This problem may be cross-checked with a timing light. Remove the valve covers. Since this test is run with the engine operating and the valve covers removed, it would be wise to purchase and install special clips that are designed to stop oil flow to the valve train. Connect a timing light to the spark plug lead of the cylinder suspected of having sticky valves. Aim the timing light at the valves of the cylinder in question. Loosen the distributor and then start the engine and watch the valves. Vary the timing slightly, smoothly, and gradually in order to observe the position of the valve at slightly different points in the rotation of the engine. If there is an erratic motion of either valve, that valve is sticking. Remember to retime the ignition system and remove the oil clips.

16·The Cooling System

How It Works

The cooling system, in spite of its compact size, handles a staggering amount of heat in order to protect the internal parts of the engine from the heat of combustion and friction. The cooling system of a modern car may remove about 6,000 BTU per minute, or considerably more heat than is required to comfortably warm a large home in extreme weather.

The coolant employed now is generally a mixture of water and ethylene glycol. Ethylene glycol is a chemical which, when mixed with water in the proper proportions, both lowers the freezing point and raises the boiling point of the solution.

Most commercial antifreezes also contain additives designed to inhibit corrosion and foaming in the system.

The water pump is the heart of the cooling system. This is usually driven off the pulley on the front of the engine crankshaft by V belts. Its bearings are usually sealed ball bearing units located in the long snout of the front pump housing. The pump's impeller is a vaned wheel which fits the inside of the water pump housing with a very close clearance. Water trapped between the vanes is forced to rotate with the impeller around the inside of the water pump housing. The resultant centrifugal force raises the pressure in the pump discharge, causing water to flow through the pump.

The coolant is discharged into the front

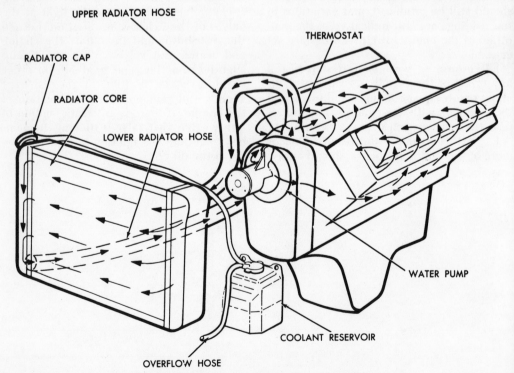

UPPER RADIATOR HOSE

THERMOSTAT

RADIATOR CAP

RADIATOR CORE

LOWER RADIATOR HOSE

WATER PUMP

COOLANT RESERVOIR

OVERFLOW HOSE

The flow of coolant through a typical V8 engine (© G.M. Corp)

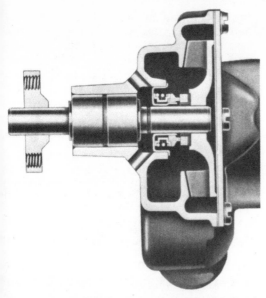

Cross-section of a typical water pump (© G.M. Corp)

of the engine block and circulates in the water jackets around the cylinders. It then makes its way upward through ports in the block, head gasket, and head to the water passages around the combustion chambers. It leaves the engine through the front of the block, passing into the thermostat housing which, in V8 engines, is a part of the intake manifold. Here, the water flow splits; part of it returning directly to the water pump inlet through an external by-pass hose or internal bypass passage, and part of it passing through the upper radiator hose.

The radiator is a heat exchanger consisting of a large number of thin water tubes fed through upper and lower or right and left side header tanks. Thin metal fins are soldered to the outside surfaces of the water tubes to increase the area of the hot metal surfaces available for transmission of heat to the air. A fan, usually driven off the water pump shaft, aids circulation of air through the radiator, especially at low speeds. Some fans have a thermostatically operated fluid drive clutch to adjust the fan speed to temperature conditions and engine speed.

A heater core, similar in construction to the radiator, receives coolant flow from the lower portion of the thermostat housing where coolant flows at all times. The heater hoses conduct the water to the core and return it to the inlet side of the water pump. The heater core is usually in a heater air duct located in the dash panel.

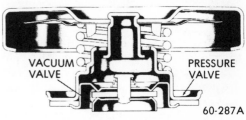

Cross-section of a radiator cap (© G.M. Corp)

A pressure cap seals the radiator against coolant leakage through the action of a sprung poppet valve whose rubber sealing ring bears against a surface inside the filler neck. The cap allows the escape of coolant when the system pressure reaches a predetermined level, usually about 15 psi, thus protecting the radiator, hoses, and other system components from excessive pressure. The cap also incorporates a vacuum relief valve which opens only during cooling of the system (when the engine is off) to prevent the formation of vacuum within the system.

The system adjusts its cooling capacity to the weather conditions, vehicle speed,

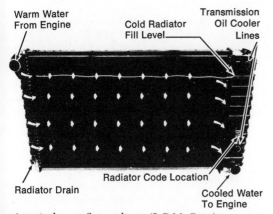

A typical cross-flow radiator (© G.M. Corp)

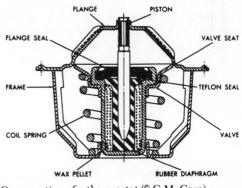

Cross-section of a thermostat (© G.M. Corp)

and engine load through the action of a thermostat. The thermostat consists of a poppet or hinged flap type of valve actuated by pressure from a fluid-filled bellows or wax pellet. The valve remains tightly closed below the rated opening temperature, forcing all the coolant discharged from the water pump to return directly to the water pump inlet. This practically eliminates loss of heat from the engine during warm-up, while protecting the system from the formation of steam at hot spots. The bypass inlet is situated near the heat-sensing portion of the thermostat so the thermostat will receive a continuous indication of the water temperature, even when none of the fluid is passing through it.

When coolant temperature reaches the specified level (usually 180–195°), the thermostat will begin opening. The valve will be opened gradually as coolant temperatures rise, and will reach a wide-open position about 25° above the opening temperature. The radiator is slightly larger than required during most operating conditions. Thus, the thermostat is usually at least part-way closed, providing a precise control of engine temperature. One exception is when the engine is idled or turned off immediately after a hard run. The cooling system's capacity to throw off heat is vastly decreased under these conditions but the great amount of heat stored up in the heavy metal of the engine block continues to warm the coolant. It is normal for the engine temperature to rise substantially under these conditions. As long as water is not discharged from the pressure cap, there is nothing wrong with the system.

RUST AND SCALE

Rust and scale cause engine cooling problems in two different ways. First, they restrict the flow of coolant which decreases the flow through the entire system. Second, they build up a layer of insulating material on all the surfaces of the system. This not only reduces the capacity of the system to throw off heat but also keeps the coolant from picking up heat in the normal manner from hot engine parts even when the coolant is running at near normal temperatures.

Rust and scale are a result of chemical reactions between the metals in the cooling system and the minute amounts of air and exhaust gases that always enter the system through the water pump shaft seal and the head gasket and the block and head. Rust and scale cause what is perhaps the most common problem in poorly maintained systems, and can cause severe overheating even when there are no leaks in the system and the engine is in good mechanical condition.

Quick Reference Guide For Cooling System Troubleshooting

A. *Inspect the system.* Check the fan and drive belt(s), coolant (level and condition) and the cap. Check for leaks. Check for operating conditions that are more severe than those for which the vehicle was designed. Check for an indication of overheating on the gauge or as indicated by the warning light. Check the thermostat. Check the circulation and listen to the water pump for excessive noise. Check the ignition timing, resetting it as necessary.

B. *Check the radiator cap with a pressure tester.*

C. *Use a radiator pressure tester to test the system's ability to hold pressure.* Check for head gasket leaks by idling the engine with the system pressurized. Test compression if necessary.

D. *Check further for leaks, keeping the system pressurized.*

E. *Check the strength of the antifreeze solution.* Most modern systems require protection to 0° to ensure protection against corrosion and boiling.

F. *Remove the thermostat and test it for proper operation.*

G. *Check the wiring to the temperature light or gauge. Replace parts as necessary.*

Cooling System Troubleshooting

A. Inspect the System.

Check the fan for bent, cracked, or broken blades and replace it as necessary. A thermostatic fan may be checked as follows:

1. Allow the engine to cool until the engine compartment is well below 150° F.

2. Cover the radiator, leaving sufficient room for circulation so air will flow through the core and fan in the normal direction.

3. Measure the temperature of the fan air discharge with a 200° F thermometer. There should be a sudden increase in noise produced by the fan between 150 and 190° F. Otherwise the unit is faulty and should be replaced.

Check the belts that drive the water pump for cracks and glazing, and replace as necessary.

NOTE: *Replace paired belts with a set, even if one looks serviceable. Use the proper size. Do not pry the belt on. Tighten to specifications.*

GAUGE

TOOL

Adjusting belt tension with a strand tension gauge (Courtesy, Chrysler Corp)

Check the belt tension and adjust it to specifications if a strand tensioning gauge is available. If not, adjust the belt so that tension exists on it at all times, and heavy thumb pressure will permit it to flex about ½ in. Tighten a new belt just a bit more snugly to allow for the tension that will be lost as the belt adapts to the pulley grooves during the first few miles of operation.

Make sure that the engine has had time to cool down, and remove the radiator cap to check the condition of the coolant.

NOTE: *Unless the engine is cold, use a heavy rag to do this. Turn the cap very slowly, pausing to allow pressure to escape.*

The coolant level should be 1–2 in. below the filler neck if the engine is warm, and about 3 in. if it is cold. If the coolant level is low, start the engine and allow it to idle while adding a 50 percent antifreeze, 50 percent water solution to the radiator.

Check the condition of the coolant. It should be clear. If there is evidence of rust and scale and the coolant is dull brown or rusty red, flush the system because clogging and poor heat transfer are probably contributing to the problem.

Check the seal in the radiator cap for cracks or torn sections. Replace it if the seal is cracked, torn or hangs out over the edges of the metal backing.

Check the radiator and hoses, especially the hose connections, for rust marks that would indicate leakage. Tighten clamps or replace hoses and clamps as necessary.

In order to conserve weight and space, most modern cooling systems are carefully sized to provide just the capacity required under normal operating conditions. If the vehicle is being used to pull a trailer that weighs more than one ton, overheating problems are probably due to the load. Installation of a trailer towing package will probably cure the problem. If the vehicle has an aftermarket air conditioner, overheating is probably due to the extra resistance to air flow, engine load, and heat produced by the unit. Install a heavy-duty radiator and fan. Finally, if your vehicle overheats during prolonged idling with the air conditioning running and the automatic transmission in gear, a change in operating habits may cure the problem. The transmission should be shifted to neutral during such idling. The heat generated in the transmission under idling conditions is passed on to a transmission oil cooler located in the radiator. Under extreme conditions, the idle speed should be increased with the throttle and the air conditioning should be turned off. Overheating should not be considered a problem unless the vehicle has trouble cooling itself under normal road operating conditions.

Allow the engine to cool until it is well below normal operating temperature. Start the engine and operate it at fast idle. The radiator should remain fairly cool for a few minutes and then suddenly turn warm. Coolant should flow through the entire radiator and both hoses, making them warm to the touch. Scattered cool spots in the radiator mean clogging. Failure of the coolant to circulate through the lower hose may mean a faulty water pump or thermostat, or severe clogging. Slow warm-up of the engine and circulation of only moderately warm water through the radiator immediately after starting means a bad thermostat that might be causing overheating.

Accelerate the engine to check to see if the radiator's lower hose collapses at higher speeds. If it does, replace it. Listen to the water pump. A loud grinding noise usually indicates worn bearings and contact between the impeller blades and water pump housing because of the improper bearing clearances. Replace a noisy pump.

Road-test the vehicle, watching the temperature gauge or light, and stopping frequently to check for coolant loss from the overflow tube.

If the gauge or light indicates overheating, and water is expelled through the overflow tube, follow through with the rest of the checks in the suggested order. If the gauge indicates overheating but there is no evidence of coolant loss, see B. If the radiator cap checks out, go on to G. If the only problem is expulsion of coolant through the overflow, with no other signs of overheating, see B. If the radiator cap checks out, go to subsection E. If the only problem is slow warm-up, replace the thermostat.

Adjust the ignition timing to specifications. Improper timing can result in overheating by reducing the efficiency of the engine.

B. Check the Radiator Pressure Cap with a Pressure Tester.

A special tester with an air pump is available for this purpose. It is the only way to adequately test a pressure cap. Check the pressure rating of the cap (which is usually stamped on the top), wet the rubber seal, and install the cap onto the tester. Pump up the pressure tester until air bleeds out from under the seal. Note the pressure. It should be within one pound of the rating on the cap. Replace the cap if pressure is released at either too high or too low a pressure; a cap which retains excess pressure can damage the system and can also make removel of the cap dangerous.

Testing the ability of the system to hold pressure (Courtesy, American Motors)

C. Use a Radiator Pressure Tester to Test the System's Ability to Hold Pressure.

Pressurize the system up to the rating of the cap. Carefully watch the pressure gauge for several minutes to see if there is

Testing the radiator cap (© G.M. Corp)

a loss of pressure. If there is no pressure loss, go on to E. If pressure is lost, idle the engine and watch the gauge carefully for fluctuations. Be sure to release pressure if there is a continuous rise after starting the engine. If there are no fluctuations but there is a slow pressure loss, proceed to D. Otherwise, remove the spark plug leads one by one to determine which cylinders are leaking. The leaking cylinder(s) will produce less fluctuation in the needle when the spark leads are removed. If obvious differences between cylinders are not noted in this test, perform a compression test as described in the previous section. Leaky cylinders must be repaired by removing the cylinder head(s) affected and replacing the head gasket.

D. Check Further for Leaks, Keeping the System Pressurized.

Keep the pressure in the system to within a pound or two of the full rating. This will cause leaks to show up that only exist under full operating pressure. Check the following parts of the system very carefully: hoses, radiator (especially at soldered joints between header tanks and water tubes), water pump (especially at the shaft seal), thermostat housing, heater core (check the floor in the passenger compartment for a light film of antifreeze), drain cocks and plugs, core plugs in block, and heater water valves (especially around valve stems). Replace any defective parts.

E. Check Strength of Antifreeze Solution.

Regardless of the climate, a modern, high-pressure system should be protected down to 0° F because ethylene-glycol antifreeze in solution with water increases the boiling point. Even with all other cooling system components in perfect condition, a weak antifreeze solution could result in boiling of coolant under difficult operating conditions.

Make the test using a special hydrometer calibrated to show the freezing point of an ethylene-glycol and water solution. Pull the solution in and out of the hydrometer several times to make sure that any residue from the last test is removed and to bring the thermometer in the hydrometer to the temperature of the solution as quickly as possible. If the unit does not have a thermometer and is not equipped

with a temperature conversion chart, a sample of coolant will have to be brought to the temperature at which the unit is calibrated to obtain an accurate reading.

The test must either be performed at the specified temperature or corrected with a conversion chart because a change in temperature will affect the reading by changing the density of the sample. If there is not adequate protection, consult an antifreeze chart, drain the coolant, and replace it with the correct antifreeze solution. Be sure to retest the new solution to ensure adequate protection.

F. Remove the Thermostat and Test It for Proper Operation.

Secure a new thermostat housing gasket before proceeding with this test, as disassembly of the housing usually ruins the old gasket. Drain coolant from the radiator down below the level of the thermostat housing. Remove the thermostat and notice whether or not the wax pellet or bellows was turned downward, toward the block. A thermostat that is upside down will respond improperly to temperature changes.

Suspend the thermostat in a pan full of water, keeping it well above the bottom so that heat will not be conducted directly to the sensing element from the bottom of the pan. Place the pan on a stove and heat it while measuring the water temperature with a 250° thermometer. The thermostat should open within 5° of its rated opening temperature (consult the owner's manual for the rating), and open fully about 25° above this temperature. (These conditions cannot be created for a 195° thermostat, but a check of opening temperature and freedom of operation can be made.) After proper opening and freedom of operation have been checked, allow the solution to cool and make sure that the thermostat closes properly.

Replace the thermostat, if necessary. In reassembly, make sure that the wax pellet or bellows is downward (toward the main portion of the block). Clean the surfaces between the upper and lower portions of the housing and replace the gasket.

If problems continue, remove the external bypass hose, if one is used, and inspect it for clogging or swelling. Replace it if it does not permit free passage of coolant.

G. Check Wiring-to-Temperature Light or Gauge. Replace Parts as Necessary.

Sometimes temperature gauges or lights will indicate overheating when there is no loss of coolant, or will fail to show overheating when coolant is lost. Failure to indicate overheating even when coolant is being lost through the overflow tube can occur because of a bad radiator cap or weak antifreeze solution. A bad sensor can cause the light or gauge to show overheating even when no problem exists.

A preliminary check of the wiring should be made in either case. Check the connection at the sensor, which is usually located in the cylinder head, to make sure it is clean and tight. Check the wiring for frayed insulation and grounds, and replace or repair it as necessary. Check the other dash gauges for normal function and, if they function normally, proceed with the checks below. If the other gauges do not work properly, there is an electrical system problem which should be rectified before blaming the cooling system gauge.

If the system pushes water out through the overflow tube, check the antifreeze solution as in subsection E. and correct a weak solution. Check the radiator pressure cap. A weak cap could cause coolant to escape even when the engine is not overheating. A cap that traps too much pressure can allow the engine to overheat without loss of coolant.

If the problem is not corrected, replace the sensor in the block. This is by far the most common source of trouble. If this does not rectify the problem, see the section on dash gauges and indicators.

Air Cooling Systems

Air cooling systems are generally trouble-free. A few problems can occur, however. If an air-cooled engine operates sluggishly after a short period of driving in warm weather, make the following checks:

A. Check the belt for glazing and cracks. If evidence of slippage exists, remove the belt to check the fan for free rotation and then replace the belt, tightening it to specifications to ensure adequate cooling.

B. Check all ducting for loose or missing screws or bent parts which might cause cracks and leaks. Check the spark plugs' rubber seals and heater hoses and clamps, and replace any parts which do not seal properly.

C. Check the ignition timing and, if applicable, the adjustment of the valves; poor tuning can cause high operating temperatures. Make sure the engine is using the right viscosity of motor oil.

D. If problems persist, check compression and check the oil pressure relief valve for proper spring tension and free plunger operation. Make repairs as necessary.

E. If the problem is still not solved, it may be necessary to remove the ducting and clean the entire engine of accumulated dirt. An oil cooler that is clogged internally can also cause overheating problems because of the importance of the oil as a coolant in an air-cooled engine. If there is evidence of sludge in the engine, it should be removed and cleaned. Check the operation and mounting of the thermostat. The thermostat should be wide open when the engine is idling after a hard run. The operation of the cooling flaps may be checked by disconnecting the bellows from the housing, and moving it back and forth to each of the extremes of the travel of the mechanism. Make sure that the mounting bracket is positioned so the bellows can fully open the cooling flaps.

17· Poor Engine Performance

Troubleshooting When The Engine Runs Poorly

When the engine refuses to start, the starting, ignition, and fuel systems, and the engine compression, should be checked as described in the preceding sections. When a minor operating problem exists, however, it frequently involves a small malfunction in one or several of the areas outlined in the preceding sections. Making a complete check of each of these aspects of engine operation would be unnecessarily time-consuming because the symptoms frequently offer clues as to the nature of the problem. Checking the appearance of the spark plugs and using a vacuum gauge will frequently reveal the nature of the problem very quickly.

This section describes how to evaluate spark plug appearance and vacuum gauge readings and contains various charts which will act as guides to using the material of the first four sections most effectively. If the engine generally runs roughly and performs poorly, carefully check the spark plugs and manifold vacuum before going to the charts. If a very minor and specific problem (e.g., hesitation on acceleration) exists, the charts should be consulted first.

It is for this type of troubleshooting that a general understanding of the operating principles of the various parts is important. For example, if a very rapid, regular misfiring occurs, it is obvious that the problem is confined to one cylinder, and that those parts which serve all the cylinders (such as the ignition points) are not at fault. If the engine runs acceptably when warmed up but refuses to start when cold, the choke is probably at fault. Keep the basic principles in mind while doing this kind of troubleshooting and you will save much time and labor.

SPARK PLUG EVALUATION

Begin this check by driving the car for several miles at reasonably high road speeds to thoroughly warm the engine. Stop the engine, clean around the plugs, remove the wires, and remove all spark plugs, keeping them in order so that, if serious problems are uncovered, the cylinders affected can be identified.

The chart below describes the appearance of the plugs and the indicated problems.

Appearance	Problem
Electrodes slightly eroded, light brown deposits. Gray or tan, glazed cinder-like lead deposits may be noticeable. Gap slightly wider than specified.	Normal wear.

Normal

161

Carbon fouling—dry, black, fluffy deposits.

On just one or two cylinders, this may indicate faulty high-tension leads or valve problems. If the problem is demonstrated on all cylinders, the fuel mixture may be too rich or the heat riser may not be functioning properly.

Carbon fouled

Oil fouling—wet black deposits.

Piston rings, valve guides, or valve seals may be worn. The condition is normal on new or recently overhauled engines.

Oil fouled

Gap bridging—heavy deposits lodged between the two electrodes.

Transfer of deposits from the combustion chamber due to a sudden change in operating conditions. The plug(s) must be replaced.

Gap bridged

Overheating—the electrodes will be burned, and the insulator will be extremely white in color and may show small black spots.

Excessive ignition advance, lean mixture, or insufficient installation torque.

Overheated

Preignition—severely burnt or melted electrodes, blistered or cracked insulator.

Melted

Plug heat range too hot, excessive ignition advance, insufficient spark plug installation torque, fuel mixture too lean, very poor compression, or fuel octane rating too low.

INTAKE MANIFOLD VACUUM TEST

Bring the engine to operating temperature. Install a vacuum guage in the intake manifold below the throttle plate. In older cars, there is usually a plugged port in the intake manifold. In newer cars, this port is used for the PCV system. Remove the plug or PCV hose from the valve and install the gauge line. Start the engine and allow it to idle. Gauge readings and their meanings are listed below:

Reading	Meaning
1. Steady, 17–22 in.	Normal reading.

Steady, from 17–22 in. Hg.

2. Low and steady, 10–15 in.	Late ignition timing, late valve timing, or uniformly low compression.

Low and steady

3. Very low, 5–10 in.	Vacuum leak.

Very low

4. Regular fluctuation as engine speed is increased.

Ignition miss, or severe compression leak—usually caused by a valve or head gasket problem.

Needle fluctuates as engine speed increases

5. Gradual drop in the reading at idle just after engine is started.

Excessive back pressure in the exhaust system.

Gradual drop in reading at idle

6. Regular fluctuation at idle speed.

Ignition miss or sticking valve.

Intermittent fluctuation at idle

7. Steadily drifting needle.

Rich idle mixture or improperly synchronized dual carburetors.

Drifting needle

8. Needle drifts around, but in a noticeably irregular manner.

Lean mixture due to improper idle mixture adjustment or intake manifold or valve guide leakage.

9. Reading steady but too high (about 25 in.).

Ignition timing too far advanced.

High and steady

ENGINE TROUBLESHOOTING CHART

This troubleshooting chart will help guide you to effective use of the "Ignition System," "Fuel System," "Compression," and "Tune-up" sections of this book for the solution of the most common of the minor engine problems that occur. Consult the chart which most nearly fits the symptoms and, if necessary, see the appropriate section to eliminate each possible cause of trouble.

Engine Troubleshooting Chart

Engine runs well, but is hard to start when cold.

√ Improper oil viscosity. Use the recommended viscosity for the prevailing temperature.

√ Choke sticks due to gum on shafts or because of a bent shaft or link.

√ Choke is improperly adjusted.

√ Ignition coil, or high-tension wires are weak, or spark plug gap is too wide.

√ Moisture shorting out ignition components. Check for frayed insulation or a cracked distributor cap. If necessary, spray with a sealing compound.

√ Ignition timing and dwell improperly adjusted.

√ Fuel pump volume and pressure inadequate, or fuel lines or strainer partially clogged.

Engine misfires at high speeds only.

√ Spark plug gaps set too wide.

√ Improper dwell angle.

√ Weak ignition coil or high-tension wires.

√ Clogged fuel filter or strainer.

√ Inadequate fuel pump pressure or volume. (Volume should be 1 pt in 30–45 seconds)

Engine idles poorly or stalls.

√ Engine idle speed or mixture improperly adjusted.

√ Carburetor jets clogged.

√ Air leak at carburetor mounting, in intake manifold, or PCV system, or other vacuum hoses.

√ Incorrect valve clearance.

√ Clogged PCV valve or hose.

√ Stuck choke, improperly adjusted choke, or improper fast idle adjustment.

√ Faulty ignition components, incorrect timing and dwell, fouled spark plugs.

√ Poor compression or badly worn valves, camshaft, or camshaft drive.

Engine misses at various speeds.

√ Water or other foreign material in fuel.

√ Clogged carburetor jets.

√ Incorrect float level.

√ Improper spring tension on points or worn or loose distributor shaft or cam.

√ Insufficient dwell angle, or late ignition timing.

√ Weak coil or condenser.

√ Weak valve spring.

Engine Troubleshooting Chart-*Continued*

Engine lacks power.

√ Improper ignition timing.

√ Improper carburetor float level.

√ Fuel pump pressure and volume inadequate.

√ Distributor shaft and bushings worn.

√ Spark plugs dirty or improperly gapped.

√ Dwell angle incorrectly adjusted.

√ Weak coil or condenser.

√ Improper valve adjustment.

√ Poor compression.

√ Ignition advance diaphragm or hose leaking.

Oil consumption.

√ Oil of too light a viscosity or oil level too high.

√ Engine overheating.

√ External leaks at fuel pump, oil pan, timing chain cover, valve covers, rear seal.

√ Valve seals worn or damaged.

√ Worn valve stems or guides.

√ Excessive bearing clearance.

√ Worn cylinder walls, rings, or ring grooves.

√ Plugged cylinder head drainback holes.

Engine detonates (pings).

√ Ignition timing too far advanced.

√ Spark plugs of too high a heat range in use.

√ Manifold heat control valve stuck open.

√ Excessive carbon deposits in combustion chambers.

√ Improper fuel in use.

Engine hesitates on acceleration.

√ Ignition timing improperly set.

√ Accelerator pump circuit dirty, or inoperative due to mechanical problems.

√ Float level too low.

√ Inadequate fuel pump pressure and volume. (Volume should be 1 pt in 30–45 seconds.)

√ Accelerator pump jets not directed properly.

Engine valves noisy.

√ Improper adjustment. (See "Tune-up" section.)

√ Incorrect engine oil level.

√ Air leaks in oil pick-up.

√ Worn or clogged hydraulic lifters.

   NOTE: *The faulty lifter(s) may be located by using a stethoscope to listen for noise while the engine is idling—with the valve cover(s) removed.*

√ Wear or breakage in valve train.

18 · The Tune-Up

Engine tune-ups are performed periodically to ensure continuous peak performance. They consist of various minor mechanical adjustments and inspection and/or replacement of worn ignition system parts.

Tune-Up Procedures

1. Test Compression.

Compression testing can reveal mechanical problems which will not be corrected by a tune-up. A careful mechanic does a compression check as the first step in a tune-up to eliminate the possibility of internal malfunctions as the cause of poor performance.

Perform a compression test as described in the section on compression. When removing spark plugs, remember to clean the area around them before removal, and to place the plugs on a workbench, in order.

2. Service the Spark Plugs.

Manufacturers generally recommend replacement of spark plugs every 12,000 miles. Replace the plugs, if necessary, with plugs of the proper heat range.

If the plugs are to be reused:

a. Inspect the electrodes for burning and check the insulators for cracks. Replace any faulty plugs.

b. Clean the electrodes with a wire brush or, if possible, sandblast them. File the center electrodes flat, and regap the spark plugs to the specified gap. (Consult a Chilton's manual or factory manual for the specified gap.) Use a wire feeler gauge to set the gap. Bend the side electrode with a spark plug tool to change the gap.

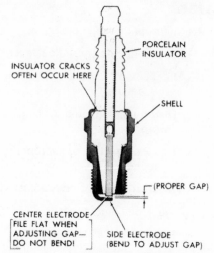

Where to measure spark plug gap (© G.M. Corp)

c. Make sure that all plugs are of the proper heat range, as specified by the manufacturer. (Consult the manual for heat range.)

NOTE: *Check the gaps on new plugs, even though some are pregapped. The gap has a great effect on engine performance.*

3. Replace the Plugs.

Use new gaskets on old plugs. Placing a drop of engine oil on the plug threads may help to ensure easy installation. *If possible, tighten the plugs with a torque wrench.* Inadequate torque causes spark plug burning, while excessive torque causes improper gap or damage to the cylinder head. All 10 mm spark plugs should be torqued to 14 ft lbs in a cast iron head, 11 ft lbs in an aluminum head. All 14 mm plugs (the most common size) should be torqued to 30 ft lbs in a cast iron head; 27 ft lbs in an aluminum head.

4. Service the Ignition Points.

Ignition points are usually replaced at 12,000 mile intervals with the spark plugs.

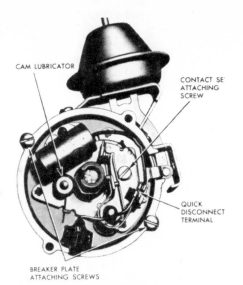

CAM LUBRICATOR

CONTACT SE
ATTACHING
SCREW

QUICK
DISCONNECT
TERMINAL

BREAKER PLATE
ATTACHING SCREWS

A typical contact set (© G.M. Corp)

The condenser is usually replaced as well. If the points are not severely burned or pitted, however, they may be reused. Used points should be removed, cleaned with a point file, and replaced.

NOTE: *This operation is performed only to remove excess carbon deposits from the points. Do not attempt to remove all roughness on the contact surfaces, or else their special, wear-resistant coating may be destroyed.*

Lubricate the cam follower with a small dab of high-melting-point grease. If the distributor uses a cam lubricator, rotate it or replace it as the manufacturer recommends. Clean all old grease from the distributor cam before reinstalling or replacing the points.

5. Adjust the Point Gap or Dwell Angle.

If a dwell meter is available, it should be used for adjusting the dwell angle. This method is more accurate than gapping the points.

a. Gapping the points. This is a good method of making a preliminary setting of the dwell angle even if a dwell meter is available. Install the points (and condenser, if it is being replaced), ensuring that all connections are pushed on or screwed together securely and, if the condenser is being replaced, that it is securely mounted to ensure a good ground. If the mounting screw on the ignition points assembly is also used to make the gap adjustment, tighten it just enough to hold the

contacts apart. Rotate the engine until the tip of one of the distributor cams sits squarely under the cam follower on the movable contact arm. Using a leaf type feeler gauge (gap the points as specified in the manual), move the base plate of the point assembly back and forth until the gauge just slips between the two contacts when it is forced straight through. If the mounting screw serves as the adjusting lock, the contact assembly may usually be moved by wedging a screwdriver blade between a slot in the contact base plate and a protrusion on the surface of the distributor plate. In assemblies with an adjusting screw which is accessible from outside the distributor, an allen wrench is inserted into the head of the adjusting screw and rotated to make the adjustment. When the points are pitted, make sure the gauge does not come in contact with the built-up portion on one of the contact surfaces. A wire feeler gauge may help to make the most accurate adjustment when the points are pitted.

NOTE: *Make sure all gauges are clean in gapping the points. An oily gauge will cause rapid point burning.*

b. Setting dwell angle. Connect the positive lead of the dwell meter to the distributor side of the coil, and the negative lead to a good ground. Make sure all wires are clear of moving parts and then start the engine. Run the engine at normal idle speed with the transmission in gear if the vehicle is equipped with an automatic

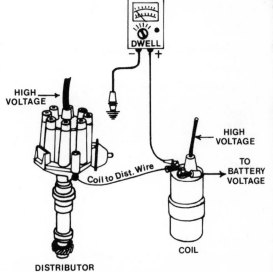

DWELL

HIGH
VOLTAGE

HIGH
VOLTAGE

TO
BATTERY
VOLTAGE

Coil to Dist. Wire

COIL

DISTRIBUTOR

Setting the dwell angle

transmission. Switch the dwell meter to the appropriate scale, according to the instructions on the dial. If the dwell is not within the range specified on the engine compartment sticker or in the manual, make the point gap narrower to increase the dwell angle, or wider to decrease it, until it falls within the specified range. If the vehicle has an automatic transmission, place it in Park. Accelerate the engine to about 2,000 rpm and watch the dwell angle. There should be very little variation in the dwell if the distributor is in good condition. If the dwell indicator moves about considerably, the distributor shaft and bushings may be badly worn. Some late-model distributors vary the dwell slightly to control emissions. However, this effect would be gradual and smooth, as contrasted with the erratic variation indicative of badly worn distributor parts.

6. Inspect the Secondary Ignition Circuit.

Inspect the inside surface of the distributor cap for cracks, carbon tracks, or badly burned contacts. To remove carbon tracks, wash the cap in soap and water and dry thoroughly. Replace the cap if it is cracked or if the contacts are badly eroded.

Inspect the rotor for cracks, excessive burning of the contacts, and mechanical damage, and replace as necessary. Slightly burned contacts should be sanded smooth.

Inspect the spark plug leads and distributor-to-coil high-tension lead for cracks, brittleness, or damaged rubber boots. Replace any deteriorated parts.

While primary wiring is less perishable than the secondary circuit, it should be checked for cracked insulation or loose connections. Tighten connections or replace wires as necessary.

7. Adjust the Ignition Timing.

Timing is adjusted at every tune-up. This is especially important because changing the dwell angle will change the ignition timing. Adjusting the contact points may throw the timing off.

On most vehicles, the engine may be timed with either a test lamp or with a stroboscopic timing light. However, manufacturer's recommendations should be consulted because some engines must be timed under certain operating conditions, while others can only be timed with the engine stopped. On emission-controlled cars, the tune-up sticker will outline the conditions under which the engine is to be timed. These instructions should be followed to the letter and, if a speed is specified, a tachometer should be used to make sure that the speed is correct before timing the engine.

Static Timing

A. Make sure the engine is at the correct temperature for timing adjustment (either fully warmed or cold, as specified in the factory manual or a Chilton's repair manual).

B. Locate no. 1 cylinder and trace its wire back to the distributor cap. Then, remove the cap.

C. Rotate the engine until the proper timing mark on the crankshaft pulley is lined up with the timing mark on the block. Observe the direction of distributor shaft rotation when the engine is turned in its normal direction of rotation.

D. Connect a test lamp from the coil terminal (the distributor side) to ground. Make sure the tip of the rotor lines up with no. 1 cylinder. If it does not, turn the engine one full revolution and line up the timing marks again.

E. Loosen the clamp that holds the distributor in position and turn the distributor body in the direction of normal shaft rotation until the points close and the test lamp goes out. Now turn the distributor in the opposite direction very slowly, just until the test lamp comes on. Tighten the distributor clamp.

F. To test the adjustment, turn the engine backward until the light again goes out, and then forward just until the light comes back on.

NOTE: *Engines with a belt-driven camshaft must not be rotated backward.*

If the timing marks are lined up, the engine is accurately timed. If the timing is too far advanced, loosen the distributor and turn it just slightly in the direction of shaft rotation, and retighten the clamp. If the timing is retarded, turn the distributor in the opposite direction and then repeat the test. Repeat this procedure until the light comes on just as the two timing marks are aligned.

Timing With a Stroboscopic Lamp

A. If the timing light operates from the battery, connect the red lead to the battery positive terminal, and the black lead to a ground. With all lights, connect the trigger lead in series with no. 1 spark plug wire.

B. Disconnect and plug the required vacuum hoses, as in the manufacturer's specifications. Connect the red lead of a tachometer to the distributor side of the coil and the black lead to ground. Start the engine, put the (automatic) transmission in gear (if required), and read the tachometer. Adjust the carburetor idle screw to the proper speed for setting the timing. Aim the timing light at the crankshaft pulley to determine where the timing point is. If the point is hard to see, it may help to stop the engine and mark it with chalk.

C. Loosen the distributor holding clamp and rotate the distributor slowly in either direction until the timing is correct. Tighten the clamp and observe the timing mark again to determine that the timing is still correct. Readjust the position of the distributor, if necessary.

D. Accelerate the engine in Neutral, while watching the timing point. If the distributor advance mechanisms are working, the timing point should advance as the engine is accelerated. If the engine's vacuum advance is engaged with the transmission in Neutral, check the vacuum advance operation by running the engine at about 1,500 rpm and connecting and disconnecting the vacuum advance hose.

8. Adjust the Carburetor.

On most vehicles manufactured before 1972, there are adjustable idle mixture screws. On emission-controlled vehicles, the instructions on the engine compartment sticker or in the manual should be followed explicitly. Generally, the idle mixture is adjusted as follows:

a. Connect a tachometer red lead to the negative terminal of the coil, and ground the black lead. Adjust the carburetor idle screw or solenoid screw to the normal idle speed or to the speed specified for mixture adjustment in the manufacturer's instructions. Solenoid screws should be adjusted with the solenoid disconnected. After adjusting the screw, reconnect the solenoid wire and open the throttle slightly to extend the plunger and check the adjustment.

b. On uncontrolled vehicles, adjust the mixture screw(s) for the highest idle speed on the tachometer. On emission-controlled vehicles, adjust the screw(s) inward from highest idle until the specified drop in rpm is attained.

c. Reset the carburetor to the specified idle speed.

9. Adjust the Valves.

Periodic valve adjustments are not required on most modern engines with hydraulic valve lifters if the engine has been well maintained and no unusual noises come from the valve train. However, the lifters may be adjusted if excessive wear has occurred in the valve train. Also, on many small engines, solid valve lifters are employed, and must be adjusted at every tune-up.

The valve adjustment is accomplished as follows:

a. Bring the engine to the conditions specified for valve adjustment (cold, hot, or hot and running) by the manufacturer.

b. Remove the valve cover(s). If the valves must be adjusted while the engine is running, oil deflector clips should be installed on each rocker arm to avoid oil spray.

c. If the valves must be adjusted with the engine stopped, follow the manufacturer's instructions for positioning the engine properly. For example, on Volkswagens, no. 1 cylinder is adjusted with no. 1 cylinder on the compression stroke at TDC, no. 2 cylinder with the crankshaft turned 180° backward, etc. If these instructions cannot be located, bring each cylinder to TDC on the compression stroke by turning the engine until both valves are closed and the piston is at TDC, before adjusting its valves.

d. Adjust solid lifters by pushing a leaf type feeler gauge of the specified thickness (consult the manual) between the valve stem and rocker arm. Loosen the locking nut and tighten the screw until a light resistance to the movement of the feeler blade is encountered. Hold the adjusting screw while tightening the locking nut. Some adjusting screws are fitted snugly into the rocker arm so no locknut is required. If the feeler is too snug, the adjustment should be loosened to permit the passage of the blade. Remember that a slightly loose adjustment is easier on the valves than an overly tight one, so adjust the valves accordingly. Always recheck the adjustment after the locknut has been tightened.

Refer to a manual for details on hydraulic valve lifter adjustment.

e. Replace the valve cover, cleaning all traces of old gasket material from both surfaces and installing a new gasket. Tighten valve cover nuts alternately, in several stages, to ensure proper seating.

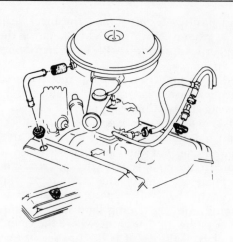

CLOSED POSITIVE
(307, 350 & 400 2-BBL)

A closed PCV system as used on Chevrolet V8 engines (© G.M. Corp)

Emission Control Checks

The PCV valve may be checked for proper function as follows:

1. Start the engine and operate it at normal idle speed.

2. Connect a tachometer between the negative coil terminal (red tach lead) and ground.

3. Note the tach reading, and then pinch off the PCV hose. There should be a drop of about 40–80 rpm. Otherwise, the PCV system is clogged, or the valve is faulty. Inspect the hoses for clogging and clean if necessary. If clogging is not found,

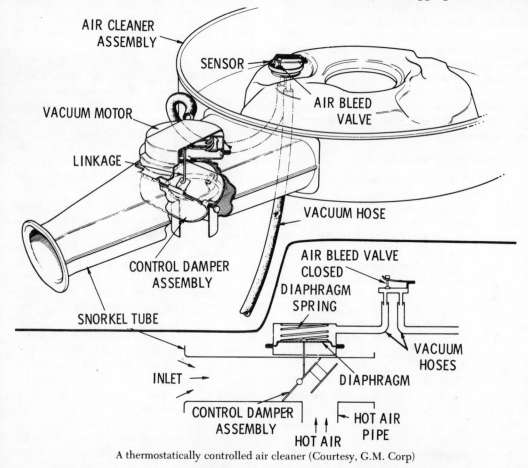

A thermostatically controlled air cleaner (Courtesy, G.M. Corp)

replace the PCV valve. If clogging is found, retest the system, replacing the valve if necessary.

All vacuum hoses should be checked for cracks or loose connections and replaced as necessary. The carburetor air preheating system may be checked by placing a small thermometer inside the air cleaner while the engine is idling. The thermometer should read 85–100° or higher. If the temperature is too low with the engine fully warmed, the thermostatic air preheating system requires repair.

If the vehicle uses an idle stop solenoid

A typical idle stop solenoid (© G.M. Corp)

(see the engine compartment sticker), the idle speed must be checked with the solenoid connected and the plunger extended. Open the throttle to allow the plunger to extend itself. After the normal idle has been checked, disconnect the solenoid. The throttle should close slightly and come to rest at the adjustment of the throttle stop screw or tang. Adjust the screw or bend the tang until the specified slow idle is attained. If the throttle does not close when the solenoid is disconnected, the solenoid or slow idle may be adjusted incorrectly or the throttle linkage may be binding. If adjustments and checking of the linkage reveal no problems, the solenoid will have to be replaced.

Many other types of emission control devices are used to position the throttle under certain operating conditions, or to interrupt and restore vacuum advance, etc. These devices, in many cases, are to be adjusted at each tune-up. It is recommended that a manual be consulted and all tune-up operations and checks required be performed at each tune-up to ensure effective control of emissions and good vehicle performance.

19· The Electrical System

Basic Electricity

Understanding just a little about the basic theory of electricity will make electrical system troubleshooting much easier. Several gauges are used in electrical troubleshooting to see inside the circuit being tested. Without a basic understanding, it will be difficult to understand testing procedures.

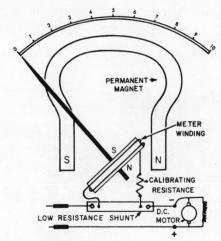

Ammeter circuit

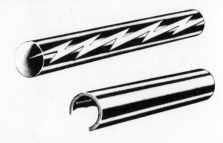

Electricity can be compared to water flowing in a pipe (© G.M. Corp)

Electricity is defined as the flow of electrons. Electrons are hypothetical particles thought to constitute the basic "stuff" of electricity. In a comparison with water flowing in a pipe, the electrons would be the water. As the flow of water can be measured, the flow of electricity can be measured. The unit of measurement is amperes, frequently abbreviated "amps". An ammeter will measure the actual amount of current flowing in the circuit.

Just as water *pressure* is measured in units such as pounds per square inch, electrical pressure is measured in volts. When a voltmeter's two probes are placed on two "live" portions of an electrical circuit with different electrical pressures, current will flow through the voltmeter and produce a reading which indicates the difference in electrical pressure between the two parts of the circuit.

While increasing the voltage in a circuit

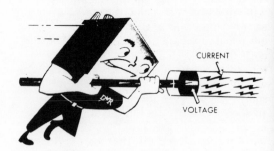

Voltage is the pressure that causes current to flow (© G.M. Corp)

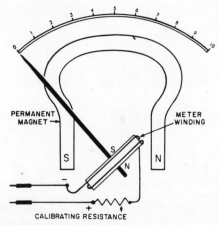

Voltmeter circuit

174

will increase the flow of current, the actual flow depends not only on voltage, but on the resistance of the circuit. The standard unit for measuring circuit resistance is an ohm, measured by an ohmmeter. The ohmmeter is somewhat similar to an ammeter, but incorporates its own source of power so that a standard voltage is always present.

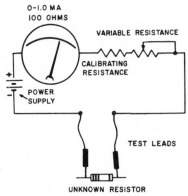

Ohmmeter circuit

An actual electric circuit consists of four basic parts. These are: the power source, such as a generator or battery; a hot wire, which conducts the electricity under a relatively high voltage or pressure to the electrical appliance supplied by the circuit; the load, such as a lamp, motor, resistor, or relay coil; and the ground wire, which carries the current back to the source under very low electrical pressure. In such a circuit, the bulk of the resistance exists between the point where the hot wire is connected to the load, and the point where the load is grounded. In an automobile, the vehicle's frame, which is made of steel, is used as a part of the ground circuit for many of the electrical devices.

Remember that, in electrical testing, the voltmeter is connected in parallel with the circuit being tested (without disconnecting any wires) and measures the difference in voltage between the locations of the two probes; that the ammeter is connected in series with the load (the circuit is separated at one point and the ammeter inserted so it becomes a part of the circuit); and that the ohmmeter is self-powered, so that all the power in the circuit should be off and the portion of the circuit to be measured contacted at either end by one of the probes of the meter.

The Charging System

How It Works

The automobile charging system provides electrical power for operation of the vehicle's ignition and starting systems and all the electrical accessories. The battery serves as an electrical surge or storage tank, storing (in chemical form) the energy originally produced by the engine-driven generator. The system also provides a means of regulating generator output to protect the battery from being overcharged and to avoid excessive voltage to the accessories.

An alternator rotor. Initial current flow comes from the battery (Courtesy of Delco-Remy)

The storage battery is a chemical device incorporating parallel lead plates in a tank containing a sulfuric acid-water solution. Adjacent plates are slightly dissimilar, and the chemical reaction of the two dissimilar plates produces electrical energy when the battery is connected to a load such as the starter motor. The chemical reaction is reversible, so that when the generator is producing a voltage (electrical pressure) greater than that produced by the battery, electricity is forced into the battery, and the battery is returned to its fully charged state.

The vehicle's generator is driven mechanically, through V belts, by the engine crankshaft. It consists of two coils of fine wire, one stationary (the "stator"), and one movable (the "rotor"). The rotor may also be known as the "armature", and consists of fine wire wrapped around an iron core which is mounted on a shaft. The electricity which flows through the two coils of wire (provided initially by the battery in some cases) creates an intense magnetic field around both rotor and stator, and the interaction between the two fields creates voltage, allowing the generator to power the accesories and charge the battery.

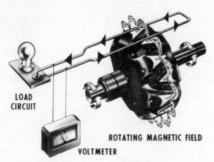

LOAD
CIRCUIT

ROTATING MAGNETIC FIELD

VOLTMETER

In an alternator, rotation of the field through the stator windings produces voltage (Courtesy of Delco-Remy)

There are two types of generators; the earlier is the direct current (DC) type. The current produced by the DC generator is generated in the armature and carried off the spinning armature by stationary brushes contacting the commutator. The commutator is a series of smooth metal contact plates on the end of the armature. The commutator plates, which are separated from one another by a very short gap, are connected to the armature circuits so that current will flow in one direction only in the wires carrying the generator output. The generator stator consists of two stationary coils of wire which draw some of the output current of the generator to form a powerful magnetic field and create the interaction of fields which generates the voltage. The generator field is wired in series with the regulator.

Newer automobiles use alternating current generators or "alternators", because they are more efficient, can be rotated at higher speeds, and have fewer brush problems. In an alternator, the field rotates while all the current produced passes only through the stator windings. The brushes bear against continuous slip rings rather than a commutator. This causes the current produced to periodically reverse the direction of its flow. Diodes (electrical one-way switches) block the flow of curent from traveling in the wrong direction. A series of diodes is wired together to permit the alternating flow of the stator to be converted to a pulsating, but unidirectional flow at the alternator output. The alternator's field is wired in series with the voltage regulator.

The regulator consists of several circuits. Each circuit has a core, or magnetic coil of wire, which operates a switch. Each switch is connected to ground through one or more resistors. The coil of wire responds directly to system voltage. When the voltage reaches the required level, the magnetic field created by the winding of wire closes the switch and inserts a resistance into the generator field circuit, thus reducing the output. The contacts of the switch cycle open and close many times each second to precisely control voltage.

While alternators are self-limiting as far as maximum current is concerned, DC generators employ a current regulating circuit which responds directly to the total amount of current flowing through the generator circuit rather than to the output voltage. The current regulator is similar to the voltage regulator except that all system current must flow through the energizing coil on its way to the various accessories.

SAFETY PRECAUTIONS

Observing these precautions will ensure safe handling of the electrical system components, and will avoid damage to the vehicle's electrical system:

A. Be *absolutely* sure of the polarity of a booster battery before making connections. Connect the cables positive to positive, and negative to negative. Connect positive cables first and then make the last connection to a ground on the body of the booster vehicle so that arcing cannot ignite hydrogen gas that may have accumulated near the battery. Even momentary

A typical alternator (© G.M. Corp)

connection of a booster battery with the polarity reversed will damage alternator diodes.

B. Disconnect both vehicle battery cables before attempting to charge a battery.

C. Never ground the alternator or generator output or battery terminal. Be cautious when using metal tools around a battery to avoid creating a short circuit between the terminals.

D. Never ground the field circuit between the alternator and regulator.

E. Never run an alternator or generator without load unless the field circuit is disconnected.

F. Never attempt to polarize an alternator.

G. Keep the regulator cover in place when taking voltage and current limiter readings.

H. Use insulated tools when adjusting the regulator.

J. Whenever DC generator-to-regulator wires have been disconnected, the generator *must* be repolarized. To do this with an externally grounded, light duty generator, momentarily place a jumper wire between the battery terminal and the generator terminal of the regulator. With an internally grounded heavy duty unit, disconnect the wire to the regulator field terminal and touch the regulator battery terminal with it.

Quick Reference Guide For Charging System Troubleshooting

A. *Inspect the system.* Check the battery electrolyte level, all electrical connections, and the generator (alternator) drive belt condition and tension.

B. *Check the battery.* Test the battery under load. Check the specific gravity of all the battery cells. Charge the battery, if necessary. Replace the battery if it will not respond to charging.

C. *Test the output of the generator (alternator).* Replace or repair if rated output is not produced.

D. *Test charging circuit resistance.* If resistance is too high, replace bad wiring or repair poor connections.

E. *Check voltage and current regulator performance.* If not to specifications, clean contacts, adjust contact gap, and readjust regulator as necessary. Replace a nonadjustable unit which does not regulate the specified voltage. Check the field circuit wiring and replace bad wires or repair poor connections before replacing the regulator.

F. *Troubleshooting chart.* Battery discharge due to electrical system short or ground, generator output drops off at high speeds, etc.

Charging System Troubleshooting

A. Inspect the System.

Check the generator mounts for cracks or loose mounting bolts, and tighten or replace parts as necessary. Check the condition and tension of the drive belt. Replace the belt if it is frayed or cracked. Tighten the belt if there is play or inadequate tension. If manufacturer's specifications and a strand tension gauge are not available, the belt should be tightened so that it can be depressed about $\frac{1}{2}$ in. for each 10 in. of length with moderate (10–15 lbs) thumb pressure.

Check the level of electrolyte in the battery cells and fill them, if necessary, with distilled water to the level of the indicator ring. Clean the surface of the battery with a rag. Replace the battery if there is a sizable crack.

Check the condition of the battery terminals. If there is corrosion, disconnect the terminals and clean them with a baking soda and water solution. Thoroughly clean the corroded material from the conducting surfaces with a wire brush. Reconnect the terminals snugly. Even if no cleaning was required, carefully tighten the terminals. Coat the terminals with clean petroleum jelly to prevent further corrosion.

All the visible wires in the charging system should then be checked for cracked or frayed insulation and loose or corroded connections. Clean any corroded connections with a wire brush or sandpaper, and reconnect them snugly. Replace any frayed wiring.

B. Check the Battery.

Check the capacity of the battery as indicated by a rating on the label in wattage or ampere-hours. Recommended battery rating for the vehicle may be found in the owner's manual. The battery capacity should be at least equal to the recommended rating.

A quick check of battery condition may be made by connecting a voltmeter across the battery posts and cranking the engine for about 15 seconds. If the voltage at the positive terminal remains at approximately 9.6 or above, the battery is most likely in good condition.

If the battery does not pass this test, test the specific gravity of the electrolyte in each of the cells. If the battery requires addition of water to bring the cells to the proper level, this should be done first. If water had to be added, the battery should be charged at a high enough rate to cause gasing (hydrogen emission) of the cells for 15 minutes to ensure thorough mixing of the electrolyte.

Test the specific gravity of each cell with a clean hydrometer. If the hydrometer has a thermometer, draw in and expel the fluid several times to make a thermometer reading. Otherwise use a battery thermometer, allowing time for the thermometer to reach the temperature of the

electrolyte. Correct the hydrometer reading by adding 0.004 to it for each 10° over 80° F, and subtracting 0.004 for each 10° below 80° F.

If the readings are more than 50 points apart, the battery should be replaced. The battery is fully charged if gravity is 1.260–1.280, half charged at about 1.210, and fully discharged at about 1.120. If the readings are inconclusive, the battery should be charged at a rate that will not bring the electrolyte to a temperature over 125° F. This should be done until the specific gravity remains constant for two hours. If at this point, all the cells are not between 1.260 and 1.280, especially if the variations exceed 50 points, the battery should be replaced.

There are various commercial battery testers available that measure output voltage while subjecting the battery to a load. They will do an excellent job.

C. Test the Output of the Generator (Alternator).

A quick and simple output test may be made using a voltmeter. Simply connect the voltmeter between the positive and negative battery terminals and measure the voltage. Then start the engine and run it at fast idle. Check the voltage again. If it has risen (usually about 2 V), the generator (alternator) and regulator are functioning.

The regulator may be easily bypassed if a field rheostat is available, in order to see whether an inadequate voltage rise as measured in the above test is due to problems in the generator (alternator) or regulator. Proceed as follows:

1. Disconnect the field wire from the F or FLD terminal on the regulator. Connect the field rheostat between the IGN terminal of the regulator and the disconnected field wire.

2. Turn the rheostat to the maximum resistance position (the low side of the scale).

3. Start the engine and operate it at fast idle. Gradually turn the rheostat control toward the decreased resistance side of the scale while watching the voltmeter. Turn the knob until the voltage read on the meter equals the manufacturer's specified maximum voltage for the generator (alternator). If it will not produce the specified voltage, it requires repair or replacement.

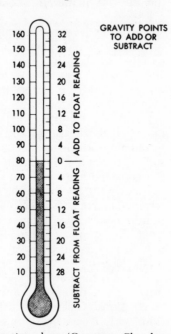

Hydrometer correction chart (Courtesy, Chrysler Corp)

In cases of questionable performance, a more accurate test of generator (alternator) condition is an amperage output test. A DC generator may be tested as described below:

a. Remove the armature and field leads from the generator. Place a jumper wire between these two terminals. Connect a 100 amp capacity ammeter between the generator armature terminal, and whichever battery lead is not grounded, with the positive ammeter lead on the generator.

b. Start the engine, and with the engine idling, move the negative ammeter lead to the positive terminal of the battery.

c. Run the engine at fast idle and note the generator output as measured on the ammeter. Compare with manufacturer's specifications. Output should be about 30 amps for regular-duty equipment, and about 50 amps for heavy-duty units.

NOTE: *Disconnect all leads as soon as the engine stops or else battery current will flow through the generator.*

Alternator output tests very according to the design of the alternator and regulator in use. For the details of testing an alternator-powered charging system, it is recommended that a Chilton manual or factory repair manual be consulted. The alternator output test is generally accomplished as follows:

a. Place an ammeter in series between the battery terminal of the alternator and the disconnected battery lead.

b. Hook up a voltmeter between the battery lead on the alternator and the battery negative terminal. Ground or connect the alternator field terminal to the battery positive post. (This will depend on the internal design of the regulator.)

c. Hook a carbon pile rheostat between the two battery posts. Connect a tachometer to the engine.

d. Start the engine and adjust to the speed specified in the test instructions. Adjust the carbon pile rheostat so the voltage at which the test is to be performed registers on the voltmeter, then read the amperage on the ammeter.

e. If amperage is below specifications, the alternator requires repairs. Some test instructions include procedures for evaluating the alternator condition and locating the problem based on the difference between rated amperage and what is found in the test.

D. Test the Charging Circuit Resistance

The charging circuit resistance test is very similar to the output test for both generators and alternators. A manual should be consulted for details of instrument hook-up and amperage settings, as well as the maximum permissible voltage drop (usually less than 1 V).

The test differs in that the voltmeter is connected between the generator battery terminal and the positive terminal of the vehicle's battery. The engine is operated at fast idle, and the carbon pile rheostat adjusted until a specified amperage is flowing to the battery. The voltage drop is then compared to specifications. If voltage drop is excessive, the connections must be carefully inspected and, if necessary, cleaned and tightened. If this fails to bring the voltage drop down to specifications, wiring must be replaced.

E. Check Voltage and Current Regulator Performance.

A very simple test of regulator performance may be made as follows:

1. Remove the high-tension lead from the coil and ground it. Crank the engine for about 30 seconds.

2. Disconnect the battery terminal of the regulator, or the alternator-to-battery cable on alternators with integral regulators, and insert an ammeter. The ammeter leads will have to be reversed (with the engine off) if the ammeter reads downscale.

3. Reconnect the distributor high-tension lead and start the engine, running it at fast idle. Watch the ammeter. The amperage reading should be high at first, and then, after two or three minutes of operation, it should fall off to a very low reading, assuming that all vehicle accessories are turned off.

If this test reveals problems, the regulator should be further tested. General test instructions follow. Manufacturer's specifications should be consulted for the exact voltage output required at various regulator temperatures.

Voltage Regulator Test

This test requires a voltmeter and ammeter. For Delco units, a 0.25 ohm resistor of 25 watt capacity is required. In the case of the Chrysler mechanical regulator with alternator, a carbon pile rheostat is required.

A. Hook up the test equipment as described below. Delco DC Generator: Connect the resistor in series between the battery and regulator by removing the line to the regulator "Batt" terminal and inserting the resistor between the terminal and the wire connection. Connect a voltmeter between the regulator terminal and a good ground.

Autolite or Ford DC Generator: Connect an ammeter between the battery and the regulator by disconnecting the line to the "Batt" terminal and inserting the ammeter. Connect the voltmeter between the armature connection on the regulator and ground.

Chrysler Mechanical Regulator with Alternator: Connect the voltmeter between the ignition terminal no. 1 of the ballast resistor and ground. Connect a carbon pile rheostat between the two battery terminals, with the resistance adjusted to the highest level.

Chrysler Electronic Regulator: Disconnect the battery during hook-up. Connect the ammeter between the alternator and

battery by disconnecting the battery-to-alternator lead and inserting the ammeter (with the positive side toward the alternator). Connect the voltmeter between the "Ign" terminal of the regulator and a good ground.

Delco 5.5 and 6.2 alternators: Connect the resistor between the battery cable (with the cable disconnected) and the battery cable connection on the junction block. Connect the voltmeter between that junction block connection and a ground on the body of the relay.

B. Start the engine and run it at fast idle (about 1,600 rpm) for 15 minutes to bring all components to operating temperature. If you are testing a Chrysler alternator with a mechanical regulator, adjust the engine speed to 1,250 rpm with a tachometer, and adjust the carbon pile rheostat so the charging rate is 15 amps. With Delcotron alternators, turn on the headlights and heater blower. With Ford DC units, turn on accessories until the generator is producing 8–10 amps. With Autolite DC units, turn accessories until one half of the generator output is being produced.

C. Place a thermometer on the regulator to measure its temperature. Stop and start

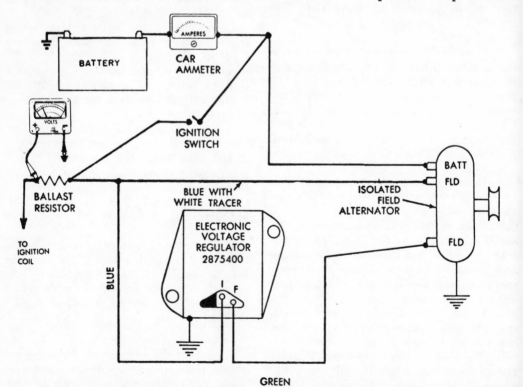

GREEN

Voltage regulator test hookup—Chrysler isolated field alternator

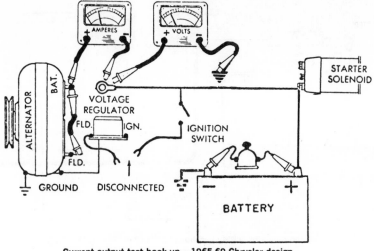

Current output test hook-up—1965-69 Chrysler design

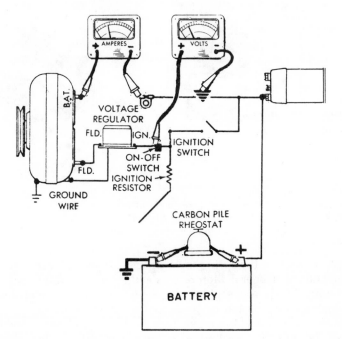

Voltage regulator test hookup—1965–69 Chrysler electro-mechanical regulator

the engine after 15 minutes to cycle the regulator off and on.

D. Read the voltage and temperature, and compare each with manufacturer's specifications. On Chrysler mechanical units with an alternator, the lower contacts must also be tested by bringing the engine speed to 2,200 rpm and adjusting the carbon pile for 7 amps charging rate.

If the results of this test do not meet specifications, or if the battery is over-charged (loses water continuously), or if starting problems are encountered with no problems in the battery or starting system, the regulator should be adjusted and ser-viced or, if necessary, replaced.

REGULATOR ADJUSTMENT

1970 and later voltage regulators are gen-erally not adjustable. For information on a specific model refer to one of Chilton's re-pair manuals for your make of car.

All mechanical units may be adjusted by either turning an adjusting screw or bending a spring mount to increase the tension of a spring to increase the voltage

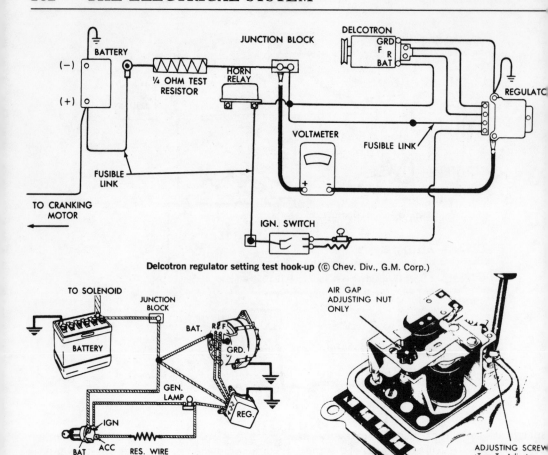

Part A. Delcotron regulator setting test hookup (Courtesy Chevrolet Div. of General Motors Corp); Part B. Typical Delcotron circuit diagram (Courtesy Chevrolet Div. of General Motors Corp); Part C. Adjusting voltage setting—mechanical regulator (Courtesy Chevrolet Div. of General Motors Corp)

and decreasing the tension of the spring to lower the output voltage. General Motors solid-state regulators which are separate from the alternator may be adjusted by removing a pipe plug in the top of the regulator and turning the adjusting screw underneath.

Specific manufacturer's instructions and specifications for each type of regulator should be consulted. All final regulator checks must be accomplished with the regulator cover in place.

If the regulator contact points are burned or pitted, they should be cleaned with a riffler file and the gap should be adjusted according to the manufacturer's

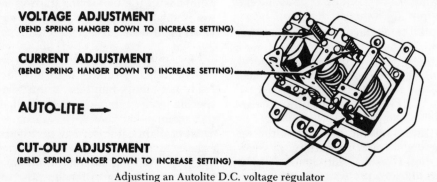

Adjusting an Autolite D.C. voltage regulator

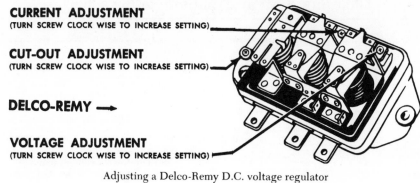

CURRENT ADJUSTMENT
(TURN SCREW CLOCK WISE TO INCREASE SETTING)

CUT-OUT ADJUSTMENT
(TURN SCREW CLOCK WISE TO INCREASE SETTING)

DELCO-REMY →

VOLTAGE ADJUSTMENT
(TURN SCREW CLOCK WISE TO INCREASE SETTING)

Adjusting a Delco-Remy D.C. voltage regulator

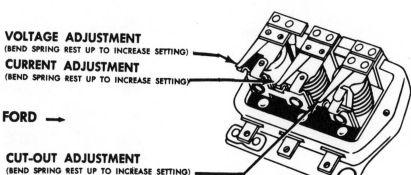

VOLTAGE ADJUSTMENT
(BEND SPRING REST UP TO INCREASE SETTING)

CURRENT ADJUSTMENT
(BEND SPRING REST UP TO INCREASE SETTING)

FORD →

CUT-OUT ADJUSTMENT
(BEND SPRING REST UP TO INCREASE SETTING)

Adjusting a Ford D.C. voltage regulator

specifications. This is done by closing the contacts and then measuring the distance between the armature and core of the regulator with a round feeler gauge. Bend the contact arm at the specified spot until the gap is correct.

In the case of DC regulators which fail to produce adequate output only under heavy load conditions, the current regulator may be checked. An ammeter is placed in series with the battery, and the amperage is read just after a very heavy load has been placed on the battery by cranking the engine for 30 seconds with the high-tension lead to the coil grounded. All accessories should be turned on for the test. The current should meet manufacturer's specifications. The current regulator is adjusted in the same way as the voltage regulator.

If the regulator produces insufficient voltage or does not regulate the voltage properly, and cannot be adjusted, it should be replaced. If voltage output is inadequate, the connections in the field circuit between the regulator and generator (alternator) should be cleaned and tightened, and the wires should be checked for continuity. Rectify any problems found by re-

placing wires or cleaning and tightening connections before condemning the regulator.

Dash Gauges and Indicators

Dash gauges and indicators permit the driver to monitor the operating conditions of his engine and charging system, and the level of fuel in his fuel tank. Generally, the engine gauges monitor the oil pressure and the coolant temperature. Engine warning lights come on if oil pressure drops to a level that cannot ensure adequate protection of the engine's moving parts from heat and wear, or if coolant temperature rises to the point where coolant will be lost through boiling. Oil and coolant gauges are usually marked to indicate safe operating ranges.

The ammeter tells the driver whether current is flowing to or from the battery, and reports the amount. Charging system warning lights tell the driver whether or not the generator is operating. They do not give an indication of charging rate.

The fuel gauge reports the level of fuel

Charging System Troubleshooting Chart

Indication:	Cause:
Generator output is good at low rpm, but suddenly drops off as speed is increased.	Loose wire in rotor slung out by centrifugal force, shorting to stator windings.
Constant slight battery drain; starting voltage is low, but only after overnight shutdown.	Ground in wiring harness or an accessory. (Disconnect battery positive cable, insert a voltmeter, and check for voltage. If there is a reading, a very small ground exists in the wiring harness.)
Battery discharges within a few hours of shutdown; a constant sizable drain.	Battery may have an internal ground: in this case, the system will show symptoms of overcharging, even though your voltage regulator is all right. Alternator may have a shorted positive diode, closing field relay and permitting constant discharge through the alternator.
Indicator light is off at all times, preventing alternator operation.	Faulty bulb, socket, or wiring. Also, regulator wiring may be at fault.
Indicator light on at all times.	Improper field relay or generator cutout adjustment, or faulty unit.
Battery slightly discharged.	Voltage limiter setting low, or generator (alternator) rating not sufficient for the accessory load. Added accessories may be the cause.
Battery overcharged.	Voltage regulator set too high for the operating conditions. Faulty resistor or coil in regulator, or poor ground between regulator and alternator.
Noisy alternator.	Loose mountings. Slipping belt. Bad bearings. Faulty rectifier (if the noise sounds electrical).
Ammeter fluctuates or headlights flicker.	Bad generator brushes, improperly set regulator, or poor connections in charging system, or faulty regulator.
Regulator points burn or stick.	Poor ground between generator and regulator, or burned regulator resistor.

in the tank, as measured by a tank float. Most such gauges are marked to indicate the level in increments of quarters of a tank.

While gauges indicate operating conditions over a wide range, warning lights are more easily noticed when trouble occurs suddenly.

Most gauge problems result from faulty wiring or connections, a faulty sensor, or a faulty gauge. In some cases a problem in several gauges at once is due to a malfunction in a special voltage regulator that supplies all the gauges. Because gauge parts are fairly inexpensive, troubleshooting in this area usually involves identifying the defective sensor, wiring, gauge, or gauge voltage regulator, and replacing the faulty unit. It should also be remembered that when many gauges malfunction at once, or repeated gauge problems occur, the voltage regulator in the charging system may be at fault.

GAUGE OPERATION

Bourdon Tube Gauges

This type of gauge is used to measure oil pressure or engine temperature. It responds to changes in pressure via a Bourdon tube which is a coil of tubing with a flattened side. As pressure rises inside the tubing, the flattened side tends to bow somewhat and straighten the coil. The

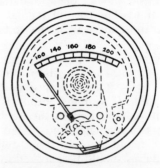

A bourdon tube type temperature gauge

gauge needle is linked directly to the end of the tube.

When used as an oil pressure gauge, the unit responds directly to the pressure generated by the oil pump, although the gauge and the line to the oil system are kept full of air to make sure that pulsations from the oil pump are dampened out. If the gauge reads accurately but pulsates, the problem may be cured by draining the oil line and gauge and reconnecting all fittings more snugly. If there is evidence of leaks, replace the faulty parts. Reconnect the line at the gauge first, and then at the engine.

If the gauge fails to respond properly, remove the line at the gauge and place it over an empty container. Then start the engine. If oil does not flow from the line after expulsion of a few bubbles, blow out the line to allow pressure to reach the gauge.

If the gauge is still in question, the best procedure is to connect a gauge of known accuracy into the system to determine that engine oil pressure is adequate and that the gauge line is clear. Replace the gauge if the good unit operates properly.

When this type of gauge is used to measure engine temperature, it responds to pressure generated by a volatile liquid sealed in a sensing bulb. The bulb is placed in or near the engine cooling water. The vapor pressure of the fluid varies directly with the temperature and the Bourdon tube and gauge are calibrated to reflect the temperature on the face of the gauge. This type of unit is entirely sealed. If the gauge simply does not move from the minimum reading, it may be assumed that the gauge, line, or sensing bulb has leaked, and the whole unit must be replaced. If readings are questionable, a unit of known accuracy may be substituted. If that unit performs accurately, the faulty unit should be replaced.

If the unit responds, but reads slightly low at all times, test the cooling system thermostat to make sure that it is operating properly. If that unit tests out, but the gauge reading has fallen substantially, the gauge unit is faulty.

Install the new unit carefully. Form a loop in the line somewhere between the engine and the gauge to minimize the effect of vibration on the gauge and sensing bulb.

Bimetal Gauges

These gauges employ a bimetallic strip to sense current flow. The two metals which make up this strip expand at different rates. As the temperature of the strip changes, therefore, the two metals work against each other, making the strip bend back and forth. The free end of the strip operates the gauge needle through a simple linkage.

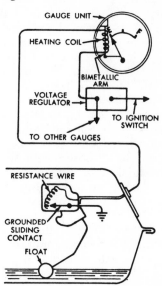

Fuel gauge circuit

In the case of a fuel tank bimetal gauge, the sensing unit consists of a resistor and sliding contact. The position of the contact is determined by a float. As the sliding contact moves across the resistor, current is sent in varying amounts to the gauge or to ground. The current which flows to the gauge passes through a resistor which surrounds the bimetal strip, so the gauge indication varies with the position of the float in the tank.

When a bimetal gauge is used to sense engine temperature, the resistor and sliding contact are replaced by a resistor which changes its resistance with temperature. The resistor unit is immersed in the cooling water or placed in direct contact with the material of the engine block.

A bimetal gauge may also be used to measure oil pressure. In this application, the sending unit's linkage to the sliding contact is activated by a diaphragm, one side of which is exposed to engine oil pressure.

The bimetal gauge may be tested by removing it from the dash and applying voltage to it with flashlight batteries. If the gauge is the type that uses a constant voltage regulator, it operates at three volts (3 V). If other gauges are also malfunctioning, the constant voltage regulator is at fault.

To test a constant voltage type gauge, apply 3 V, using two flashlight cells in series and jumper wires. If the gauge operates at line voltage, use four batteries in series to provide 6 V. Under these conditions, the 3 V gauge will read full scale, while the 12 V unit will read half-scale. Replace the unit if it fails to read properly.

If the gauge checks out, or if replacing a faulty unit fails to correct the problem, the sending unit should be tested. Fuel gauge sending units should be removed from the tank and tested for continuity (with an ammeter) through the full range of float movement. If the unit shows zero resistance at any or all positions, it should be replaced. The float should also be checked for leaks. Check the mechanism for binding. Repair or replace the unit as necessary.

The only way to test oil pressure and temperature gauge sending units used with bimetal gauges is to substitute a good unit in place of the suspected one and operate the engine to check for normal response.

If the sending unit proves faulty, it must be replaced. If the problem does not lie in the sending unit, the wire between the sending unit and the gauge should be checked for continuity with an ohmmeter. Check also for bad connections. Clean and tighten connections or replace wiring as necessary.

Magnetic Gauges

The magnetic gauge employs two electromagnetic coils of different sizes to influence the position of the gauge pointer. The smaller coil, located on the left side of the gauge and known as the battery coil, pulls the needle toward the downscale side at all times. This coil receives a constant supply of current directly from the ignition switch. The larger coil, known as the ground coil, receives all of the current passing through the unit to ground when full scale readings are required. Under all other circumstances, varying amounts of the current are passed through the sending unit to ground. When less than full current passes through the ground coil, the battery

coil pulls the pointer over toward the low side of the scale. The sending units for fuel and temperature gauges of this type work on the same principles that apply to the sending units used with bimetal fuel and temperature gauges. The two types of sending units resemble one another closely. However, units designed for one type of gauge cannot be used with the other. It is, therefore, necessary to use only the proper sending unit for the particular gauge.

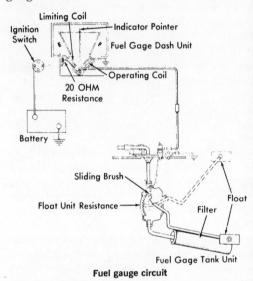

Fuel gauge circuit

Fuel gauge circuit

TESTING GAUGES

Magnetic Fuel Gauges

To test the dash gauge, use a tank unit of known accuracy. Pull the wire from the tank unit and install it on the unit being used for the test. Ground the body of the unit being used for the test. Moving the float arm through its entire range should produce a consistent response from the gauge, with the needle moving from empty to full positions.

If the gauge reads properly, the problem is in the tank unit. Remove it and check for a gas-logged float, binding float, or lack of continuity somewhere in the operating range of the float arm. Replace or repair parts of the unit as necessary.

If the problem does not lie in the sending unit, check all the connections between the sending unit and the dash gauge. Also, check the wire between the dash gauge and the tank unit for continu-

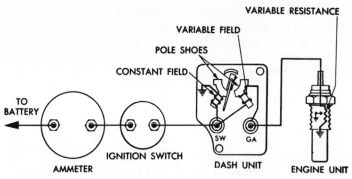

Water temperature gauge

ity. If wiring and connections are all right, or if rectifying problems in them does not give accurate readings, replace the dash gauge.

Magnetic Temperature Gauges

First, disconnect the wire at the sending unit. The gauge hand should be in the cold position. Ground the wire which goes to the sending unit. The gauge should move to the hot position.

If the gauge does not read cold when the wire to the sending unit is disconnected, either the gauge is defective or the wire is grounded somewhere. Disconnect the wire that goes to the sending unit at the gauge. If the gauge now reads cold, replace the wire. Otherwise, replace the gauge unit.

If the gauge reads to the cold side when the wire is disconnected, but does not move to the hot side when it is grounded, ground the sending unit terminal of the gauge. If this causes the gauge to read to the hot side, replace the wire that goes to the sending unit.

If there is no response from the gauge when the sending unit terminal is grounded, test for voltage with a voltmeter or test lamp at the ignition switch terminal of the gauge. If there is no voltage here, test for voltage at the ignition switch accessory terminal. If there is voltage at the ignition switch terminal, replace the wire between this terminal and the gauge. Otherwise, replace the ignition switch.

If this does not produce accurate readings, remove the engine thermostat and test it for proper operation as described in the cooling system troubleshooting section. If the thermostat is all right, or if replacing it does not rectify the problem, substitute a good sending unit for the one pres-

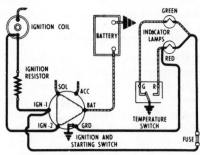

Temperature indicator circuit

ently in the engine block. If this does not produce good readings, replace the dash gauge.

WARNING LIGHTS

Warning lights continuously receive voltage whenever the ignition switch is turned on. The circuit is completed to ground whenever the sending unit contacts close, allowing current to flow through the light.

Oil pressure warning light sending units consist of a diaphragm which responds to about five lbs oil pressure, opening the contacts when that pressure level is exceeded. Water temperature warning lights are energized when a bimetal element closes the contacts in the sending unit at a predetermined water temperature.

TESTING WARNING LIGHTS

Oil Pressure Warning Lights

If the oil light is on all the time, remove the connection at the sending unit. If the light is still on, the problem is a ground between the light and sending unit. Replace the wire between these two units.

If the light goes off when the wire is removed, connect a pressure gauge into the fitting where the oil pressure sending unit is normally installed. If the oil pressure exceeds five lbs, replace the sending unit. Otherwise, there is a mechanical problem causing low oil pressure.

If the light never operates, remove the wire from the sending unit and ground it. If this causes the light to come on, replace the sending unit. If there is no response, check for voltage at both terminals of the lamp socket and at the ignition switch accessory terminal. The faulty unit lies between a hot and a dead terminal. If the lamp socket is suspected, replace the lamp with one that is known to operate. If this produces no response, replace the socket.

Temperature Warning Lights

See the cooling system service section for procedures on testing this system. If the light does not operate in spite of coolant loss, the antifreeze strength, radiator cap, and cooling system pressure tests should be performed. If the light operates even though no coolant is lost, check the radiator cap and thermostat, and, if necessary, clean the system.

If these system tests do not uncover the problem, the light should be tested as outlined for the oil pressure light test above. If the system is known to operate properly, but the light comes on when it should not, or does not come on when overheating occurs, the sending unit should be replaced.

Fuses, Circuit Breakers, and Fusible Links

Fuses are replaceable electrical conductors sealed in small glass cylinders for protection against dust and corrosion. The conducting portion of the fuse is made of a metal with a low melting point. The fuse is designed so that if the amperage passing through it exceeds its rated capacity, the conducting material will melt and interrupt the flow of current through the circuit.

Circuit breakers are electrical switches that employ bimetallic elements to open the circuit whenever current exceeds a specified level. The heat from the passage of current through the unit bends the bimetallic arm to open the contacts of the

switch. After a short period of cooling, the contacts close again.

Circuit breakers are usually used to protect heavy-duty electric motors that can be operated only intermittently. These motors power such auxiliaries as power windows, convertible tops, and tailgates.

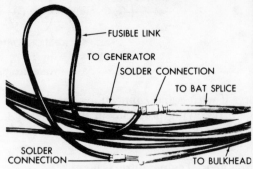

A typical fusible link (© G.M. Corp)

Fusible links are sections of vehicle wiring designed to protect the wiring itself, as well as individual accessories. The links consist of wiring sections about four gauges smaller (larger numerically) than the regular wiring. If a severe overload occurs, the link will burn out entirely before the regular vehicle wiring is damaged.

Repair a burned out fusible link as follows:

A. Disconnect the battery. Cut out all remaining portions of the burned out link. Strip the main wiring insulation back about ½ in. on either end.

B. Solder in a 10 in. long link of wire that is four gauges smaller than the wire to be protected. Use resin core solder only.

C. Tape all exposed portions of the wire securely. Reconnect the battery.

Windshield Wiper Systems

Most windshield wipers are powered by small electric motors of either the permanent magnet or electromagnet type. Some systems are powered by hydraulic pressure from the power steering pump or by intake manifold vacuum.

The wiper systems usually provide two or three operating speeds. Speed is controlled by inserting a resistor into the circuit in the lower speed or speeds. The resistance element may either be located on

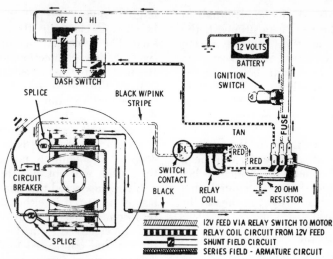

OFF LO HI

DASH SWITCH

SPLICE

BLACK W/PINK STRIPE

CIRCUIT BREAKER

SPLICE

SWITCH CONTACT

BLACK

RELAY COIL

12 VOLTS
BATTERY

IGNITION SWITCH

TAN

RED

RED

FUSE

20 OHM RESISTOR

12V FEED VIA RELAY SWITCH TO MOTOR
RELAY COIL CIRCUIT FROM 12V FEED
SHUNT FIELD CIRCUIT
SERIES FIELD - ARMATURE CIRCUIT

General Motors round motor low-speed circuit (Courtesy G.M. Corp)

the wiper switch or on the wiper motor itself. Most electrical systems employ a circuit breaker which may be located on either the switch or the motor.

If the system does not operate at all, make sure that the blades are not frozen in place or adjusted so the motor cannot reach a park position. Pull the blades outward, then turn on the ignition and wiper switches and check the response. If the blades now move, adjust the blades so that when the motor is parked, they just reach the bottom of the windshield.

If the system does not operate at all, or does not park properly, an electrical check should be made to see if the problem is in the wiring, switch, or motor. If the motor operates but there is no response from the wipers, the gearbox on the motor is at fault.

Locate the wiper switch and test the terminal for the wire from the ignition switch for voltage. If there is no voltage, check for voltage at each connection between the wiper switch and the ignition switch and replace fuses or wiring as necessary.

If there is voltage to the switch but the system does not operate, remove the switch from the dash. Locate a factory manual for the vehicle. Perform a continuity test with an ohmmeter according to the instructions in the manual. This will involve testing for continuity between various terminals with the wiper switch in different positions. Replace the switch if continuity does not exist in one of the tests.

If the switch is good and the wipers still do not perform properly, check the wiring between the switch and the wiper motor. Each wire should be checked for continuity. If all wires are good, or if replacing any defective wire does not rectify the problem, the problem is a mechanical or electrical malfunction in the wiper motor.

Lighting, Turn Signals, and Warning Flashers

The first step in checking any lighting problem is to inspect all wiring and connectors. Make sure all insulation is sound and that all connectors in the circuits involved are securely connected. Also, make sure that the battery and charging systems are in good condition.

TROUBLESHOOTING

Headlamps

If a headlamp does not operate on one or both dimmer positions, substitute a lamp that is known to be good (perhaps the one from the other side of the car), or check for voltage at all terminals of the connector. All should have voltage in at least one of the dimmer positions. If all have voltage, replace the lamp.

If the connector at the lamp does not check out, check for voltage at the dimmer switch. Regardless of the type of switch, voltage should exist at all the terminals in at least one of the switch positions. If the dimmer switch is all right, replace wiring or correct loose connections between the switch and the headlight connector. If there is voltage anywhere in the switch, but one or more of the terminals has no voltage in either switch position, replace the switch.

If there is no voltage to the switch, check for voltage at each connection back to the battery. The faulty component is between a hot connection and a dead one. Replace wiring, fuses, or the headlight switch as necessary.

Direction Signals and Warning Flashers

If one of the direction signal lamps fails to operate, turn on the four-way flasher and check all lamps for operation. If the lamps operate with the flasher on, the defect is in the direction signal flasher or connections.

If the same lamp(s) fails to operate, substitute a lamp that is known to be good for the faulty lamp in each case. If this fails to correct the problem, check for voltage at each connection right back to the flasher. Also check for a corroded socket which might prevent proper grounding of the lamp, and clean up the socket as necessary. The faulty connector or wire is between a hot connection and a dead one. Replace wiring as necessary.

If all the lamps operate, and the direction signal or four-way flasher does not flash, replace the flasher unit. Remember that the unit flashes on and off by means of a bimetal strip that is heated by current flow. If any lamp is not getting current, the flasher will not operate properly.

If it is suspected that the flasher is faulty, it may be tested in either of two ways. If a replacement flasher is available, the wires may be removed from the one installed in the car and connected to the replacement flasher without removing the original unit. If this flasher works properly, replace the original one.

The flasher may also be tested for continuity by consulting a factory service manual for a table that lists which terminals should have continuity in the various switch positions.

If the flasher is not at fault, the wiring between the flasher and the battery or ignition switch should be tested for continuity. Replace wiring, fuses, or connectors as necessary.

20 · The Air Conditioning System

How It Works

The automotive air conditioning system's basic purpose is to reverse the normal flow of heat. Heat normally flows from an area at a certain temperature to any cooler area. The car's air conditioning system must keep the passenger compartment below the outside temperature by continuously removing heat.

This is accomplished by a mechanical compressor which is driven off the engine's crankshaft to compress a material which can be readily changed from a liquid to a gas state. The refrigerant in automotive applications is R-12 which has a $-27°$ F boiling point at atmospheric pressure.

The R-12 is metered into a cooling coil (very similar in construction to a car radiator) at about 30 psi. The refrigerant is in liquid form at this point in the cycle. Its boiling point at 30 psi is just above the

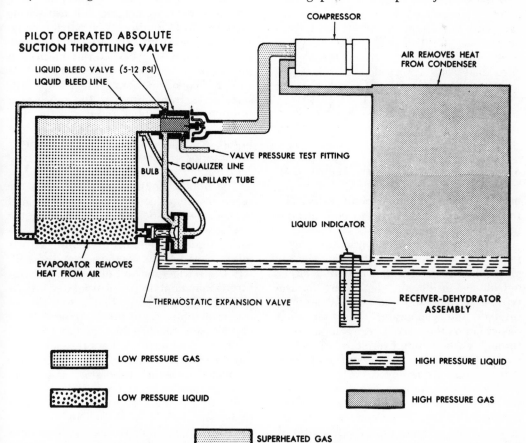

The refrigeration cycle (© G.M. Corp)

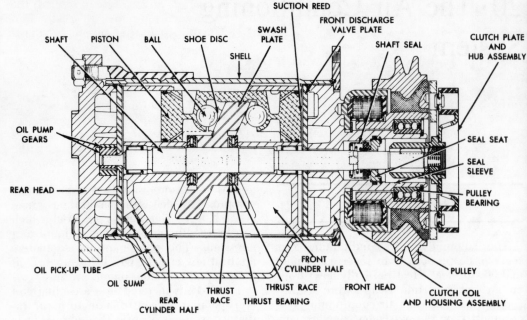

A General Motors type compressor (© G.M. Corp)

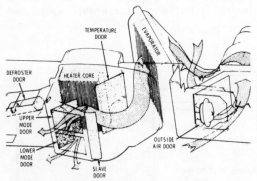

Air flow through the evaporator (Courtesy, G.M. Corp)

normal freezing temperature of water. The refrigerant therefore tends to boil, absorbing heat from the coil.

The cooling coil is known as the evaporator. It is normally located inside the car or on the firewall. A blower forces either outside or inside air, depending on the type of system and the control settings, through the evaporator. The air then passes into the passenger compartment through dash-mounted registers. As the air passes through the evaporator coil, heat and moisture are removed.

The refrigerant boils completely inside the evaporator and then passes into the compressor where its pressure is vastly increased. The pressure on the refrigerant as it leaves the compressor is usually 200 psi or more.

The refrigerant then enters the condenser, a heat exchanging coil usually located in front of the car's radiator. The very high pressure generated in the compressor is put to work at this point and raises the boiling point of the R-12 to over 150° F. When the cooling effect of the outside air is transmitted to the refrigerant through the thin tubes and fins of the condenser coil, it cools and changes back to a liquid, losing the heat it picked up from the interior of the car in the boiling process.

The liquified refrigerant then enters the receiver-drier, a small black tank located next to the condenser or on one of the fender wells. This unit has the job of separating liquid refrigerant from any gas that might have left the condenser, and also filters the refrigerant and absorbs any moisture it may contain. It incorporates a sight glass, in most systems, that allows the refrigerant returning to the evaporator to be checked for the presence of gas bubbles.

The refrigerant then flows through a liquid line to the expansion valve. This valve is located near the evaporator, usually (on most factory systems) on or near the firewall. On aftermarket systems, it is located under the dash. It is shaped like a mushroom, and in some systems incorporates the sight glass. This is the valve which controls the flow of refrigerant to the evaporator. The flow is controlled to supply only that amount the evaporator can handle.

The compressor incorporates a magnetic clutch to permit it to be turned off when it is not required. The clutch is operating whenever the flat portion on the front is turning with the belt-driven pulley located on the front of the compressor.

WARNING: *Because of the dangerous pressures and temperatures associated with the escape of refrigerant, repairs involving a line or fitting that contains refrigerant should always be left to trained servicemen.*

Air Conditioning System Troubleshooting

A. Check the Compressor Belts.

Inspect the compressor belts for cracks or glazing. Cracks that will affect operation of the belt appear as a separation of a large portion of the lower section of the belt. Glazing is the result of slippage, and is indicated by an absolutely smooth appearance of the two belt surfaces that bear against the pulley grooves.

If the belt is cracked or glazed, replace it. Use only the belt specified for the application. Replace multiple belts with new, matched sets, even if one of the belts is still serviceable.

When replacing the belt:

1. Loosen the mounting bolts of the compressor and move the unit toward the fan so that the new belt can be installed without prying.

2. Tighten the belt by pulling the compressor away from the fan, prying it carefully with a breaker bar or, if the mount is provided with a square hole, by applying torque on the mount with the square end of a socket drive. Position the compressor and then tighten all the mounting bolts.

Belts should be tightened so that there is no slack and so they have a springy feel. Applying moderate thumb pressure should cause the belt to yield about $1/2$–$3/4$ in. for each 10 in. between the two pulleys. New belts should be slightly tighter to allow for tension loss during break-in.

Tighten all belts to these specifications, even if there is no evidence of wear. If the belt is noisy, the problem is usually slippage which can be cured by proper adjustment or replacement.

B. Make Sure the Compressor Is Turning.

The front portion of the clutch remains stationary when the clutch is disengaged, even when the car's engine is operating. If that portion of the clutch turns with the pulley and belts, the compressor is operating.

If the compressor is not running, make sure that the air conditioning is turned on and that the controls are set for full cold. Also, the compressor of many units will not run if outside temperature is below 50° F. If all the switches are set properly and the weather is warm, the compressor should run at least intermittently. If there is no response, pull the wire from the connection on the clutch and test for voltage with a voltmeter. If voltage exists, the clutch is faulty and will have to be replaced. If there is no voltage, trace the wiring back toward the ignition switch. If the wire leads to a device mounted onto the receiver drier, or mounted on the firewall and electrically connected to the back of the compressor, the system has a low refrigerant protection system. If voltage exists on the ignition switch side of this unit but not on the clutch side, the system's refrigerant has leaked out. In this instance, repair by a professional air conditioning mechanic is required.

Otherwise, check each connection for voltage all the way back to the ignition switch. Lack of current can be caused by faulty wiring, bad connections, a blown fuse, or an inoperative thermostat (located right behind the temperature control). Fuses may be checked by removing them and checking for continuity with an ohmmeter. The faulty component lies between the last dead connection and the first to show voltage. Repair wiring, fuses, or switches as necessary.

C. Inspect the Condenser and Fan.

Inspect the condenser for bent fins or foreign material. Straighten the fins and clean them, if necessary.

NOTE: *Be careful, when straightening fins, not to allow the tools being used to damage the condenser tubing.*

Check the fan for bent blades or improper operation caused by slipping belts or a faulty fan clutch. See the cooling system troubleshooting section. Any cooling system problem can contribute to inferior air conditioner performance.

D. Check for Leaks.

Refrigerant system leaks show up as oily areas on the various components because the compressor oil is transported around the entire system along with the refrigerant. Look for oily spots on all the hoses and lines and at the hose and tubing connections, especially. If there are oily deposits, the system may have a leak and should be checked as in subsection E. A small area of oil on the front of the compressor is normal.

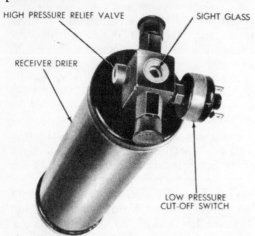

HIGH PRESSURE RELIEF VALVE

SIGHT GLASS

RECEIVER DRIER

LOW PRESSURE
CUT-OFF SWITCH

A receiver-drier showing location of the sight glass (Courtesy, Chrysler Corporation)

E. Check the Appearance of the Sightglass.

Start the engine and put the idle speed screw on one of the lower steps of the fast idle cam. Set the blower for high speed and set the thermostat for the lowest possible setting. Locate the sightglass, remove any protective covers, and clean it with a rag. Have someone turn on the air conditioner while you watch the sightglass. The glass should foam and then become clear. After a few minutes of operation, the glass should be entirely clear unless outside temperature is below 70° F. A few bubbles will be present at cooler temperatures, even if the system is in perfect condition. If a few bubbles appear at warm temperatures, the system has probably leaked

slightly and should be tested and recharged. If the glass shows severe bubbling or remains completely clear throughout the test, the refrigerant charge may be low, and unit operation should be discontinued immediately after making the test in F. If the sight glass foamed and then remained clear, go on to G.

F. Check the Temperature of the Lines.

Feel along the small, liquid line that runs from the condenser to the expansion valve. This line should be warm along its entire length. If there is a sudden drop in temperature before reaching the expansion valve, the line is clogged at the point where the temperature changes. The line will have to be removed and cleaned by a professional refrigeration mechanic. If the temperature drop occurs at the receiver-drier, this unit will have to be replaced because of saturation with moisture or dirt.

While the liquid line between the condenser and the expansion valve is the most common location for clogging, a sudden drop in temperature in the condenser or in the compressor discharge line will also indicate clogging. Be careful when feeling either the line between the compressor and condenser, or the condenser itself, as the temperature may be very high.

If the compressor discharge and suction lines are at about the same temperature and the sight glass does not foam even at start up, the entire refrigerant charge has probably leaked out.

G. Check System Performance and Blower Operation.

Operate the system with the blower at high speed and the temperature control set at the lowest setting. The engine should be operated at a fast idle (over 1,100 rpm).

The temperature at the discharge ducts varies with the weather and other conditions. However, most systems will maintain a comfortable temperature in all but the most extreme weather. If the temperature exceeds 90° F, a slight reduction in performance may be expected.

If system performance is inadequate, the problem may be in the blower, refrigeration system, or temperature control system.

If the blower operates on all speeds and changes its speed every time the blower speed switch is moved, it is probably operating properly. If it operates only on one or two of the positions, the blower resistor may be at fault. This resistor is usually located in the engine compartment on the evaporator housing. Remove the resistor and check it for burned or shorted resistor coils. If there is any evidence of burning, separation, or bending of the coils, replace the resistor.

If the blower does not operate at all, run a jumper wire from the battery positive terminal to the blower motor terminal to see if the motor will operate. If it does not run, check the ground strap. If the ground is all right, replace the blower motor. If the blower operates, check each connection between the motor and the air conditioning switch to isolate the faulty wire or connection.

If the system output is inadequate, even though the blower operates properly, the temperature control system may be at fault. Have someone move the temperature control lever back and forth while you look under the hood and dash for a moving control cable. The cable operates either an air mixing door or a water valve. If no cable movement is apparent and shifting the temperature control back and forth has a direct effect on the operation of the compressor, have the thermostatic switch checked by a professional air conditioning mechanic.

If the temperature control lever is moving a water valve or air door linkage, inspect the linkage to see that it is operating properly. The most common problem is an improper adjustment or slipping adjusting screw. The adjustment is usually made on

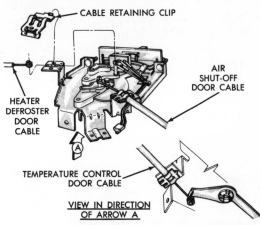

Adjustment of a typical heater control cable (© Ford Motor Co)

the clamp which holds the cable in place. Adjust the cable's position so that the door or water valve will move to the fully closed or maximum cooling position just before the temperature control reaches the full cold setting. Where a vacuum-operated water valve is used to stop coolant flow through the heater core at maximum cooling only, check the vacuum line to the valve. If the vacuum line is not cracked and is tightly connected to the valve, have the valve checked by a professional. Otherwise, replace or tighten the line as necessary.

If the air conditioner performs satisfactorily for 20–40 minutes and then begins to perform less efficiently, the evaporator core is freezing. The suction throttling valve or de-icing switch is malfunctioning. Have a professional air conditioning man adjust or repair the unit.

21 · Manual Transmission and Clutch

How They Work

Because of the way the gasoline engine breathes, it can produce torque, or twisting force, only within a narrow speed range. Most modern engines must turn at about 2,500 rpm to produce their peak torque. By 4,500 rpm they are producing so little torque that continued increases in engine speed produce no power increases.

The transmission and clutch are employed to vary the relationship between engine speed and the speed of the wheels so that adequate engine power can be produced under all circumstances. The clutch

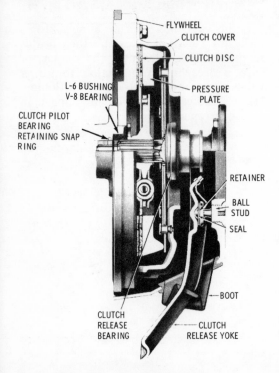

A typical clutch assembly (© G.M. Corp)

allows engine torque to be applied to the transmission input shaft gradually, due to mechanical slippage. The car can, consequently, be started smoothly from a full stop.

The transmission changes the ratio between the rotating speeds of the engine and the wheels by the use of gears. Three-speed or four-speed transmissions are most common. The lower gears allow full engine power to be applied to the rear wheels during acceleration at low speeds.

The clutch driven plate is a thin disc, the center of which is splined to the transmission input shaft. Both sides of the disc are covered with a layer of material which is similar to brake lining and which is capable of allowing slippage without roughness or excessive noise.

The clutch cover is bolted to the engine flywheel and incorporates a diaphragm spring which provides the pressure to engage the clutch. The cover also houses the pressure plate. The driven disc is sandwiched between the pressure plate and the smooth surface of the flywheel when the clutch pedal is released, thus forcing it to turn at the same speed as the engine crankshaft.

The transmission contains a mainshaft which passes all the way through the transmission, from the clutch to the driveshaft. This shaft is separated at one point, so that front and rear portions can turn at different speeds.

Power is transmitted by a countershaft in the lower gears and reverse. The gears of the countershaft mesh with gears on the mainshaft, allowing power to be carried from one to the other. All the countershaft gears are integral with that shaft, while several of the mainshaft gears can either rotate independently of the shaft or be locked to it. Shifting from one gear to the

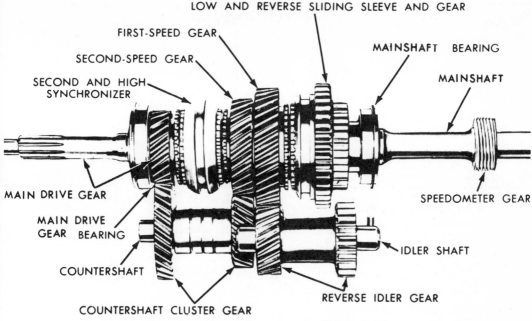

LOW AND REVERSE SLIDING SLEEVE AND GEAR

FIRST-SPEED GEAR

SECOND-SPEED GEAR

SECOND AND HIGH SYNCHRONIZER

MAINSHAFT BEARING

MAINSHAFT

SECOND AND HIGH SYNCHRONIZER

MAIN DRIVE GEAR

MAIN DRIVE GEAR BEARING

COUNTERSHAFT

COUNTERSHAFT CLUSTER GEAR

SPEEDOMETER GEAR

IDLER SHAFT

REVERSE IDLER GEAR

The inner workings of a transmission (© G.M. Corp)

next causes one of the gears to be freed from rotating with the shaft, and locks another to it. Gears are locked and unlocked by internal dog clutches which slide between the center of the gear and the shaft. The forward gears usually employ synchronizers: friction members which smoothly bring gear and shaft to the same speed before the toothed dog clutches are engaged.

The clutch is operating properly if:

1. It will stall the engine when released with the vehicle held stationary.

2. The shift lever can be moved freely between first and reverse gears when the vehicle is stationary and the clutch disengaged.

A clutch pedal free-play adjustment is incorporated in the linkage. If there is about 1–2 in. of motion before the pedal begins to release the clutch, it is adjusted properly. Inadequate free-play wears all parts of the clutch releasing mechanisms and may cause slippage. Excessive free-play may cause inadequate release and hard shifting of gears.

Some clutches use a hydraulic system in place of mechanical linkage. If the clutch fails to release, fill the clutch master cylinder with fluid to the proper level and pump the clutch pedal to fill the system with fluid. Bleed the system in the same way as a brake system. If leaks are located, tighten loose connections or overhaul the master or slave cylinder as necessary.

Clutch Troubleshooting Chart

SLIPPAGE

Insufficient free-play
(Pedal linkage causing constant pressure against release mechanisms.)
Binding pedal linkage
Driven disc covered with oil
Driven disc worn
(This causes a lack of spring tension.)
Spring tension poor due to heat-weakened springs
Pressure plate warped from heat
Driven plate not seated (brand new)
Clutch overheated, due to extreme operating conditions

CLUTCH FAILS TO RELEASE— HARD SHIFTING

Excessive clutch pedal free-play
Clutch plate binding on transmission input shaft
Severely warped driven disc or pressure plate
Transmission input shaft binding in the pilot bearing

Clutch Engagement Rough

Linkage requires lubrication
Worn or loose engine or transmission mounts
Loose clutch cover mounting bolts
Oil on flywheel
Disc hub binding on transmission input shaft
Pressure plate distorted or cracked

Clutch Noisy

(Noise occurs constantly)
Insufficient free-play
Worn linkage return spring
(Noise occurs whenever pedal is depressed)
Worn or poorly lubricated throwout bearing

Poor Clutch Facing Life

Insufficient pedal free-play
Riding the clutch (driving with foot on pedal)
Hard usage
Rough surface on flywheel or pressure plate
Oil or water on facing
Weak pressure plate springs
(causing constant slippage)

Transmission Troubleshooting Chart

Jumping Out of Gear

Transmission not aligned with clutch housing

Gearshift linkage out of adjustment
Mechanical interference with linkage
Insufficient spring tension on shifter rail plunger
End-play in main shaft
Bent shaft
Bent shifter fork
Synchronizer clutch teeth worn

Gears do not Synchronize

If only high gear synchronizes:
Binding main shaft pilot bearing
Clutch not releasing fully
Improper lubrication
Scored or worn synchronizer cones
If only one lower gear synchronizes:
Worn bearings in that mainshaft gear only

Sticking in Gear

Clutch not releasing fully
Binding shifter rail
Burred transmission mainshaft
Frozen synchronizer clutch
Inadequate or improper lubrication
Corroded transmission parts
Defective mainshaft pilot bearing

Transmission Noisy

Improper or inadequate lubrication
Worn thrust washers in countershaft gear
Loose synchronizer hub spline
Damaged or worn gear teeth
Loose transmission bearings

22 · The Automatic Transmission

How It Works

The automatic transmission allows engine torque and power to be transmitted to the rear wheels within a narrow range of engine operating speeds. The transmission will allow the engine to turn fast enough to produce plenty of power and torque at very low speeds, while keeping it at a sensible rpm at high vehicle speeds. The transmission performs this job entirely without driver assistance.

The transmission uses a light fluid as the medium for the transmission of power. This fluid also works in the operation of various hydraulic control circuits and as a lubricant. Because the transmission fluid performs all of these three functions, trouble within the unit can easily travel from one part to another. For this reason, and because of the complexity and unusual operating principles of the transmission, a very sound understanding of the basic principles of operation will simplify troubleshooting.

THE TORQUE CONVERTER

The torque converter replaces the conventional clutch. It has three functions:

1. It allows the engine to idle with the vehicle at a standstill—even with the transmission in gear.

2. It allows the transmission to shift from range to range smoothly, without requiring that the driver close the throttle during the shift.

3. It multiplies engine torque to an increasing extent as vehicle speed drops and throttle opening is increased. This has the effect of making the transmission more responsive and reduces the amount of shifting required.

The torque converter is a metal case which is shaped like a sphere that has been flattened on opposite sides. It is bolted to the rear end of the engine's crankshaft. Generally, the entire metal

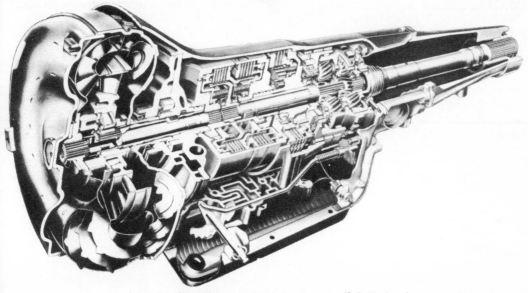

Cutaway of a modern automatic transmission (© G.M. Corp)

199

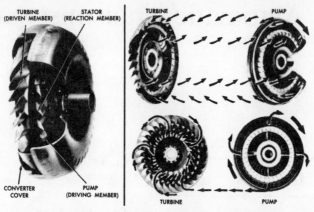

Cutaway view of a torque converter (© G.M. Corp)

case rotates at engine speed and serves as the engine's flywheel.

The case contains three sets of blades. One set is attached directly to the case. This set forms the torus or pump. Another set is directly connected to the output shaft, and forms the turbine. The third set is mounted on a hub which, in turn, is mounted on a stationary shaft through a one-way clutch. This third set is known as the stator.

A pump, which is driven by the converter hub at engine speed, keeps the torque converter full of transmission fluid at all times. Fluid flows continuously through the unit to provide cooling.

Under low-speed acceleration, the torque converter functions as follows:

The torus is turning faster than the turbine. It picks up fluid at the center of the converter and, through centrifugal force, slings it outward. Since the outer edge of the converter moves faster than the portions at the center, the fluid picks up speed.

The fluid then enters the outer edge of the turbine blades. It then travels back toward the center of the converter case along the turbine blades. In impinging upon the turbine blades, the fluid loses the energy picked up in the torus.

If the fluid were now to immediately be returned directly into the torus, both halves of the converter would have to turn at approximately the same speed at all times, and torque input and output would both be the same.

In flowing through the torus and turbine, the fluid picks up two types of flow, or flow in two separate directions. It flows through the turbine blades, and it spins

with the engine. The stator, whose blades are stationary when the vehicle is being accelerated at low speeds, converts one type of flow into another. Instead of allowing the fluid to flow straight back into the torus, the stator's curved blades turn the fluid almost 90° toward the direction of rotation of the engine. Thus the fluid does not flow as fast toward the torus, but is already spinning when the torus picks it up. This has the effect of allowing the torus to turns much faster than the turbine. This difference in speed may be compared to the difference in speed between the smaller and larger gears in any gear train. The result is that engine power output is higher, and engine torque is multiplied.

As the speed of the turbine increases, the fluid spins faster and faster in the direction of engine rotation. As a result, the ability of the stator to redirect the fluid flow is reduced. Under cruising conditions, the stator is eventually forced to rotate on its one-way clutch in the direction of engine rotation. Under these conditions, the torque converter begins to behave almost like a solid shaft, with the torus and turbine speeds being almost equal.

THE PLANETARY GEARBOX

The ability of the torque converter to multiply engine torque is limited. Also, the unit tends to be more efficient when the turbine is rotating at relatively high speeds. Therefore, a planetary gearbox is used to carry the power output of the turbine to the driveshaft to make the most efficient use of the converter.

Planetary gears function very similarly to conventional transmission gears. However, their construction is different in that

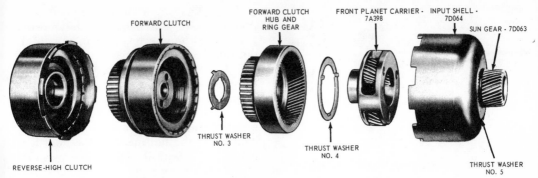

FORWARD CLUTCH

FORWARD CLUTCH
HUB AND
RING GEAR

FRONT PLANET CARRIER -
7A398

INPUT SHELL -
7D064

SUN GEAR - 7D063

REVERSE-HIGH CLUTCH

THRUST WASHER
NO. 3

THRUST WASHER
NO. 4

THRUST WASHER
NO. 5

Exploded view of a planetary gearset (Courtesy, Ford Motor Co)

three elements make up one gear system, and in that all three elements are different from one another. The three elements are: an outer gear that is shaped like a hoop, with teeth cut into the inner surface; a sun gear, mounted on a shaft and located at the very center of the outer gear; and a set of three planet gears, held by pins in a ring-like planet carrier and meshing with both the sun gear and the outer gear. Either the outer gear or the sun gear may be held stationary, providing more than one possible torque multiplication factor for each set of gears. Also, if all three gears are forced to rotate at the same speed, the gearset forms, in effect, a solid shaft.

Most modern automatics use the planetary gears to provide either a single reduction ratio of about 1.8:1, or two reduction gears: a low of about 2.5:1, and an intermediate of about 1.5:1. Bands and clutches are used to hold various portions of the gearsets to the transmission case or to the shaft on which they are mounted. Shifting is accomplished, then, by changing the portion of each planetary gearset which is held to the transmission case or to the shaft.

THE SERVOS AND ACCUMULATORS

The servos are hydraulic pistons and cylinders. They resemble the hydraulic actuators used on many familiar machines, such as bulldozers. Hydraulic fluid enters the cylinder, under pressure, and forces the piston to move to engage the band or clutches.

The accumulators are used to cushion the engagement of the servos. The transmission fluid must pass through the accumulator on the way to the servo. The accumulator housing contains a thin piston which is sprung away from the discharge passage of the accumulator. When fluid passes through the accumulator on the way to the servo, it must move the piston against spring pressure, and this action smooths out the action of the servo.

THE HYDRAULIC CONTROL SYSTEM

The hydraulic pressure used to operate the servos comes from the main transmission oil pump. This fluid is channeled to the various servos through the shift valves. There is generally a manual shift valve which is operated by the transmission selector lever and an automatic shift valve for each automatic upshift the transmission provides: i.e., two-speed automatics have a low-high shift valve, while three-speeds will have a 1–2 valve, and a 2–3 valve.

There are two pressures which effect the operation of these valves. One is the governor pressure which is affected by vehicle speed. The other is the modulator pressure

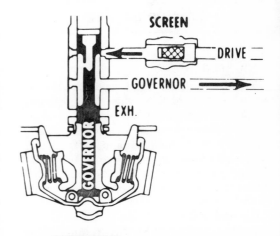

SCREEN

DRIVE

GOVERNOR

EXH.

GOVERNOR

Schematic of a governor (© G.M. Corp)

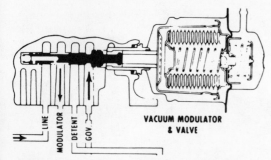

Schematic of a vacuum modulator (© G.M. Corp)

which is affected by intake manifold vacuum or throttle position. Governor pressure rises with an increase in vehicle speed, and modulator pressure rises as the throttle is opened wider. By responding to these two pressures, the shift valves cause the upshift points to be delayed with increased throttle opening to make the best use of the engine's power output.

Most transmissions also make use of an auxiliary circuit for downshifting. This circuit may be actuated by the throttle linkage or the vacuum line which actuates the modulator, or by a cable or solenoid. It applies pressure to a special downshift surface on the shift valve or valves.

The transmission modulator also governs the line pressure, used to actuate the servos. In this way, the clutches and bands will be actuated with a force matching the torque output of the engine.

Automatic Transmission Troubleshooting

A. Check the Transmission Fluid Level.

The transmission fluid level should always be checked first when troubleshooting for transmission slippage or failure to engage either forward or reverse gears. Loss of only a small amount of fluid can cause air to be drawn into the transmission oil pump pick-up. The resultant foaming of the oil prevents proper engagement of the clutches and bands.

Check the fluid as follows:

1. Operate the vehicle for 15 miles or so to bring the transmission to normal operating temperature. If the transmission gears will not engage, add at least enough oil to produce a measurement on the dipstick.

2. Place the selector lever in each of the positions, and then place it in Park.

3. Check the fluid level by removing the dipstick, wiping it, reinserting it, and then removing it for a reading. Make sure the dipstick is all the way in during the final insertion into the transmission. Bring the fluid up to the full mark. If the fluid level is too high, drain fluid from the pan until it is within the proper range. Excess fluid will cause foaming within the transmission. The gears will pick up the fluid and throw it around inside the housing.

If the transmission leaks fluid, the leak should be repaired. Leaks should be detected as follows:

1. Operate the vehicle until the transmission fluid is at operating temperature.

2. Thoroughly remove all oil and grease from the bottom of the transmission.

3. Look for the leak with the engine operating.

4. If no leak is detected with the engine in operation, check again with the engine stopped, after fluid has had a chance to drain back into the transmission sump.

Leaks occur at the seam between the oil pan and transmission case because of improperly torqued pan bolts, a faulty pan gasket, or a gasket mounting face that is rough. The front and rear seals, and all seals where shafts, cables, and filler pipes pass through the case should be checked.

In some cases, leaks are caused by porosity of the transmission case. These leaks may frequently be repaired with epoxy cement.

B. Check the Engine Condition and Linkage Adjustments.

If the transmission shifts are consistently late (at too high a speed) and rough or harsh, and performance is sluggish, the engine may be at fault. An engine which is out of tune, or has mechanical problems such as low compression will suffer reduced torque at high throttle openings and low manifold vacuum levels. Since the transmission measures either manifold vacuum or throttle position in order to determine shift points and line pressure, an abnormal engine condition will affect the transmission. Also, an engine which performs poorly will prevent the torque converter from working at its best, resulting in very poor performance. Make sure that the engine has good compression on all cylinders and is in good tune before condemning the transmission.

An improperly adjusted mechanical linkage to the modulator valve, or an improperly adjusted vacuum modulator can cause late and harsh shifts, or early, sluggish shifts. Vacuum leaks in the manifold or in the line to the vacuum modulator valve can also cause problems.

Factory manuals provide adjustment specifications for mechanical linkages. However, if these specifications are not readily available, the linkage may be adjusted to see if the problem is merely improper adjustment at assembly or last overhaul. Adjust as follows:

1. Examine the linkage to see which way it moves as the engine throttle is opened.

2. Remove the cotter pin or other locking device.

3. Turn the adjustment so that the transmission linkage will move farther in the direction of open throttle for later, harsher shifts, or toward closed throttle for earlier, smoother shifts.

4. Replace the locking device.

Vacuum modulators are adjustable if an adjusting screw protrudes from the cover. Turn the screw inward (clockwise) for earlier, smoother shifts, and outward for later, harsher shifts.

It would be wise to consult the specifications tables provided by the factory regarding proper shift points. Early, smooth shifts can cause premature clutch wear.

C. Check the Torque Converter.

Torque converter problems are usually characterized by either of the following:

1. Low engine rpm at lower speeds, and sluggish acceleration until cruising speeds are reached.

2. Normal performance until cruising conditions are reached, at which time the engine races, and fuel economy is very poor.

The first problem is caused by a slipping stator clutch, while the second results if the clutch is frozen. The first symptom may be checked further by running a stall test according to the manufacturer's instructions. This involves measuring engine revolutions with the transmission in gear, the vehicle stationary, and the throttle

wide open. Make sure, if the second symptom is noticed, that the problem is not failure of the transmission to shift into high gear.

Improper stall speed or other torque converter problems can be cured only by replacement of the complete converter unit.

D. The Line Pressure Test.

This test is accomplished by operating the vehicle with a 200 lbs pressure gauge installed in a special fitting in the side of the transmission. A long hose is used with the gauge so it may be read while the mechanic is riding inside the passenger compartment of the car. Most factory manuals have a line pressure chart which lists proper pressure under various operating conditions. Finding whether the line pressure is normal, low, or high helps considerably in troubleshooting internal transmission problems.

Troubleshooting Chart

Consult the chart below to locate various transmission problems.

FAILURE TO UPSHIFT

Low fluid level
Incorrect linkage adjustment
Faulty or sticking governor
Leaking valve body
Leak in vacuum lines to vacuum modulator
Faulty modulator
Stuck shift valve, detent cable, or downshift solenoid
Faulty clutches, servos, or oil pump

FAILURE TO DOWNSHIFT (KICK-DOWN)

Improperly adjusted throttle linkage
Sticking downshift linkage or cable
Faulty modulator
Stuck shift valve
Faulty downshift solenoid or wiring
Faulty detent valve
Faulty clutches or servos

HIGH LINE PRESSURE

Vacuum leak or modulator leak or malfunction

FAULTY PRESSURE REGULATOR

Improper pressure regulator adjustment
Faulty valve body

LOW LINE PRESSURE

Low fluid level
Faulty modulator
Faulty oil pump
Clogged strainer
Faulty seals in accumulators or clutches
Faulty transmission case

SLIPPAGE

Low oil level
Low line pressure (see above)
Faulty accumulator seals
Faulty servo piston seals
Clutch plates worn or burned
Incorrect shift linkage adjustment

NOISE

Low oil level
Clogged strainer
Faulty oil pump
Water in oil
Valve body malfunction (buzzing)

23 · The Rear Axle

How It Works

The rear axle is a special type of transmission that reduces the speed of the drive from the engine and transmission and divides the power to the rear wheels.

Power enters the rear axle from the drive-shaft via the companion flange. The flange is mounted on the drive pinion shaft. The drive pinion shaft and gear which carry the power into the differential turn at engine speed. The gear on the end of the pinion shaft drives a large ring gear the axis of rotation of which is 90° away from that

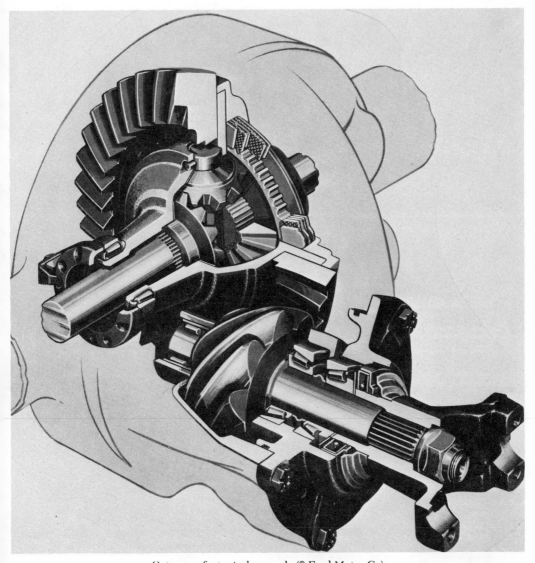

Cutaway of a typical rear axle (© Ford Motor Co)

of the pinion. The pinion and gear reduce the speed and multiply the power by the gear ratio of the axle, and change the direction of rotation to turn the axle shafts which drive both wheels. The rear axle gear ratio is found by dividing the number of pinion gear teeth into the number of ring gear teeth.

The ring gear drives the differential case. The case provides the two mounting points for the ends of a pinion shaft on which are mounted two pinion gears. The pinion gears drive the two side gears, one of which is located on the inner end of each axle shaft.

By driving the axle shafts through this arrangement, the differential allows the outer drive wheel to turn faster than the inner drive wheel in a turn.

The main drive pinion and the side bearings, which bear the weight of the differential case, are shimmed to provide proper bearing preload, and to position the pinion and ring gears properly.

NOTE: *The proper adjustment of the relationship of the ring and pinion gears is critical. It should be attempted only by those with extensive equipment and/or experience.*

Limited-slip differentials include clutches which tend to link each axle shaft to the differential case. Clutches may be engaged either by spring action or by pressure produced by the torque on the axles during a turn. During turning on a dry pavement, the effects of the clutches are overcome, and each wheel turns at the required speed. When slippage occurs at either wheel, however, the clutches will transmit some of the power to the wheel

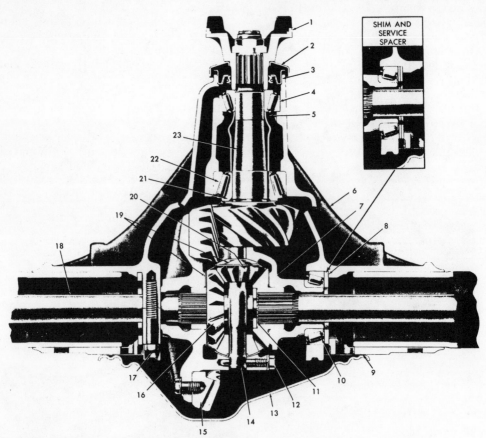

Typical General Motors rear axle—C type (Courtesy of Chevrolet Div. of G.M. Corp)

1. Companion flange	7. Differential case	13. Cover	19. Thrust washer
2. Deflector	8. Shim	14. Pinion shaft	20. Differential pinion
3. Pinion oil seal	9. Gasket	15. Ring gear	21. Shim
4. Pinion front bearing	10. Differential bearing	16. Slide gear	22. Pinion rear bearing
5. Pinion bearing spacer	11. C Lock	17. Bearing cap	23. Drive pinion
6. Differential carrier	12. Pinion shaft lockbolt	18. Axle shaft	

which has the greater amount of traction. Because of the presence of clutches, limited-slip units require a special lubricant. Consult a Chilton Manual or factory information for unit identification and lubricant recommendations.

Diagnosing Noises

To diagnose noises, first warm up the differential thoroughly, and then operate the vehicle on a very smooth, blacktop surface. Note the types of noises produced and the vehicle speeds at which they occur. Then, stop the vehicle and operate the engine at the approximate speeds at which it was turning during the production of noise on the road. If the same noises occur, poor engine, transmission, or exhaust system mounts may be at fault.

If the noises do not recur, pump up the tires to about 50 psi and repeat the test. If the noises recur, the tires are not at fault.

If the tires are not causing the problem, repeat the test, changing the position of the throttle gradually to subject the differential to drive, coast, and overrun conditions. If radical changes are noted, the problem lies in the rear axle gears or bearings.

If the noises occur only while cornering, even if the cornering is fairly gentle, the problem probably lies in the differential side gears or pinions, as these parts work against each other only on turns. Use of the wrong lubricant in limited-slip differentials will produce chattering noises on turns.

Wheel bearing noise will usually diminish slightly when the brakes are applied. A cross-check may be made by jacking up the car and spinning the front wheels to check for noise. Rear wheel bearing noise will usually change as the car is swerved from side to side, while rear axle noises tend to remain constant.

Check all parts of the rear suspension for metal-to-metal contact which might telegraph normal axle noise. Replace any faulty bushings.

Defective bearings in the rear axle generally produce a rough noise that is constant in pitch, while gearing problems generally produce a noise that cycles and varies in pitch with the speed.

Gear noises can frequently be caused by low lubricant level or improperly adjusted ring and pinion gears.

Troubleshooting Chart

NOISES

Inadequate amount of lubricant
Improper lubricant
Wheels loose on drums
Improper ring gear and pinion adjustment
Excessively worn ring and pinion gear teeth
Drive bearing preload improperly adjusted
Differential bearing preload improperly adjusted
Loose companion flange (flange should be turned 90° before tightening)
Worn pinion shaft
Worn keyways or splines in axle shafts

LEAKAGE

Excessive fluid
Clogged vent
Loose housing bolts or cover screws
Worn drive pinion oil seal (may be caused by a rough companion flange)
Worn axle shaft oil seals
Cracked housing

OVERHEATING

Insufficient lubricant
Too light a lubricant in use
Bearings adjusted too tightly
Insufficient ring-to-pinion clearance
Gears very badly worn

WHEELS FIGHT EACH OTHER ON TURNS (LIMITED-SLIP)

Use of too light a lubricant

ONLY ONE WHEEL SPINS (LIMITED-SLIP)

Use of too heavy a lubricant
Worn clutches
Clutches improperly assembled

DIAGNOSING DRIVESHAFT AND UNIVERSAL JOINT NOISES

Install a tachometer on the vehicle and operate it at the speed at which vibration occurs. Then slow the vehicle and shift it to a lower gear. Operate the vehicle at the same engine speed at which the vibration occurs in high gear.

If the vibration recurs, it is in the transmission or engine. If it does not appear, or is at a much lower frequency, it is in the drive line.

Driveshaft and Universal Joint Troubleshooting Chart

VIBRATION

Undercoating on driveshaft
Missing balance weights

Loose U-joint flange bolts
Worn U-joints
Excessive U-joint bolt torque
Excessively tight U-joints
Damaged companion flange
Drive shaft or companion flange unbalanced
Incorrect rear joint angle due to improper riding height or other rear suspension defects

NOISES

Worn U-joints
Loose companion flange
Loose control arm bushing (coil type rear springs)

24 · The Front Suspension and Wheel Alignment

How the Front Suspension Works

Most front suspensions include two control arms (an upper and a lower) which are attached to the chassis by hinges. The hinges permit the outer ends of the control arms to move up and down in relation to the chassis as the vehicle travels over bumps in the road surface, while keeping the outer ends from moving forward or backward.

The outer ends of the control arms are kept an equal distance apart by steering knuckles. The steering knuckles are held in place, at top and bottom, by ball joints. The wheel spindles extend outward from about the middle of the steering knuckles. The ball joints permit the upward and downward motion of the steering knuckles and the turning motion required for cornering, while keeping them vertical. Tie rods link them to the steering gear.

The upper and lower ends of the steering knuckles are not the same distance from the chassis; the upper end is closer. Therefore, the wheel spindles tend to angle downward and lift the vehicle slightly whenever the wheels are not pointed straight ahead.

A list of various terms used in wheel alignment, with their definitions, follows.

Camber

The wheel is not positioned vertically on most vehicles, but is angled so that the upper edge is further away from the chassis than is the lower edge. Angling the wheel in this manner makes better use of the tire tread during cornering.

Caster

The vehicle has caster if the upper end of the steering knuckle is positioned slightly behind the lower end. Caster helps the vehicle's steering return to the

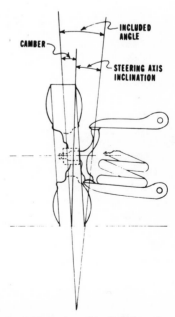

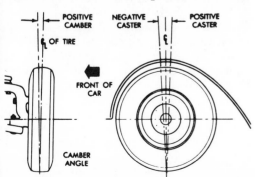

Caster and Camber angles

Camber, steering axis and included angle

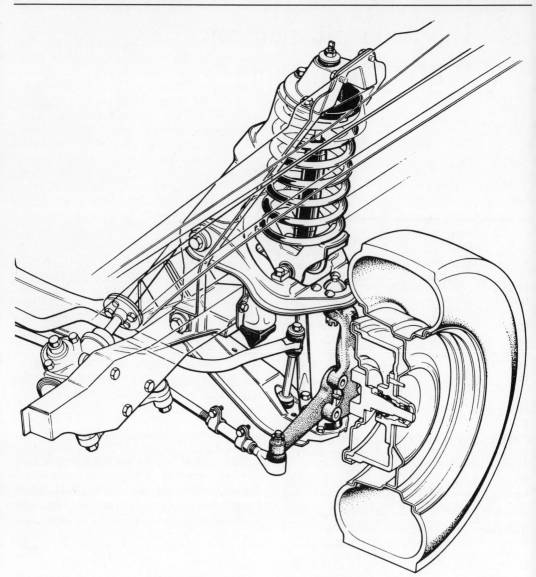

A typical front suspension system (© Ford Motor Co)

straight-ahead position, and improves directional stability.

Steering Axis Inclination

Steering axis inclination results from the fact that the upper end of the steering knuckle is closer to the chassis than the lower end. This angular mounting is what causes the vehicle to lift slightly during cornering. The car's weight thus tends to help the steering return to the center and to aid directional stability.

Included Angle

The included angle is the sum of the steering axis inclination and the caster an-gles. It is the angle between a line drawn between the two mounting points of the steering knuckle and a line drawn verti-cally through the center of the wheel.

In each of the above definitions, an imag-inary angle between the vertical and the centerline of the wheel or the steering knuckle is described. On an alignment chart, these angles are referred to in de-grees of positive caster, camber, etc. If the angle is listed as zero, the unit in question is to be perfectly vertical. If a figure of less than zero is listed, the unit should be an-gled in the opposite direction. For exam-ple, negative caster refers to an adjustment which positions the upper end of the steer-

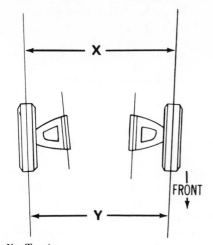

X − Y = Toe-in

ing knuckle ahead of the lower end, rather than behind.

Toe-In

On most vehicles, when the front wheels are stationary, they are closer together at the front than at the rear. Aligning the wheels in this manner compensates for various frictional forces that alter the angles between the wheels when the vehicle is moving. Thus, the wheels are brought into a parallel position, relative to each other, as the vehicle gains speed. Toe-in is measured in inches; the difference between the distance separating the front and rear centerlines of the wheels.

Toe-Out

The steering is designed so that the inner wheel turns more sharply toward the center of the turn than the outer wheel turns. This compensates for the fact that

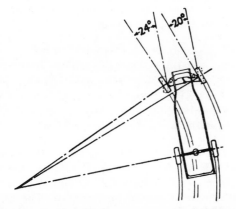

Toe-out. Inside wheel turns a greater number of degrees

the inner wheel actually travels a shorter distance during the turn. Designing the steering in this manner avoids having the front wheels fight each other, thus improving tire life and aiding stability. Where toe-out is to be checked, angles are given for the inner and outer wheel relative to travel in a straight line. Thus, in a left-hand turn, the left (inner) wheel might be 24° from straight ahead, and the right (outer) wheel 20° from straight ahead. For a right turn, the figures would be reversed.

Tracking

During straight-line operation, the vehicle's rear wheels must duplicate, or run parallel to, the paths of the front wheels. To measure the accuracy of a vehicle's tracking, measure the distance from the right-side lower ball joint to a point on the left side of the rear axle, and repeat the measurement for the left-side lower ball joint and a similar point on the right side of the rear axle. You may wish to drop a plumb line from each of these four points to the ground and mark the spots in order to avoid interference from various parts of the vehicle's undercarriage. The two diagonal lines should be equal in length to within ¼ in. Otherwise, the frame of the vehicle is bent or the rear axle is off center.

The rear wheels may also be checked for toe-in or toe-out by measuring between the inner surfaces of the tires at front and rear. Toe-in or toe-out in excess of manufacturer's specifications indicates a bent rear axle.

There is a special machine designed to check the alignment of the front wheels. Caster is first adjusted to specifications by moving the upper control arm. This may be accomplished by repositioning shims, changing the length of a strut with adjusting nuts, or by repositioning the mounting point of a strut on the frame. Camber is then accomplished by pulling the entire control arm toward the frame or forcing it further away. This involves repositioning shims equally at the front and rear of the control arm, turning adjusting nuts an equal amount, or repositioning a strut.

There are exceptions to these general rules. For example, on 1965–66 Thunderbirds, these adjustments affect the lower control arm, and on Vegas, camber is adjusted before caster. Consult a manual for

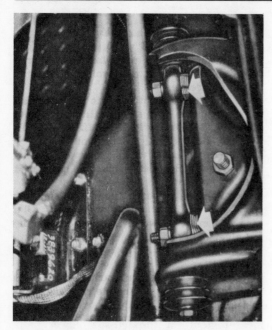

Caster and camber adjusting shim installation (Courtesy of Chevrolet Div. of G.M. Corp)

the precise method to be used for the vehicle in question.

On all vehicles, toe-in is adjusted after caster and camber are correct by turning the adjusting sleeves on the tie rods. These sleeves should be turned in equal amounts in opposite directions in order to keep the steering wheel centered. If the wheel is off center, it may be centered without affecting toe-in by turning both adjusting sleeves in the same direction.

When caster, camber, and toe-in have been adjusted, steering axis inclination and toe-out figures should be correct. If not, a worn ball joint or bent suspension or steering part is at fault.

Alignment Troubleshooting Chart

FRONT WHEEL SHIMMY

1. Tire inflation uneven or low
2. Tires improperly mounted or wheels improperly balanced
3. Incorrect caster
4. Incorrect toe-in
5. Uneven tire wear

6. Excessively worn wheel bearings
7. Worn ball joints
8. Bent steering knuckle(s)
9. Inoperative shock absorbers

EXCESSIVE TIRE WEAR

1. Both edges wear: insufficient pressure
2. Center wears: excessive pressure
3. One edge wears evenly: incorrect camber or toe-in, or damaged suspension parts
4. One edge wears unevenly: incorrect camber or toe-in, insufficient pressure, improper wheel balance, or loose steering linkage
5. Unequal wear between tires: unequal pressures or tire size, incorrect camber or toe-in, loose or bent steering linkage

VEHICLE WANDERS

1. Tire pressures incorrect or unequal
2. Incorrect caster, camber, or toe-in
3. Loose or worn bushings anywhere in front suspension
4. Rear axle position improper or frame bent
5. Badly worn shock absorbers

CAR PULLS TO ONE SIDE

1. Uneven tire pressures
2. Incorrect caster, camber, or toe-in
3. Brakes improperly adjusted
4. Wheel bearings improperly adjusted
5. Bent steering knuckle or other suspension component
6. Improper tracking

HARD STEERING

1. Low tire pressures
2. Inadequate front-end lubrication
3. Incorrect caster
4. Improper steering gear adjustment
5. Sagging front spring

CHECKING BALL JOINTS

Support the car as follows:
If the front spring or torsion bar is supported by the lower control arm, locate the jackstand under the lower control arm. Otherwise, support the vehicle by the crossmember or frame.

The ball joint which supports the load should permit a very slight up-and-down motion, and radial play of about 1/4 in. Otherwise it should be replaced. The unloaded ball joint should not have any perceptible play at all.

REAR SUSPENSION ALIGNMENT

Tracking of the rear wheels should be checked for cars with solid rear axles as described above. These vehicles will have rear wheel alignment problems only rarely, as the rear axle assembly can be bent only by a severe collision.

Corvettes, however, employ a fully independent type of rear suspension which requires setting of the camber and toe-in. The camber is set by adjusting the position of an eccentric cam and bolt located at the inboard mounting of the suspension strut rod.

The toe-in is adjusted by shimming the torque control arm pivot bushing. The shims are inserted on both sides of the bushing inside the frame side member.

25 · Brakes

Hydraulic Systems

Hydraulic systems are used to actuate the brakes of all modern automobiles. The system transports the power required to force the frictional surfaces of the braking system together from the pedal to the individual brake units at each wheel. A hydraulic system is used for two reasons. First, fluid under pressure can be carried to all parts of an automobile by small hoses—some of which are flexible—without taking up a significant amount of room or posing routing problems. Second, a great mechanical advantage can be given to the brake pedal end of the system, and the foot pressure required to actuate the brakes can be reduced by making the surface area of the master cylinder pistons smaller than that of any of the pistons in the wheel cylinders or calipers.

The master cylinder consists of a fluid reservoir and either a single or double cylinder and piston assembly. Double type master cylinders are designed to separate the front and rear braking systems hydraulically in case of a leak.

Steel lines carry the brake fluid to a point on the vehicle's frame near each of the vehicle's wheels. The fluid is then carried to the slave cylinders by flexible tubes in order to allow for suspension and steering movements.

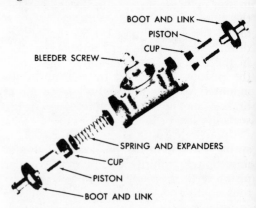

Wheel cylinder (Courtesy of Chevrolet Div. of G.M. Corp)

In drum brake systems, the slave cylinders are called wheel cylinders. Each wheel cylinder contains two pistons, one at either end, which push outward in opposite directions. In disc brake systems, the slave cylinders are part of the calipers. One or four cylinders are used to force the brake pads against the disc, but all cylinders contain one piston only. All slave cylinder pistons employ some type of seal, usually made of rubber, to minimize the leakage of fluid around the piston. A rubber dust boot seals the outer end of the cylinder against dust and dirt. The boot fits around the outer end of the piston on disc brake calipers, and around the brake actuating rod on wheel cylinders.

The hydraulic system operates as fol-

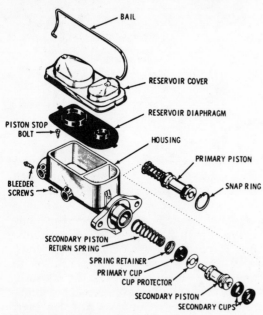

Bendix dual master cylinder (Courtesy of Oldsmobile Div. of G.M. Corp)

214

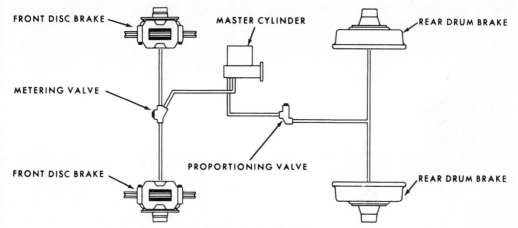

FRONT DISC BRAKE

METERING VALVE

FRONT DISC BRAKE

MASTER CYLINDER

PROPORTIONING VALVE

REAR DRUM BRAKE

REAR DRUM BRAKE

Disc brake hydraulic system

lows: When at rest, the entire system, from the piston(s) in the master cylinder to those in the wheel cylinders or calipers, is full of brake fluid. Upon application of the brake pedal, fluid trapped in front of the master cylinder piston(s) is forced through the lines to the slave cylinders. Here, it forces the pistons outward, in the case of drum brakes, and inward toward the disc, in the case of disc brakes. The motion of the pistons is opposed by return springs mounted outside the cylinders in drum brakes, and by internal springs or spring seals, in disc brakes.

Upon release of the brake pedal, a spring located inside the master cylinder immediately returns the master cylinder piston(s) to the normal position. The pistons contain check valves and the master cylinder has compensating ports drilled in it. These are uncovered as the pistons reach their normal position. The piston check valves allow fluid to flow toward the wheel cylinders or calipers as the pistons withdraw. Then, as the return springs force the brake pads or shoes into the released position, the excess fluid returns to the master cylinder fluid reservoir through the compensating ports. It is during the time the pedal is in the released position that any fluid that has leaked out of the system will be replaced through the compensating ports.

Dual circuit master cylinders employ two pistons, located one behind the other, in the same cylinder. The primary piston is actuated directly by mechanical linkage from the brake pedal. The secondary piston is actuated by fluid trapped between the two pistons. If a leak develops in front

of the secondary piston, it moves forward until it bottoms against the front of the master cylinder, and the fluid trapped between the pistons will operate the rear brakes. If the rear brakes develop a leak, the primary piston will move forward until direct contact with the secondary piston takes place, and it will force the secondary piston to actuate the front brakes. In either case, the brake pedal moves farther when the brakes are applied, and less braking power is available.

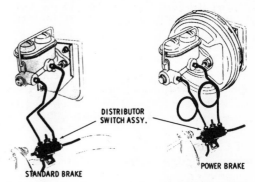

DISTRIBUTOR SWITCH ASSY.

STANDARD BRAKE   POWER BRAKE

A typical distributor switch assembly (Courtesy, G.M. Corp)

All dual-circuit systems use a distributor switch to warn the driver when only half of the brake system is operational. This switch is located in a valve body which is mounted on the firewall or the frame below the master cylinder. A hydraulic piston receives pressure from both circuits, each circuit's pressure being applied to one end of the piston. When the pressures are in balance, the piston remains stationary. When one circuit has a leak, however, the greater pressure in that circuit during application of the brakes will push the piston to one side, closing the distributor switch and activating the brake warning light.

In disc brake systems, this valve body also contains a metering valve and, in some cases, a proportioning valve. The metering valve keeps pressure from traveling to the disc brakes on the front wheels until the brake shoes on the rear wheels have contacted the drums, ensuring that the front brakes will never be used alone. The proportioning valve throttles the pressure to the rear brakes so as to avoid rear wheel lock-up during very hard braking.

These valves may be tested by removing the lines to the front and rear brake systems and installing special brake pressure testing gauges. Front and rear system pressures are then compared as the pedal is gradually depressed. Specifications vary with the manufacturer and design of the brake system.

Brake system warning lights may be tested by depressing the brake pedal and holding it while opening one of the wheel cylinder bleeder screws. If this does not cause the light to go on, substitute a new lamp, make continuity checks, and, finally, replace the switch as necessary.

The hydraulic system may be checked for leaks by applying pressure to the pedal gradually and steadily. If the pedal sinks very slowly to the floor, the system has a leak. This is not to be confused with a springy or spongy feel due to the compression of air within the lines. If the system leaks, there will be a gradual change in the position of the pedal with a constant pressure.

Check for leaks along all lines and at wheel cylinders. If no external leaks are apparent, the problem is inside the master cylinder.

Hydraulic System Troubleshooting Chart

Low Pedal

1. Brake fluid level low
(If fluid is low, check all lines and wheel cylinders for leaks, and repair as necessary.)
2. Air in system

(This will be accompanied by a spongy feel at the pedal, and by a low fluid level. Check as above.)
3. Master cylinder primary cup damaged, or cylinder bore worn or corroded
4. Use of improper fluid
(Fluid boils from the heat and the resulting gas compresses during pedal application.)

Spongy Pedal

1. Air trapped in system
(This may include the master cylinder. Check for leaks as described above.)
2. Use of improper fluid
3. Clogged compensating port in master cylinder
(This may be checked for by watching for motion of fluid in master cylinder fluid reservoir during early part of brake pedal stroke. If no fluid motion, the port is clogged.)
4. Hoses soft
(Expanding under pressure.)

One Wheel Drags

1. Wheel cylinder piston cups swollen
2. Clogged line

All Brakes Drag

1. Clogged compensating port in master cylinder
2. Mineral oil in system

High Pedal Pressure Required

1. Corroded wheel cylinder
2. Clogged line
3. Clogged compensating port in master cylinder

Power Brake Boosters

Power brakes operate just as standard brake systems except in the actuation of the master cylinder pistons. A vacuum diaphragm is located on the front of the master cylinder and assists the driver in applying the brakes, reducing both the effort and travel he must put into moving the brake pedal.

The vacuum diaphragm housing is connected to the intake manifold by a vacuum hose. A check valve is placed at the point where the hose enters the diaphragm hous

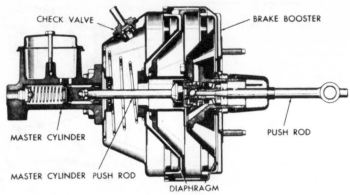

CHECK VALVE

BRAKE BOOSTER

MASTER CYLINDER

PUSH ROD

MASTER CYLINDER PUSH ROD

DIAPHRAGM

Cutaway view of brake booster and master cylinder (© G.M. Corp)

ing, so that during periods of low manifold vacuum brake assist vacuum will not be lost.

Depressing the brake pedal closes off the vacuum source and allows atmospheric pressure to enter on one side of the diaphragm. This causes the master cylinder pistons to move and apply the brakes. When the brake pedal is released, vacuum is applied to both sides of the diaphragm, and return springs return the diaphragm and master cylinder pistons to the released position. If the vacuum fails, the brake pedal rod will butt against the end of the master cylinder actuating rod, and direct mechanical application will occur as the pedal is depressed.

The hydraulic and mechanical problems that apply to conventional brake systems also apply to power brakes, and should be checked for if the tests and chart below do not reveal the problem.

Test for a system vacuum leak as described below:

1. Operate the engine at idle with the transmission in Neutral without touching the brake pedal for at least one minute.

2. Turn off the engine, and wait one minute.

3. Test for the presence of assist vacuum by depressing the brake pedal and releasing it several times. Light application will produce less and less pedal travel, if vacuum was present. If there is no vacuum, air is leaking into the system somewhere.

Test for system operation as follows:

1. Pump the brake pedal (with engine off) until the supply vacuum is entirely gone.

2. Put a light, steady pressure on the pedal.

3. Start the engine, and operate it at idle with the transmission in Neutral. If the system is operating, the brake pedal should fall toward the floor if constant pressure is maintained on the pedal.

Power brake systems may be tested for hydraulic leaks just as ordinary systems are tested, except that the engine should be idling with the transmission in Neutral throughout the test.

Power Brake Booster Troubleshooting Chart

HARD PEDAL

1. Faulty vacuum check valve
2. Vacuum hose kinked, collapsed, plugged, leaky, or improperly connected
3. Internal leak in unit
4. Damaged vacuum cylinder
5. Damaged valve plunger
6. Broken or faulty springs
7. Broken plunger stem

GRABBING BRAKES

1. Damaged vacuum cylinder
2. Faulty vacuum check valve
3. Vacuum hose leaky or improperly connected
4. Broken plunger stem

PEDAL GOES TO FLOOR

Generally, when this problem occurs, it is not caused by the power brake booster. In rare cases, a broken plunger stem may be at fault.

Brake Mechanical Problems

Drum brakes employ two brake shoes mounted on a stationary backing plate to force the brake linings against the inside of the drum which rotates with the wheel. The shoes are held in place by springs; this allows them to slide toward the drums while keeping the linings and drums in alignment. The wheel cylinder's two actuating links force the tops of the shoes outward toward the inner surface of the drum. This action forces the bottoms of the two shoes to contact either end of the adjusting screw. When pressure within the wheel cylinder is relaxed, return springs pull the shoes back, away from the drum.

Most modern drum type brakes are designed to adjust themselves during application when the vehicle is moving in reverse. This motion causes both shoes to rotate very slightly with the drum, rocks an adjusting lever, and thus causes rotation of the adjusting screw by means of a star wheel.

Generally, the rear drum type brakes are used in parking. Cables link the pedal or lever in the passenger compartment to the actuating mechanism inside the drum. Generally, this consists of a lever and strut combination that forces one of the linings outward at the top. This action forces the other lining to contact the drum via the adjusting screw.

Disc brakes employ a double-walled disc rotating with the wheel in place of the drum. The two walls of the disc are

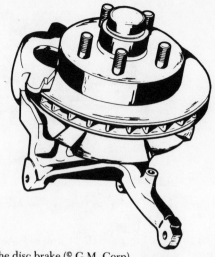

The disc brake (© G.M. Corp)

separated by struts which allow cooling air to flow between them. This superior cooling combined with the fact that the disc does not tend to warp away from the brake pads as drums do, makes the disc brake superior in terms of fade resistance.

The brake pads (linings) used with disc brakes are forced against either side of the disc in a squeezing action by a brake caliper. The caliper may employ only one piston and slide along mounting bushings in order to squeeze the two brake pads against the disc. Or, it may employ a movable piston or pistons on either side of the disc. In this design, the caliper is fixed in place by its mounting bolts.

Disc brakes are inherently self-adjusting. After each application, the pad is pulled away from the disc only far enough to ensure that the brakes do not drag. Thus, the

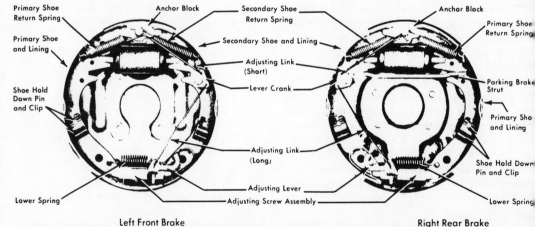

Left Front Brake   Right Rear Brake

Wagner compound self-adjusting brake (Courtesy of American Motors Corp)

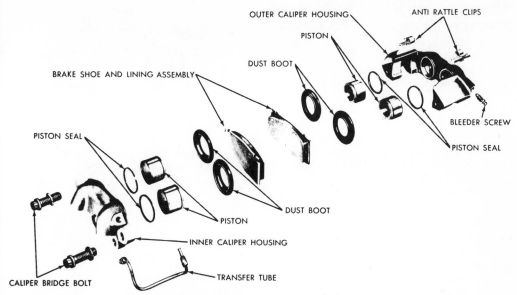

Kelsey-Hayes four piston disc brake (© G.M. Corp)

released position of the piston is continuously adjusted as the pad lining wears.

Parking brakes generally do not require adjustment if the automatic adjusters are working properly. If adjustment is required, proceed as follows:

1. Put the vehicle on a lift so neither rear wheel is touching the ground.

2. Engage the parking brake about halfway.

3. Loosen the locknut on the equalizer yoke, located under the ear, and then turn the adjusting nut just until a drag can be felt on both rear wheels.

4. Release the brake and check for free rotation of the rear wheels.

On systems where a floor-mounted handlever is used, the adjustment is usually contained under the rubber boot which covers the base of the lever. Tighten each of the adjusting nuts on these systems until an equal, slight torque is required to turn each rear drum.

Mechanical Problem Troubleshooting Chart

Low Pedal

1. Automatic adjusters not working, or brakes improperly adjusted

2. Linings or pads excessively worn
3. Drums excessively worn

Spongy Pedal

1. Brake drums too thin
2. Brakes improperly adjusted
3. Brake shoes bent

One Wheel Drags

1. Parking brake improperly adjusted
2. Shoe return springs weak
3. Brakes improperly adjusted
4. Loose front wheel bearings
5. Shoe pads rough or grooved
6. Support plate loose or worn
7. Corroded automatic adjuster parts

All Wheels Drag

1. Pedal linkage sticking
(Check stop light switch.)
2. Automatic adjuster parts corroded
3. Linings or pads distorted
4. Shoes and pads rough or grooved

High Pedal Pressure Required

1. Brakes improperly adjusted
2. Linings or pads soiled with grease or oil
3. Improper linings in use
4. Pedal linkage binding

Car Pulls to One Side

1. Brake shoes or pads of unequal quality, or unequally worn, installed

2. Shoes or pads on one side soiled with grease or oil
3. Caliper loose
4. Linings or drums charred or scored
5. Tire pressures unequal
6. Improper alignment

1. Linings not fully broken in
2. Disc with excessive lateral run-out
3. Disc imperfectly cast
4. Use of improper lining or pad

26 · Steering Systems

Power Steering

Power steering units are mechanical steering gear units incorporating a power assist. A worm shaft, which is rotated by the shaft coming down from the steering wheel via a flexible coupling, causes a rack piston nut to slide up and down inside the housing. This motion is changed into rotating force by the action of an output shaft sector gear. The rack piston nut is forced up and down inside the housing by the ro-

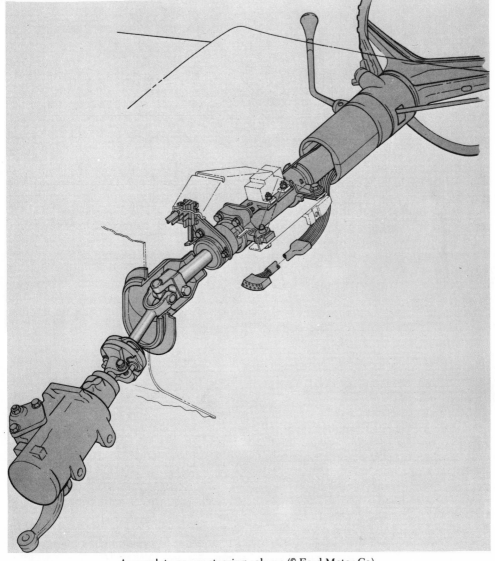

A complete power steering column (© Ford Motor Co)

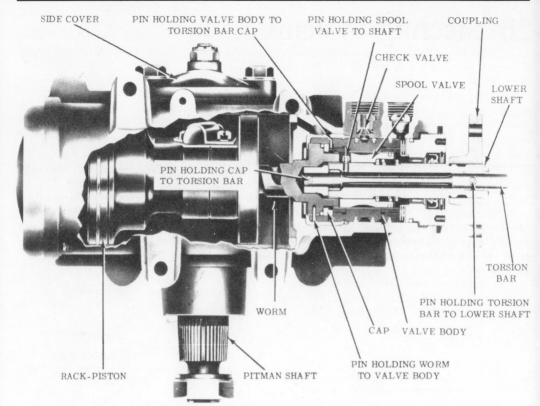

SIDE COVER   PIN HOLDING VALVE BODY TO   PIN HOLDING SPOOL   COUPLING
TORSION BAR CAP   VALVE TO SHAFT

CHECK VALVE

SPOOL VALVE

LOWER
SHAFT

PIN HOLDING CAP
TO TORSION BAR

TORSION
BAR

PIN HOLDING TORSION
BAR TO LOWER SHAFT

WORM

CAP   VALVE BODY

RACK-PISTON   PITMAN SHAFT   PIN HOLDING WORM
TO VALVE BODY

A typical power steering unit (© Ford Motor Co)

tation of the worm gear, which forces the nut to move through the action of recirculating balls. The nut fits tightly inside the housing, and is sealed against the sides of the housing by a ring type seal. Power assist is provided by forcing hydraulic fluid into the housing on one side or the other of the rack piston nut.

The hydraulic pressure is supplied by a rotary vane pump, driven by the engine via V belts. The pump incorporates a flow control valve that bypasses the right amount of fluid for the proper operating pressure. The pump contains a fluid reservoir, located above the main body of the pump. The same fluid lubricates all parts of the power steering unit.

A rotary valve, spool valve, or pivot lever, located in the steering box, senses the rotation of the steering wheel and channels fluid to the upper or lower surface of the rack piston nut.

When power steering problems occur, the pump fluid level should first be checked. Note that two levels are given. The lower level is correct if the pump and fluid are at room temperature, after having been inoperative for some time. The upper

level is correct if the system has been in operation (about 175°).

The drive belt should also be checked for looseness, cracks, or glazing. Replace the belt if it is damaged, or tighten it if necessary.

A quick check of the power steering pump oil pressure relief valves may be made by turning the wheel to either stop. There should be a buzzing or swishing noise caused by flow of fluid through bypass valves.

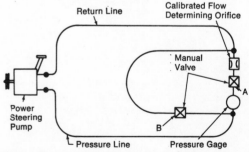

Power Steering pump test circuit diagram (Courtesy of Ford Motor Co)

If steering is difficult, the power steering pump pressure may be tested. A special set of valves and gauges is required. Perform the test as follows:

1. With the engine off, remove the two hoses at the pump and install the gauges and valves.

2. Open both valves, and then start the engine and operate it at idle. The fluid must be brought up to 165–170° F. Closing valve B to build up 350 lbs pressure will speed the process.

3. When the fluid is fully warmed, close valve B. The pressure should be 620 psi or more, or else the pump is faulty.

4. Close both valve A and valve B. *Do not keep valves closed for more than five seconds.* This should raise the pressure level to the manufacturer's specifications for this type of test.

This test measures the ability of the pump to produce pressure. It does not test the pump's pressure regulating valve, a malfunction of which can also cause lack of steering assist.

5. Binding in steering linkage
6. Steering unit valve (rotary valve, spool valve, or pivot lever) malfunctioning
7. Worn ball joints

Power Steering Noisy

1. Belts loose or glazed
2. Fluid level low
3. Air in system
4. Kinked hydraulic lines
5. Foreign matter clogging hydraulic lines
6. Flow control valve sticking
7. Steering unit valve (rotary valve, spool valve, or pivot lever) worn
8. Worn pump parts
9. Steering gear mountings loose
10. Interference in front end

Poor Return of Steering

1. Tires overinflated
2. Improper caster adjustment
3. Bind in steering column
4. Improper front-end lubrication
5. Steering gear adjustments too tight

Power Steering Troubleshooting Chart

Hard Steering

1. Improper (low) tire pressure
2. Loose or glazed pump drive belt
3. Low fluid level
4. Poorly lubricated front-end parts
5. Bind in steering column
6. Inadequate pump output pressure, due to worn pump parts or malfunctioning pressure regulator valve
7. Obstructions in pump lines
8. Excessive caster
9. Cross-shaft adjustment too tight

Car Veers to One Side

1. Tire pressures or tread wear unequal
2. Improper front-end alignment
3. Improperly adjusted brakes
4. Faulty shock absorbers or springs

Car Wanders

1. Tire pressures improper
2. Improper front-end alignment
3. Play in pitman arm
4. Loose wheel bearings

Manual Steering

Manual steering units convert the rotating force of the steering wheel into a slower, higher torque rotation of the pitman arm. The force of the arm is then transmitted to the wheels by tie rods. Generally, a flexible coupling connects the shaft coming down from the steering wheel to the worm shaft of the steering box.

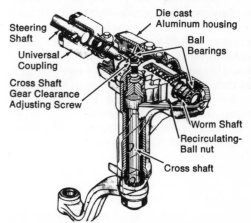

Chrysler steering gear, recirculating ball type (Courtesy of Chrysler Corp)

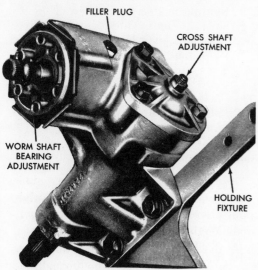

FILLER PLUG

CROSS SHAFT
ADJUSTMENT

WORM SHAFT
BEARING
ADJUSTMENT

HOLDING
FIXTURE

Steering gear adjustment locations (Courtesy of Chrysler Corp)

The worm shaft rotates the cross-shaft or pitman shaft by having the worm gear on the worm shaft rotate the sector gear, mounted on the cross-shaft. In many designs, the efficiency of the unit is increased by using a ball nut incorporating recirculating balls to transmit the rotating force from the worm to the sector gear.

The bearings which carry the worm shaft are usually adjustable, to compensate for wear. In some designs, an adjusting screw is employed, while in others shims may be used to provide the proper bearing preload. Generally, preload is measured by rotating the steering wheel with a spring scale with the pitman arm disconnected from the lower portions of the steering gear.

An adjusting screw is also provided for positioning the cross-shaft for proper meshing of the worm or ball nut and sector gear. After worm bearing preload is adjusted, play is removed from the unit with the cross-shaft adjusting screw, and a recheck of turning effort is made. The adjusting screw must then be backed off slightly if too great a steering wheel turning torque is required. Consult the manufacturer's instructions to make these ad-justments because of variations in actual procedures and torque specifications.

Before beginning to troubleshoot manual steering problems, check the condition and pressure of the tires, and the lubrication of the steering gear. Consult the manufacturer's specifications for proper lubricant. It is usually a heavy oil like that used in rear axles. If there is uneven tire wear, it might be wise to align the front end before trying to track down steering malfunctions.

Manual Steering Troubleshooting Chart

HARD STEERING

1. Improper (low) tire pressure
2. Inadequate lubricant
3. Inadequately lubricated front-end parts
4. Bind in steering column
5. Excessive caster
6. Cross-shaft adjustment too tight

CAR VEERS TO ONE SIDE

1. Tire pressures or tread wear unequal
2. Improper front-end alignment
3. Improperly adjusted brakes
4. Faulty shock absorbers or springs

CAR WANDERS

1. Tire pressures improper
2. Improper front-end alignment
3. Play in pitman arm
4. Loose wheel bearings
5. Binding in steering linkage
6. Steering box loose on frame
7. Worn ball joints

POOR RETURN OF STEERING

1. Tires overinflated
2. Improper caster adjustment
3. Bind in steering column
4. Improper front-end lubrication. Steering gear adjustments too tight

27 · Tires

Types of Tires

Bias Ply

Bias ply tires are the most basic and simple design available. The plies of fabric cord which strengthen the tire are applied in a criss-cross fashion for strength. The plies run from rim-edge to rim-edge to help increase the tire's resistance to bruises, and to the forces of braking and cornering.

Belted Bias

These tires are constructed very similarly to the bias-ply tires—with the plies applied in a criss-cross fashion. However, circumferential belts are applied just under the tread to strengthen it and keep it as flat as possible. Thus, the life and performance of the tire are improved. Because the construction is somewhat more complex than that of bias ply tires, belted bias tires are slightly more expensive.

TYPES OF TIRE CONSTRUCTION

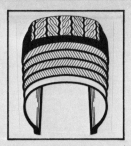
Bias-Ply

Belted-Bias

Radial

NOTE: Each tire has an air-tight inner-liner under the body plies. The belted-bias and the radial tires also have under-tread belts, which are shown with a gray tone.

RESULTS OF IMPROPER CARE

Suspension Neglect

Over-Inflation

Under-Inflation

Extreme Cornering

The Firestone Tire & Rubber Company

Radial

Radial tires are the most expensive and best tires made. They offer both improved cornering and improved tread life over belted bias and bias ply tires. The body plies run from rim to rim in a hoop fashion, and the tire employs circumferential belts. The result is that the tread is kept still more perfectly flat and open than with belted bias tires.

There is a relationship between a tire's cornering ability and its ability to provide long tread wear. A tread that remains flat and does not squirm or close up when under heavy load wears more evenly and suffers less from scuffing. Therefore, most manufacturer's recommend that the tire buyer consider purchase of a belted bias or radial tire, claiming that the cost per mile will be lower.

Of course, if the buyer does not plan to keep his car until the new rubber is fully worn out, a less expensive tire should be considered. However, if long mileage is desired, especially under rough cornering or heavy loading conditions, the more expensive designs may prove to be more economical.

If good cornering is desired, the radial is the obvious choice. The cornering characteristics of these tires are so significantly superior to those of other types that mixing radials and other types of tires on the same vehicle is not recommended. The differences in traction between the types can cause undesirable cornering characteristics.

from the outer edges to wear more than the others on bias belted tires.

TIRES WORN ON ONE SIDE ONLY

1. Improper toe-in adjustment: This is the problem if both outer edges or both inner edges are worn
2. Improper camber adjustment.
3. Hard cornering: In addition to wearing the outer edges more than the center, this will round off the edges.

TIRES WORN IN SEVERAL SPOTS AROUND THE CIRCUMFERENCE OF THE TREAD

1. Underinflation combined with improper toe-in adjustment.
2. Improperly balanced tires and wheels.
3. Worn shock absorbers.
4. Worn suspension components.
5. Out-of-round brake drums.

NOISES

1. Irregular wear.
2. Low pressure.
3. Bulges due to faulty construction or structural damage.

NOTE: *Inflating tires to 50 pounds pressure for test purposes tends to stop noises. Driving the car on a very smooth road and inflating the tires to a very high pressure, one at a time, will isolate the noisy tire.*

Tire Troubleshooting Chart

TIRE WORN IN CENTER OF TREAD

Overinflation: Excess pressure causes the center of the tread to contact the road, while the edges ride free.

TIRE WORN ON OUTER EDGES ONLY

Underinflation: Underinflation causes the tread to bow, lifting the center off the road. This also increases flexing and heat, and may result in weakening of the tire cords. Note, however, that it is normal for the two sections of tread just one section

Tire Care

Because the tire employs air under pressure as part of its structure, it is designed around the supporting strength of a gas at a specified pressure. For this reason, running a tire with either too high or too low a pressure actually undermines its structural strength, and, in effect, makes its shape improper for the job to be done.

Not only will improper inflation pressure keep the tread from properly laying on the road, it will reduce the tire's ability to resist damage from road shock. It can also increase operating temperatures.

Tire pressures should, therefore, be carefully checked *at least* once a month. A hand tire gauge of good quality should be used.

In almost all cases, the manufacturer's recommendations for pressures should be followed. While manufacturers tended to recommend low pressures several years ago, in order to achieve good ride characteristics, their recommendations from about 1968 are generally quite accurate. Remember that the differential between pressures at front and rear is of particular importance in maintaining stability on the road. The recommended differential should be maintained, and where higher pressures are recommended for high speeds or heavy loads, pressures should be tailored to the operating conditions. Check the tires when they are cold in order to ensure accurate pressure measurement. Do not bleed air out of hot tires to maintain the recommended pressure level. Remember to use valve caps to keep dirt out of the valve core.

Tires should be rotated about every 6,000 miles. This will even out wear that might otherwise destroy a small segment of the tread prematurely, thereby wasting the remainder. The spare tire should be included in the rotation, as inactivity is harmful to a tire.

The tires should be statically and dynamically balanced at the first sign of ride roughness. Static balance means that the tire would remain in any selected position without turning itself on the wheel bearings with the vehicle on a lift. Dynamic balance refers to distribution of weight from side to side of the tire. Static balance is performed with the tire at rest; dynamic balance is done with the tire in motion.

Generally, new tires should not be balanced until they have been operated for several hundred miles to ensure a minimal further change in weight distribution in the tire.

Tire Selection

Higher-priced tires do not necessarily increase cost per operating mile. Radial tires offer the longest mileage, and belted bias tires last longer than bias ply designs. The increased manufacturing cost is not usually as great as the gain in mileage.

If possible, all four tires on an automobile should be of the same type. If mixing is necessary, make sure that tires on one axle are not of different designs.

These precautions are particularly important with radial tires, which have vastly different cornering characteristics. If radials and another design *must* be mixed, put the radials on the rear axle.

Rims are generally 5–5½ in wide, with some optional rims, as on station wagons, going as wide as 6 in. Super wide tires sometimes use rims up to 7 in. wide. Generally, it is permissible to go one range wider than original equipment without changing the rims. In other words, an E78 or E70 tire may use a 5½ in. rim with good results. In going to E60 tires, however, wider (7–8 in.) rims are recommended. Tire dealers have charts showing recommended rim widths for various tire sizes.

It should be remembered that, when

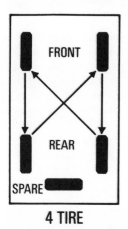

4 TIRE

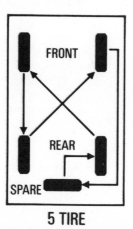

5 TIRE

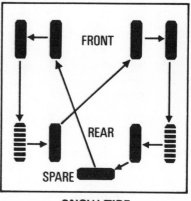

SNOW TIRE

Various methods of tire rotation (Courtesy of Firestone Tire & Rubber Co)

wider rims and tires are used, wheel bearing wear may be increased due to the increased load on the bottom of the outer bearing and the top of the inner bearing.

Tire Size Designation Chart *

The tire industry recently changed its tire size designations from a numerical to a combination alphabetical-numerical system.

For example, it's no longer an 8.25-15. That size is now known as G78-15. Basically, the higher the letter the larger the tire size, as the accompanying chart illustrates. The following numerals show the relationship of tire width to height. The last two numbers show the wheel size.

E78-14	7.35-14
F78-14	7.75-14
G78-14	8.25-14
H78-14	8.55-14
E78-15	7.35-15
G78-15	8.25-15
H78-15	8.55-15
J78-15	8.85-15
L78-15	9.15-15

* Courtesy of Firestone Tire & Rubber Co.

Appendix

General Conversion Table

Multiply by	To convert	To	
2.54	Inches	Centimeters	.3937
30.48	Feet	Centimeters	.0328
.914	Yards	Meters	1.094
1.609	Miles	Kilometers	.621
.645	Square inches	Square cm.	.155
.836	Square yards	Square meters	1.196
16.39	Cubic inches	Cubic cm.	.061
28.3	Cubic feet	Liters	.0353
.4536	Pounds	Kilograms	2.2045
4.546	Gallons	Liters	.22
.068	Lbs./sq. in. (psi)	Atmospheres	14.7
.138	Foot pounds	Kg. m.	7.23
1.014	H.P. (DIN)	H.P. (SAE)	.9861
——	To obtain	From	Multiply by

Note: 1 cm. equals 10 mm.; 1 mm. equals .0394″.

Conversion—Common Fractions to Decimals and Millimeters

INCHES			INCHES			INCHES		
Common Fractions	Decimal Fractions	Millimeters (approx.)	Common Fractions	Decimal Fractions	Millimeters (approx.)	Common Fractions	Decimal Fractions	Millimeters (approx.)
1/128	.008	0.20	11/32	.344	8.73	43/64	.672	17.07
1/64	.016	0.40	23/64	.359	9.13	11/16	.688	17.46
1/32	.031	0.79	3/8	.375	9.53	45/64	.703	17.86
3/64	.047	1.19	25/64	.391	9.92	23/32	.719	18.26
1/16	.063	1.59	13/32	.406	10.32	47/64	.734	18.65
5/64	.078	1.98	27/64	.422	10.72	3/4	.750	19.05
3/32	.094	2.38	7/16	.438	11.11	49/64	.766	19.45
7/64	.109	2.78	29/64	.453	11.51	25/32	.781	19.84
1/8	.125	3.18	15/32	.469	11.91	51/64	.797	20.24
9/64	.141	3.57	31/64	.484	12.30	13/16	.813	20.64
5/32	.156	3.97	1/2	.500	12.70	53/64	.828	21.03
11/64	.172	4.37	33/64	.516	13.10	27/32	.844	21.43
3/16	.188	4.76	17/32	.531	13.49	55/64	.859	21.83
13/64	.203	5.16	35/64	.547	13.89	7/8	.875	22.23
7/32	.219	5.56	9/16	.563	14.29	57/64	.891	22.62
15/64	.234	5.95	37/64	.578	14.68	29/32	.906	23.02
1/4	.250	6.35	19/32	.594	15.08	59/64	.922	23.42
17/64	.266	6.75	39/64	.609	15.48	15/16	.938	23.81
9/32	.281	7.14	5/8	.625	15.88	61/64	.953	24.21
19/64	.297	7.54	41/64	.641	16.27	31/32	.969	24.61
5/16	.313	7.94	21/32	.656	16.67	63/64	.984	25.00
21/64	.328	8.33						

Conversion—Millimeters to Decimal Inches

mm	inches	mm	inches	mm	inches	mm	inches	mm	inches
1	.039 370	31	1.220 470	61	2.401 570	91	3.582 670	210	8.267 700
2	.078 740	32	1.259 840	62	2.440 940	92	3.622 040	220	8.661 400
3	.118 110	33	1.299 210	63	2.480 310	93	3.661 410	230	9.055 100
4	.157 480	34	1.338 580	64	2.519 680	94	3.700 780	240	9.448 800
5	.196 850	35	1.377 949	65	2.559 050	95	3.740 150	250	9.842 500
6	.236 220	36	1.417 319	66	2.598 420	96	3.779 520	260	10.236 200
7	.275 590	37	1.456 689	67	2.637 790	97	3.818 890	270	10.629 900
8	.314 960	38	1.496 050	68	2.677 160	98	3.858 260	280	11.032 600
9	.354 330	39	1.535 430	69	2.716 530	99	3.897 630	290	11.417 300
10	.393 700	40	1.574 800	70	2.755 900	100	3.937 000	300	11.811 000
11	.433 070	41	1.614 170	71	2.795 270	105	4.133 848	310	12.204 700
12	.472 440	42	1.653 540	72	2.834 640	110	4.330 700	320	12.598 400
13	.511 810	43	1.692 910	73	2.874 010	115	4.527 550	330	12.992 100
14	.551 180	44	1.732 280	74	2.913 380	120	4.724 400	340	13.385 800
15	.590 550	45	1.771 650	75	2.952 750	125	4.921 250	350	13.779 500
16	.629 920	46	1.811 020	76	2.992 120	130	5.118 100	360	14.173 200
17	.669 290	47	1.850 390	77	3.031 490	135	5.314 950	370	14.566 900
18	.708 660	48	1.889 760	78	3.070 860	140	5.511 800	380	14.960 600
19	.748 030	49	1.929 130	79	3.110 230	145	5.708 650	390	15.354 300
20	.787 400	50	1.968 500	80	3.149 600	150	5.905 500	400	15.748 000
21	.826 770	51	2.007 870	81	3.188 970	155	6.102 350	500	19.685 000
22	.866 140	52	2.047 240	82	3.228 340	160	6.299 200	600	23.622 000
23	.905 510	53	2.086 610	83	3.267 710	165	6.496 050	700	27.559 000
24	.944 880	54	2.125 980	84	3.307 080	170	6.692 900	800	31.496 000
25	.984 250	55	2.165 350	85	3.346 450	175	6.889 750	900	35.433 000
26	1.023 620	56	2.204 720	86	3.385 820	180	7.086 600	1000	39.370 000
27	1.062 990	57	2.244 090	87	3.425 190	185	7.283 450	2000	78.740 000
28	1.102 360	58	2.283 460	88	3.464 560	190	7.480 300	3000	118.110 000
29	1.141 730	59	2.322 830	89	3.503 903	195	7.677 150	4000	157.480 000
30	1.181 100	60	2.362 200	90	3.543 300	200	7.874 000	5000	196.850 000

To change decimal millimeters to decimal inches, position the decimal point where desired on either side of the millimeter measurement shown and reset the inches decimal by the same number of digits in the same direction. For example, to convert .001 mm into decimal inches, reset the decimal behind the 1 mm (shown on the chart) to .001; change the decimal inch equivalent (.039″ shown) to .00039″).

Tap Drill Sizes

	National Fine or S.A.E.				National Coarse or U.S.S.		
Screw & Tap Size	Threads Per Inch	Use Drill Number		Screw & Tap Size	Threads Per Inch	Use Drill Number	
No. 5	44	37		No. 5	40	39	
No. 6	40	33		No. 6	32	36	
No. 8	36	29		No. 8	32	29	
No. 10	32	21		No. 10	24	25	
No. 12	28	15		No. 12	24	17	
1/4	28	3		1/4	20	8	
5/16	24	1		5/16	18	F	
3/8	24	Q		3/8	16	5/16	
7/16	20	W		7/16	14	U	
1/2	20	29/64		1/2	13	27/64	
9/16	18	33/64		9/16	12	31/64	
5/8	18	37/64		5/8	11	17/32	
3/4	16	11/16		3/4	10	21/32	
7/8	14	13/16		7/8	9	49/64	
1 1/8	12	1 3/64		1	8	7/8	
1 1/4	12	1 11/64		1 1/8	7	63/64	
1 1/2	12	1 27/64		1 1/4	7	1 7/64	
				1 1/2	6	1 11/32	

Decimal Equivalent Size of the Number Drills

Drill No.	Decimal Equivalent	Drill No.	Decimal Equivalent	Drill No.	Decimal Equivalent
80	.0135	53	.0595	26	.1470
79	.0145	52	.0635	25	.1495
78	.0160	51	.0670	24	.1520
77	.0180	50	.0700	23	.1540
76	.0200	49	.0730	22	.1570
75	.0210	48	.0760	21	.1590
74	.0225	47	.0785	20	.1610
73	.0240	46	.0810	19	.1660
72	.0250	45	.0820	18	.1695
71	.0260	44	.0860	17	.1730
70	.0280	43	.0890	16	.1770
69	.0292	42	.0935	15	.1800
68	.0310	41	.0960	14	.1820
67	.0320	40	.0980	13	.1850
66	.0330	39	.0995	12	.1890
65	.0350	38	.1015	11	.1910
64	.0360	37	.1040	10	.1935
63	.0370	36	.1065	9	.1960
62	.0380	35	.1100	8	.1990
61	.0390	34	.1110	7	.2010
60	.0400	33	.1130	6	.2040
59	.0410	32	.1160	5	.2055
58	.0420	31	.1200	4	.2090
57	.0430	30	.1285	3	.2130
56	.0465	29	.1360	2	.2210
55	.0520	28	.1405	1	.2280
54	.0550	27	.1440		

Decimal Equivalent Size of the Letter Drills

Letter Drill	Decimal Equivalent	Letter Drill	Decimal Equivalent	Letter Drill	Decimal Equivalent
A	.234	J	.277	S	.348
B	.238	K	.281	T	.358
C	.242	L	.290	U	.368
D	.246	M	.295	V	.377
E	.250	N	.302	W	.386
F	.257	O	.316	X	.397
G	.261	P	.323	Y	.404
H	.266	Q	.332	Z	.413
I	.272	R	.339		

To Increase the Freezing Protection of Anti-Freeze Solutions Already Installed

Cooling System Capacity Quarts	Number of Quarts of **ETHYLENE GLYCOL** Anti-Freeze Required to Increase Protection													
	From +20°F. to					From +10°F. to					From 0°F. to			
	0°	−10°	−20°	−30°	−40°	0°	−10°	−20°	−30°	−40°	−10°	−20°	−30°	−40°
10	1¾	2¼	3	3½	3¾	¾	1½	2¼	2¾	3¼	¾	1½	2	2½
12	2	2¾	3½	4	4½	1	1¾	2½	3¼	3¾	1	1¾	2½	3¼
14	2¼	3¼	4	4¾	5½	1¼	2	3	3¾	4½	1	2	3	3½
16	2½	3½	4½	5¼	6	1¼	2½	3½	4¼	5¼	1¼	2¼	3¼	4
18	3	4	5	6	7	1½	2¾	4	5	5¾	1½	2½	3¾	4¾
20	3¼	4½	5¾	6¾	7½	1¾	3	4¼	5½	6½	1½	2¾	4¼	5¼
22	3½	5	6¼	7¼	8¼	1¾	3¼	4¾	6	7¼	1¾	3¼	4½	5½
24	4	5½	7	8	9	2	3½	5	6½	7½	1¾	3½	5	6
26	4¼	6	7½	8¾	10	2	4	5½	7	8¼	2	3¾	5½	6¾
28	4½	6¼	8	9½	10½	2¼	4¼	6	7½	9	2	4	5¾	7¼
30	5	6¾	8½	10	11½	2½	4½	6½	8	9½	2¼	4¼	6¼	7¾

Test radiator solution with proper hydrometer. Determine from the table the number of quarts of solution to be drawn off from a full cooling system and replace with undiluted anti-freeze, to give the desired increased protection. For example, to increase protection of a 22-quart cooling system containing Ethylene Glycol (permanent type) anti-freeze, from +20°F. to −20°F. will require the replacement of 6¼ quarts of solution with undiluted anti-freeze.

1977 EPA RATINGS

Subcompact Cars

Model	Engine Size/ cylinders	Transmission	Fuel System	City MPG	Highway MPG	Combined MPG
American Motors						
Gremlin	232/6	M	1	20	27	23
	232/6	A	1	18	24	20
	258/6	M	2	17	26	20
	258/6*	A	2	17	23	19
Audi						
Fox	97/4*	M	F1	24	36	28
	97/4*	A	F1	24	33	28
Buick						
Opel by Isuzu	111/4*	M	2	23	36	27
	111/4*	A	2	24	30	26
Skyhawk	231/6	M	2	18	29	21
	231/6	A	2	19	26	21
Chevrolet						
Camaro	250/6	M	1	18	25	20
	250/6	A	1	17	22	19
	305/8	M	2	16	22	19
	305/8	A	2	16	21	18
	350/8	M	4	14	18	15
	350/8	A	4	15	20	17
Chevette	85/4	M	1	28	42	33
	85/4	A	1	25	35	29
	98/4	M	1	31	43	36
	98/4	A	1	26	36	30
Monza	140/4	M	2	24	33	28
	140/4	A	2	21	28	24
	305/8	M	2	16	22	18
	305/8	A	2	17	25	20
Vega	140/4	M	2	24	33	28
	140/4	A	2	21	28	24
Datsun						
B-210	85/4*	M	2	29	41	34
	85/4*	A	2	26	33	29
F-10	85/4*	M	2	29	41	34
Dodge						
Celeste	98/4*	M	2	26	39	31
	98/4*	A	2	26	35	30
	122/4*	M	2	20	33	24
	122/4*	A	2	21	28	24
Colt	98/4*	M	2	29	45	35
	98/4*	A	2	26	35	30
	122/4*	M	2	20	33	24
	122/4*	A	2	21	28	24
Ford						
Maverick	200/6	M	1	21	28	24
	200/6	A	1	18	24	20
	250/6	M	1	21	28	24
	250/6	A	1	17	22	19
	302/8	A	2	17	22	19

Subcompact Cars

Model	Engine Size/ cylinders	Transmission	Fuel System	City MPG	Highway MPG	Combined MPG
Mustang II	140(2.3L)/4	M	2	23	33	26
	140(2.3L)/4	A	2	21	29	24
	171(2.8L)/6	M	2	20	27	23
	171(2.8L)/6	A	2	17	23	19
	302/8	M	2	16	21	18
	302/8	A	2	17	22	19
Pinto	140(2.3L)/4	M	2	26	37	30
	140(2.3L)/4	A	2	23	32	26
	171(2.8L)/6	A	2	18	23	20
Lincoln-Mercury						
Bobcat	140(2.3L)/4	M	2	26	37	30
	140(2.3L)/4	A	2	23	32	26
	171(2.8L)/6	A	2	18	23	20
Comet	200/6	M	1	21	28	24
	200/6	A	1	18	24	20
	250/6	M	1	21	28	24
	250/6	A	1	17	22	19
	302/8	A	2	17	22	19
Mazda						
Cosmo	80/2*	M	4	20	32	25
	80/2*	A	4	18	26	21
RX-4	80/2*	M	4	20	32	25
	80/2*	A	4	18	26	21
808	78/4	M	2	35	42	38
	97/4*	M	2	23	33	27
	97/4*	A	2	23	30	26
Oldsmobile						
Starfire	140/4	M	2	24	33	28
	140/4	A	2	21	28	24
	231/6	M	2	18	29	21
	231/6	A	2	19	26	21
Plymouth						
Arrow	98/4*	M	2	26	39	31
	98/4*	A	2	26	35	30
	122/4*	M	2	20	33	24
	122/4*	A	2	21	28	24
Cricket	98/4*	M	2	28	42	33
	98/4*	A	2	26	35	30
	122/4*	M	2	20	33	24
	122/4*	A	2	21	28	24
Pontiac						
Astre	140/4	M	2	24	33	28
	140/4	A	2	21	28	24
	151/4	M	2	26	37	30
	151/4	A	2	24	32	27
Firebird	231/6	M	2	16	26	19
	231/6	A	2	17	25	20
	301/8	M	2	15	23	18
	301/8	A	2	17	23	19
	350/8	A	4	16	22	18

* Not equipped with catalyst

The 1977 EPA ratings are reprinted from the United States Environmental Protection Agency booklet 1977 Gas Mileage Guide, September 1976.

* Not equipped with catalyst

Extra copies are available from: Fuel Economy, Pueblo, Colorado 81009.

Subcompact Cars

Model	Engine Size/cylinders	Transmission	Fuel System	City MPG	Highway MPG	Combined MPG
Firebird	400/8	M	4	12	19	15
	400/8	A	4	15	20	17
Sunbird	151/4	M	2	26	37	30
	151/4	A	2	24	32	27
	231/6	M	2	18	29	21
	231/6	A	2	19	26	21
Subaru						
Subaru	97/4*	M	2	28	41	32
	97/4*	A	2	24	31	26
Toyota						
Celica	134/4*	M	2	21	35	26
	134/4*	A	2	22	29	25
Corolla	71/4	M	2	36	49	41
	97/4*	M	2	28	39	32
	97/4*	A	2	25	31	27
Corona	134/4*	M	2	21	35	25
	134/4*	A	2	22	29	24
Volkswagen						
Beetle	97/4*	M	F1	23	33	26
Dasher	97/4*	M	F1	24	36	28
	97/4*	A	F1	24	33	28
Dasher Diesel	90/4*	M	F1	35	47	40
Rabbit	97/4	M	1	29	43	34
	97/4*	M	F1	24	37	28
	97/4*	A	F1	24	33	27
Rabbit Diesel	90/4*	M	F1	39	52	44
Scirocco	97/4	M	1	29	43	34
	97/4*	M	F1	24	37	28
	97/4*	A	F1	24	33	27

Compact Cars

Model	Engine Size/cylinders	Transmission	Fuel System	City MPG	Highway MPG	Combined MPG
American Motors						
Hornet	232/6	M	1	18	23	20
	232/6	A	1	18	23	20
	258/6	M	2	17	24	19
	258/6*	A	2	17	23	19
Pacer	232/6	M	1	18	23	20
	232/6	A	1	18	23	20
	258/6	M	2	17	24	19
	258/6*	A	2	17	23	19

Compact Cars

Model	Engine Size/cylinders	Transmission	Fuel System	City MPG	Highway MPG	Combined MPG
Audi						
100LS	114/4*	M	F1	18	27	21
	114/4*	A	F1	17	23	19
Buick						
Skylark	231/6	M	2	16	26	19
	231/6	A	2	18	25	20
	301/8	A	2	17	23	19
	305/8	A	2	16	21	18
Cadillac						
Seville	350/8	A	F1	14	19	16
Chevrolet						
Monte Carlo	305/8	A	2	16	20	17
	350/8	A	4	14	19	16
Nova	250/6	M	1	19	27	22
	250/6	A	1	18	23	20
	305/8	M	2	16	22	19
	305/8	A	2	16	21	18
	350/8	M	4	14	18	15
	350/8	A	4	15	20	17
Dodge						
Aspen	225/6	M	1	20	29	23
	225/6	A	1	18	24	20
	225/6	M	2	17	24	20
	225/6	A	2	16	21	18
	318/8	M	2	15	25	19
	318/8	A	2	15	20	17
	360/8	A	2	14	19	16
	360/8	A	4	11	17	13
Ford						
Granada	200/6	M	1	21	28	24
	250/6	M	1	21	28	24
	250/6	A	1	18	23	20
	302/8	M	2	16	24	18
	302/8	A	2	16	22	18
Thunderbird	302/8	A	2	15	19	17
	351/8	A	2	14	20	16
	400/8	A	2	13	18	15
Lincoln-Mercury						
Monarch	200/6	M	1	21	28	24
	250/6	M	1	21	28	24
	250/6	A	1	18	23	20
	302/8	M	2	16	24	18
	302/8	A	2	16	22	18
Oldsmobile						
Omega	231/6	M	2	16	27	20
	231/6	A	2	19	26	21
	260/8	A	2	17	23	19
	305/8	M	2	16	22	19
	305/8	A	2	16	21	18

* Not equipped with catalyst

Compact Cars

Model	Engine Size/cylinders	Transmission	Fuel System	City MPG	Highway MPG	Combined MPG
Plymouth						
Volare	225/6	M	1	20	29	23
	225/6	A	1	18	24	20
	225/6	M	2	17	24	20
	225/6	A	2	16	21	18
	318/8	M	2	15	25	19
	318/8	A	2	15	20	17
	360/8	A	2	14	19	16
	360/8	A	4	11	17	13
Pontiac						
Grand Prix	301/8	A	2	16	23	19
	350/8	A	4	14	21	17
	400/8	A	4	14	21	17
Ventura	151/4	M	2	22	34	26
	151/4	A	2	21	29	24
	231/6	M	2	17	27	20
	231/6	A	2	18	26	21
	301/8	M	2	15	23	18
	301/8	A	2	17	23	19
	305/8	A	2	16	22	18

Mid-Size Cars

Model	Engine Size/cylinders	Transmission	Fuel System	City MPG	Highway MPG	Combined MPG
Buick						
Century/Regal	231/6	M	2	16	26	19
	231/6	A	2	17	25	20
	350/8	A	2	15	20	17
	350/8	A	4	15	22	17
Cadillac						
Eldorado	425/8	A	4	11	18	14
Chevrolet						
Malibu	250/6	M	1	18	25	20
	250/6	A	1	17	22	19
	305/8	A	2	16	21	17
	350/8	A	4	14	19	16
Chrysler						
Cordoba	318/8	A	2	13	18	15
	360/8	A	2	14	20	16
	400/8	A	4	11	19	14

Mid-Size Cars

Model	Engine Size/cylinders	Transmission	Fuel System	City MPG	Highway MPG	Combined MPG
Dodge						
Charger SE	318/8	A	2	13	18	15
	360/8	A	2	14	20	16
	400/8	A	4	11	19	14
Monaco	225/6	A	1	17	22	19
	225/6	A	2	16	21	18
	318/8	M	2	14	23	17
	318/8	A	2	13	18	15
	360/8	A	2	14	20	16
	360/8	A	4	11	16	12
	400/8	A	4	11	19	14
	440/8	A	4	9	17	11
Ford						
LTD II	302/8	A	2	15	19	17
	351/8	A	2	14	20	16
	400/8	A	2	13	18	15
Lincoln-Mercury						
Continental Mark V	400/8	A	2	13	18	15
	460/8	A	4	11	16	13
Cougar/Cougar XR-7	302/8	A	2	15	19	17
	351/8	A	2	14	20	16
	400/8	A	2	13	18	15
Oldsmobile						
Cutlass	231/6	M	2	16	26	19
	231/6	A	2	17	25	20
	260/8	M	2	17	28	20
	260/8	A	2	16	21	18
	350/8	A	4	16	21	18
	403/8	A	4	15	21	18
Plymouth						
Fury	225/6	A	1	17	22	19
	225/6	A	2	16	21	18
	318/8	M	2	14	23	17
	318/8	A	2	13	18	15
	360/8	A	2	14	20	16
	360/8	A	4	11	16	12
	400/8	A	4	11	19	14
	440/8	A	4	9	17	11
Pontiac						
Lemans	231/6	M	2	16	26	19
	231/6	A	2	17	25	20
	301/8	A	2	16	23	19
	350/8	A	4	14	21	17
	400/8	A	4	14	21	17

Large Cars

Model	Engine Size/cylinders	Transmission	Fuel System	City MPG	Highway MPG	Combined MPG
American Motors						
Matador	258/6	A	1	15	21	17
	304/8	A	2	13	17	15
	360/8	A	2	13	16	14
Buick						
Electra	350/8	A	4	15	22	17
	403/8	A	4	15	21	18
Lesabre	231/6	A	2	17	25	20
	301/8	A	2	17	23	19
	350/8	A	4	16	22	18
	403/8	A	4	15	21	18
Riviera	350/8	A	4	15	22	17
	403/8	A	4	15	21	18
Cadillac						
Cadillac	425/8	A	4	14	18	16
Limousine	425/8	A	4	12	18	14
Chevrolet						
Chevrolet	250/6	A	1	17	22	19
	305/8	A	2	16	21	18
	350/8	A	4	15	20	17
Chrysler						
Chrysler	360/8	A	2	12	18	14
	400/8	A	4	11	18	13
	440/8	A	4	10	16	12
Dodge						
Royal Monaco	318/8	A	2	13	18	15
	360/8	A	2	12	18	14
	400/8	A	4	11	18	13
	440/8	A	4	9	17	11
Ford						
Ford	302/8	A	2	15	19	17
	351/8	A	2	13	19	15
	400/8	A	2	13	18	15
	460/8	A	4	11	16	13
Lincoln-Mercury						
Lincoln Continental	400/8	A	2	13	18	15
	460/8	A	4	11	16	13
Mercury	400/8	A	2	13	18	15
	460/8	A	4	11	16	13
Oldsmobile						
Delta 88	231/6	A	2	17	25	20
	260/8	A	2	17	23	19
	350/8	A	4	16	22	18
	403/8	A	4	15	21	18
Oldsmobile 98	350/8	A	4	16	21	18
	403/8	A	4	15	21	18
Toronado	403/8	A	4	13	19	16
Plymouth						
Gran Fury	318/8	A	2	13	18	15
	360/8	A	2	12	18	14
	400/8	A	4	11	18	13
	440/8	A	4	9	17	11

Large Cars

Model	Engine Size/cylinders	Transmission	Fuel System	City MPG	Highway MPG	Combined MPG
Pontiac						
Pontiac	231/6	A	2	17	25	20
	301/8	A	2	17	23	19
	350/8	A	4	16	22	18
	403/8	A	4	15	21	18

Two Seaters

Model	Engine Size/cylinders	Transmission	Fuel System	City MPG	Highway MPG	Combined MPG
Chevrolet						
Corvette	350/8	M	4	14	18	15
	350/8	A	4	15	20	17
Datsun						
280Z	168/6*	M	F1	18	27	21
	169/6*	A	F1	18	22	20
Porsche						
Turbo Carrera	183/6*	M	F1	14	24	17
911S	164/6*	M	F1	15	24	18
	164/6*	S	F1	16	21	18
924	121/4*	M	F1	17	31	21

* Not equipped with catalyst

Small Station Wagons

Model	Engine Size/cylinders	Transmission	Fuel System	City MPG	Highway MPG	Combined MPG
American Motors						
Hornet Wagon	232/6	M	1	18	23	20
	232/6	A	1	18	23	20
	258/6*	A	2	17	23	19

Small Station Wagons

Model	Engine Size/cylinders	Transmission	Fuel System	City MPG	Highway MPG	Combined MPG
Pacer						
Wagon	232/6	M	1	18	23	20
	232/6	A	1	18	23	20
	258/6	M	2	17	24	19
	258/6*	A	2	17	23	19
Audi						
Fox						
Wagon	97/4*	M	F1	24	36	28
	97/4*	A	F1	24	33	28
Chevrolet						
Vega						
Wagon	140/4	M	2	24	33	28
	140/4	A	2	21	28	24
Datsun						
F-10						
Wagon	85/4*	M	2	29	41	34
Dodge						
Colt						
Wagon	98/4*	M	2	24	37	28
	122/4*	M	2	20	33	24
	122/4*	A	2	21	28	24
Ford						
Pinto						
Wagon	140(2.3L)/4	M	2	23	33	26
	140(2.3L)/4	A	2	21	29	24
	171(2.8L)/6	A	2	18	23	20
Lincoln-Mercury						
Bobcat						
Wagon	140(2.3L)/4	M	2	23	33	26
	140(2.3L)/4	A	2	21	29	24
	171(2.8L)/6	A	2	18	23	20
Mazda						
RX-4						
Wagon	80/2*	M	4	20	32	25
	80/2*	A	4	18	26	21
808						
Wagon	78/4	M	2	33	42	36
	97/4*	M	2	23	33	27
	97/4*	A	2	23	30	26
Plymouth						
Cricket						
Wagon	98/4*	M	2	24	37	28
	122/4*	M	2	20	33	24
	122/4*	A	2	21	28	24
Pontiac						
Astre						
Safari						
Wagon	151/4	M	2	26	37	30
	151/4	A	2	24	32	27
Subaru						
Subaru						
Wagon	97/4*	M	2	28	38	32
	97/4*	A	2	25	31	27

* Not equipped with catalyst

Small Station Wagons

Model	Engine Size/cylinders	Transmission	Fuel System	City MPG	Highway MPG	Combined MPG
Toyota						
Corolla						
Wagon	97/4*	M	2	28	39	32
	97/4*	A	2	25	31	27
Corona						
Wagon	134/4*	M	2	21	35	25
	134/4*	A	2	22	29	24
Volkswagen						
Dasher						
Wagon	97/4*	M	F1	24	36	28
	97/4*	A	F1	24	33	28
Dasher						
Wagon						
Diesel	90/4*	M	F1	35	47	40

* Not equipped with catalyst

Mid-Size Station Wagons

Model	Engine Size/cylinders	Transmission	Fuel System	City MPG	Highway MPG	Combined MPG
Buick						
Century						
Wagon	350/8	A	4	14	19	16
Chevrolet						
Malibu						
Wagon	305/8	A	2	16	20	17
	350/8	A	4	13	17	14
Dodge						
Aspen						
Wagon	225/6	M	2	17	24	20
	225/6	A	2	16	21	18
	318/8	M	2	15	24	18
	318/8	A	2	15	20	17
	360/8	A	2	14	20	16
	360/8	A	4	11	16	12
Monaco						
Wagon	360/8	A	2	12	18	14
	400/8	A	4	11	18	13
Ford						
LTD II						
Wagon	351/8	A	2	13	19	15
	400/8	A	2	13	18	15
Lincoln-Mercury						
Cougar						
Wagon	351/8	A	2	13	19	15
	400/8	A	2	13	18	15

Mid-Size Station Wagons

Manu-facturers	Vehicle Description			Fuel Economy		
Model	Engine Size/cylinders	Transmission	Fuel System	City MPG	Highway MPG	Combined MPG
Oldsmobile						
Vista						
Cruiser						
Wagon	350/8	A	4	14	19	16
	403/8	A	4	13	19	15
Plymouth						
Fury						
Wagon	360/8	A	2	12	18	14
	400/8	A	4	11	18	13
Volare						
Wagon	225/6	M	2	17	24	20
	225/6	A	2	16	21	18
	318/8	M	2	15	24	18
	318/8	A	2	15	20	17
	360/8	A	2	14	20	16
	360/8	A	4	11	16	12
Pontiac						
Lemans						
Safari						
Wagon	301/8	A	2	16	23	19
	400/8	A	4	13	18	15

Large Station Wagons

Manu-facturers	Vehicle Description			Fuel Economy		
Model	Engine Size/cylinders	Transmission	Fuel System	City MPG	Highway MPG	Combined MPG
American Motors						
Matador						
Wagon	304/8	A	2	13	17	15
	360/8	A	2	13	16	14
Buick						
Estate						
Wagon	350/8	A	4	16	21	18
	403/8	A	4	15	21	18
Chevrolet						
Chevrolet						
Wagon	305/8	A	2	16	20	17
	350/8	A	4	14	19	16
Chrysler						
Chrysler						
Wagon	400/8	A	4	10	16	12
	440/8	A	4	10	16	12
Dodge						
Royal						
Monaco						
Wagon	400/8	A	4	10	16	12
	440/8	A	4	10	16	12
Ford						
Ford						
Wagon	400/8	A	2	13	18	15
	460/8	A	4	11	16	13
Lincoln-Mercury						
Mercury						
Wagon	400/8	A	2	13	18	15
	460/8	A	4	11	16	13
Oldsmobile						
Custom						
Cruiser						
Wagon	350/8	A	4	16	21	18
	403/8	A	4	15	21	18
Plymouth						
Gran						
Fury						
Wagon	400/8	A	4	10	16	12
	440/8	A	4	10	16	12
Pontiac						
Pontiac						
Safari						
Wagon	301/8	A	2	16	23	19
	403/8	A	4	15	21	18

Small Pickup Trucks

Manu-facturers	Vehicle Description			Fuel Economy		
Model	Engine Size/cylinders	Transmission	Fuel System	City MPG	Highway MPG	Combined MPG
Chevrolet						
Luv						
Pickup	111/4*	M	2	23	33	26
	111/4*	A	2	21	29	24
Datsun						
Pickup	119/4*	M	2	22	32	25
	119/4*	A	2	22	27	24
Toyota						
Hilux	134/4*	M	2	24	34	28
	134/4*	A	2	23	28	25

* Not equipped with catalyst

Standard Pickup Trucks

Manu-facturers	Vehicle Description			Fuel Economy		
Model	Engine Size/cylinders	Transmission	Fuel System	City MPG	Highway MPG	Combined MPG
GMC						
Pickup	250/6	M	1	18	24	20
	250/6	A	1	17	21	19
	305/8	M	2	16	21	18
	305/8	A	2	16	19	17
	350/8	M	4	14	20	16
	350/8	A	4	14	19	16
Sprint	250/6	M	1	18	25	20
	250/6	A	1	17	22	19
	305/8	A	2	16	21	17
	350/8	A	4	14	19	16

Standard Pickup Trucks

Manu-facturers	Vehicle Description			Fuel Economy		
Model	Engine Size/cylinders	Transmission	Fuel System	City MPG	Highway MPG	Combined MPG
Chevrolet						
El						
Camino	250/6	M	1	18	25	20
	250/6	A	1	17	22	19
	305/8	A	2	16	21	17
	350/8	A	4	14	19	16
Pickup	250/6	M	1	18	24	20
	250/6	A	1	17	21	19
	305/8	M	2	16	21	18
	305/8	A	2	16	19	17
	350/8	M	4	14	20	16
	350/8	A	4	14	19	16
Dodge						
Pickup	225/6	M	1	18	24	20
	225/6	A	1	17	22	19
	318/8	M	2	14	23	17
	318/8	A	2	14	20	16
	360/8	A	2	13	20	16
Ford						
Pickup	300/6	M	1	19	26	22
	300/6	A	1	18	26	21
	302/8	M	2	17	24	19
	302/8	A	2	16	22	19
	351/8	M	2	14	20	16
	351/8	A	2	14	20	16
	400/8	A	2	13	18	15
Ranchero	302/8	A	2	15	19	17
	351/8	A	2	14	20	16
	400/8	A	2	13	18	15

Vans/Special Purpose Trucks

Manu-facturers	Vehicle Description			Fuel Economy		
Model	Engine Size/cylinders	Transmission	Fuel System	City MPG	Highway MPG	Combined MPG
Chevrolet						
Van	250/6	M	1	18	25	21
	250/6	A	1	17	21	18
	305/8	M	2	16	21	18
	305/8	A	2	16	20	18
	350/8	M	4	14	19	16
	350/8	A	4	14	19	16
Dodge						
Utility	225/6	M	1	14	20	16
	225/6	A	1	17	22	19
	318/8	M	2	14	21	16
	318/8	A	2	13	20	15
	360/8	A	2	13	20	16
Van	225/6	M	1	18	24	20
	225/6	A	1	17	22	19
	318/8	M	2	15	25	18
	318/8	A	2	14	20	16
	360/8	A	2	13	20	16
Ford						
Bronco	302/8	M	2	17	24	19
	302/8	A	2	16	22	19
Van (Econo-line/Club Wagon)	300/6	M	1	18	25	21
	300/6	A	1	18	25	20
	351/8	M	2	14	20	16
	351/8	A	2	14	20	16

Vans/Special Purpose Trucks

Manu-facturers	Vehicle Description			Fuel Economy		
Model	Engine Size/ cylinders	Transmission	Fuel System	City MPG	Highway MPG	Combined MPG
GMC						
Van	250/6	M	1	18	25	21
	250/6	A	1	17	21	18
	305/8	M	2	16	21	18
	305/8	A	2	16	20	18
	350/8	M	4	14	19	16
	350/8	A	4	14	19	16
Jeep						
Jeep	232/6*	M	1	17	20	18
	258/6*	M	1	17	21	18
	258/6*	A	1	16	19	17
	304/8	M	2	15	19	17
	304/8	A	2	13	17	14
Plymouth						
Utility	225/6	M	1	14	20	16
	225/6	A	1	17	22	19
	318/8	M	2	14	21	16
	318/8	A	2	13	20	15
	360/8	A	2	13	20	16
Van	225/6	M	1	18	24	20
	225/6	A	1	17	22	19

Vans/Special Purpose Trucks

Manu-facturers	Vehicle Description			Fuel Economy		
Model	Engine Size/ cylinders	Transmission	Fuel System	City MPG	Highway MPG	Combined MPG
Van	318/8	M	2	14	22	17
	318/8	A	2	14	20	16
	360/8	A	2	13	20	16
Toyota						
Hilux Cab Chassis	134/4*	M	2	20	28	23
Land Cruiser	258/6*	M	2	13	19	15
Land Cruiser Wagon	258/6*	M	2	12	17	14
Volkswagen						
Bus (Wagon, Kombi, Camp-mobile)	120/4*	M	F1	20	28	23
	120/4*	A	F1	19	25	21

* Not equipped with catalyst

NOTES

Chapter One

1. United States Department of Transportation, Federal Highway Administration, *Cost of Operating an Automobile*, Washington, D.C., April, 1972.

Chapter Two

1. "The Fastest Man on Earth," *Bicycling*, November, 1973, p. 20.

2. Jack C. Cornell, *Passenger Car Fuel Economy Characteristics on Modern Superhighways*, SAE Report No. 650862. Report to the National Fuels and Lubricants Meeting, Society of Automotive Engineers, Tulsa, Oklahoma, November 2–4, 1965 (New York: Society of Automotive Engineers, 1965), cited in Motor Vehicle Manufacturers Association of the United States, *Automobile Fuel Economy*, September 21, 1973, p. 7.

3. *Ibid.*

4. Thomas C. Austin and Karl H. Hellman, *Passenger Car Fuel Economy—Trends and Influencing Factors*, SAE Report No. 730790, Report to National Combined Farm, Construction, and Industrial Machinery and Fuels and Lubricants Meetings, Milwaukee, Wisconsin, September 10–13, 1973. (New York: Society of Automotive Engineers, 1973.), p. 16.

5. Cummins Engine Company, *Answers to Questions about Diesels*, Bulletin No. 952760, August, 1970, p. 19.

6. William D. Bowman, *The Present Status of Automobile Aerodynamics in Automobile Engineering and Development*, Proceedings of the AIAA Symposium on the Aerodynamics of Sport and Competition Vehicles, April, 1968, p. 71.

7. Firestone Tire and Rubber Company, Promotional Announcement, 1973.

8. Cornell, *Passenger Car Fuel Economy Characteristics on Modern Superhighways*, cited in Motor Vehicle Manufacturers Association, p. 7.

9. Motor Vehicle Manufacturers Association, *Automobile Fuel Economy*, September 21, 1973, p. 4.

10. Carl E. Burke, Larry H. Nagler, E. C. Campbell, W. E. Zierer, H. L. Welch, L. C. Lundstrom, T. D. Kaiser, and W. A. McConnell, "Where Does All The Power Go?", *SAE Transactions*, 65 (57), cited in Motor Vehicle Manufacturers Association, p. 10.

11. United States Environmental Protection Agency, *A Report on Automotive Fuel Economy*, Washington, D.C., Government Printing Office, October, 1973, p. 30.

12. *Ibid.*

13. *Ibid.*
14. Chrysler Corporation, "Drive More, Pay Less," Detroit, Michigan, May 24, 1973 (News Release), cited in Motor Vehicle Manufacturers Association, p. 15.

Chapter Three
1. United States Environmental Protection Agency, p. 10.
2. G. H. Huebner, Jr., and D. J. Gasser, "General Factors Affecting Vehicle Fuel Consumption" (Paper presented at National Automobile Engineering Meeting, Society of Automotive Engineers, Detroit, Michigan, May 15, 1973), cited in Motor Vehicle Manufacturers Association, p. 6.
3. *Ibid.*
4. Jack C. Cornell, "Car Size Chiefly Responsible for Low MPG at High MPH," *SAE Journal*, April, 1966, p. 37.
5. United States Environmental Protection Agency, p. 21.
6. *Ibid.*
7. Huebner and Gasser, cited in Motor Vehicle Manufacturers Association, p. 16.
8. United States Environmental Protection Agency, p. 14.
9. *Ibid.*
10. Cornell, *Passenger Car Fuel Economy Characteristics on Modern Superhighways,* cited in Motor Vehicle Manufacturers Association, p. 13.
11. Huebner and Gasser cited in Motor Vehicle Manufacturers Association, p. 13.
12. Harold C. MacDonald, "Remarks" (speech presented to 1973 Engineering Meeting, Society of Automotive Engineers, Detroit, Michigan, May 15, 1973), cited in Motor Vehicle Manufacturers Association, p. 5.
13. Cornell, *Passenger Car Fuel Economy Characteristics on Modern Superhighways,* cited in Motor Vehicle Manufacturers Association, p. 12.
14. Firestone Tire and Rubber Company, and the United States Environmental Protection Agency, p. 14.
15. American Petroleum Institute, "Gasoline, Questions-Answers," Publication No. 1580, Washington, D.C., April, 1972, p. 5.
16. *Ibid.*
17. American Society for Testing and Materials, *Standard Specifications for Automotive Gasoline,* Designation D439-73, Oct., 1973.
18. United States Department of the Interior, Bureau of Mines, *Thermal Properties of Petroleum Products,* report no. M97, Washington, D.C., Government Printing Office, 1973., cited in Motor Vehicle Manufacturers Association, p. 18.
19. American Petroleum Institute, *Motor*

Oil Guide, Publication No. 1551-fourth edition; Washington, D.C., January, 1972, p. 33.
20. *Ibid.*
21. Rubber Manufacturers Association, *Care and Service of Automobile Tires,* New York, 1972, p. 5.
22. Firestone Tire and Rubber Company.
23. *Ibid.*
24. Ronald A. Hingst, "Meter Provides Readout of Fuel Miles per Gallon," *Automotive News,* December 31, 1973, p. 33.

Chapter Four
1. Huebner and Gasser, cited in Motor Vehicle Manufacturers Association, p. 19.
2. United States Department of Transportation, Federal Highway Administration, *The Effect of Speed on Automobile Gasoline Consumption Rates,* Washington, D.C., Government Printing Office, October, 1973, p. 8.
3. Daimler-Benz, A. G., Statement Before the Senate Public Works Committee, Subcommittee on Air and Water Pollution, May 18, 1973. Figure 7, p. 48.
4. Chrysler Corporation, cited in Motor Vehicle Manufacturers Association, p. 20.
5. Ronald M. Weiers, *Licensed To Kill,* Chilton Book Company, Philadelphia, Pa., 1968, p. 35.
6. Huebner and Gasser, cited in Motor Vehicle Manufacturers Association, p. 12.
7. United States Department of Transportation, Federal Highway Admininistration, *The Effect of Speed on Automobile Gasoline Consumption Rates,* p. 8.
8. Cornell, *Passenger Car Fuel Economy Characteristics on Modern Superhighways,* cited in Motor Vehicle Manufacturers Association, p. 9.

Chapter Five
1. United States Environmental Protection Agency, p. 29.
2. Joseph C. Brabetz and Donald S. Pike, "Engines Like To Be Warm," *SAE Journal,* January, 1965, p. 70.
3. *Ibid.*
4. American Petroleum Institute, "Gasoline Saving Tips," Washington, D.C., not dated.
5. *Ibid.*
6. *Ibid.*
7. Chrysler Corporation, cited in Motor Vehicle Manufacturers Association, p. 21.
8. P. N. Gammelgard, statement presented to U.S. Senate Subcommittee on Air and Water Pollution, Washington, D.C., June 26, 1973, cited in Motor Vehicle Manufacturers Association, p. 14.

9. American Petroleum Institute, "Gasoline Saving Tips."

10. United States Department of Commerce, National Bureau of Standards, *Tires, Their Selection and Care*, Government Printing Office, Washington, D.C., March, 1971, p. 4.

11. Chrysler Corporation, cited in Motor Vehicle Manufacturers Association, p. 21.

Chapter Six

1. Charles E. Scheffler and George W. Niepoth, *Customer Fuel Economy Estimated from Engineering Tests*, SAE report no. 650861, Report to the National Fuel and Lubricants Meeting, Society of Automotive Engineers, Tulsa, Oklahoma, November 2–4, 1965 (New York: Society of Automotive Engineers, 1965), cited in Motor Vehicle Manufacturers Association, p. 20.

2. MacDonald, cited in Motor Vehicle Manufacturers Association, p. 5.

Appendix One

1. Cummins Engine Company, *Trucker's Guide to Fuel Savings*, Bulletin 952880, Columbus, Indiana, October, 1973, p. 5.

2. *Ibid.*

3. "Aerodynamically-Styled Paymaster Offers Tremendous Fuel Savings," *Diesel Equipment Superintendent*, October, 1973, p. 26.

4. Cummins, *Trucker's Guide to Fuel Savings*, pp. 11, 20.

5. *Ibid.*, p. 14.

6. *Ibid.*, p. 15.

7. *Ibid.*, p. 13.

8. *Ibid.*, p. 17.

9. *Ibid.*, p. 19.

10. *Ibid.*, p. 10.

11. *Ibid.*, p. 8.

12. *Ibid.*, p. 9.

13. *Ibid.*, p. 12.

14. *Ibid.*, p. 7.

15. *Ibid.*, p. 20.

16. Cummins Engine Company, *Answers to Questions About Diesels*, p. 8.

17. George C. Nield, "Light Diesels Give Promise in Mail Service," *SAE Journal*, July, 1966, p. 77.

18. Source: Motorcycle Industry Council, 1973.

19. Motorcycle Industry Council, "Cost of Operating a Motorcycle Compared to the Cost of Operating an Automobile," news release, Washington, D.C., 1973.

Appendix Two

1. United States Environmental Protection Agency, p. 21.

2. American Honda Motor Company, *Description of Honda CVCC Engine*, technical news release, December, 1972.

3. United States Environmental Agency, p. 21.

4. *Ibid.*

5. Cummins Engine Company, *Answers to Questions About Diesels*, p. 7.

6. *Ibid.*, p. 8.

7. Daimler-Benz, A. G., Figure 7, p. 48.

8. *Chemical and Engineering News*, Dec. 24, 1973. American Chemical Society.

9. "News Notes," *Research/Development*, January, 1974, p. 8.

BIBLIOGRAPHY

1. American Honda Motor Company, *Description of Honda CVCC Engine,* technical news release, December, 1972.

2. American Petroleum Institute, "Gasoline, Questions-Answers," publication no. 1580, Washington, D.C. April, 1972.

3. American Petroleum Institute, "Gasoline Savings Tips," Washington, D.C., not dated.

4. American Petroleum Institute, *Motor Oil Guide,* Publication no. 1551-fourth edition, Washington, D.C., January, 1972.

5. American Society for Testing and Materials, *Standard Specifications For Automotive Gasoline,* Designation D 439-73, Oct., 1973.

6. Austin, Thomas C. and Karl H. Hellman, *Passenger Car Fuel Economy—Trends and Influencing Factors,* SAE Report No. 730790, Report to National Combined Farm, Construction, and Industrial Machinery and Fuels and Lubricants Meetings, Milwaukee, Wisconsin, September 10–13, 1973 (New York: Society of Automotive Engineers, 1973.)

7. *Bicycling,* "The Fastest Man On Earth," November, 1973.

8. Bowman, William D., *The Present Status of Automobile Aerodynamics in Automobile Engineering and Development,* Proceedings of the AIAA Symposium on the Aerodynamics of Sport and Competition Vehicles, April, 1968.

9. Brabetz, Joseph C., and Donald S. Pike, "Engines Like To Be Warm," *SAE Journal,* January, 1965.

10. *Chemical and Engineering News,* December 24, 1973.

11. Cornell, Jack C., "Car Size Chiefly Responsible for Low MPG at High MPH," *SAE Journal,* April, 1966.

12. Cummins Engine Company, *Answers to Questions About Diesels,* Bulletin no. 952760, August, 1970.

13. Cummins Engine Company, *Truckers' Guide to Fuel Savings,* Bulletin 952880, Columbus, Indiana, October, 1973.

14. Daimler-Benz, A. G., Statement Before the Senate Public Works Committee, Subcommittee on Air and Water Pollution, May 18, 1973.

15. *Diesel Equipment Superintendent,* "Aerodynamically-Styled Paymaster Offers Tremendous Fuel Savings," October, 1973.

16. Firestone Tire and Rubber Company, Promotional Announcement, 1973.

17. Hingst, Ronald A., "Meter Provides Readout of Fuel Miles Per Gallon," *Automotive News,* December 31, 1973.

18. Motorcycle Industrial Council, "Cost of

Operating a Motorcycle Compared to the Cost of Operating an Automobile," news release, Washington, D.C., 1973.

19. Motor Vehicle Manufacturers Association, *Automobile Fuel Economy*, September 21, 1973.

20. Nield, George C., "Light Diesels Give Promise in Mail Service," *SAE Journal*, July, 1966.

21. *Research/Development*, "News Notes," January, 1974.

22. Rubber Manufacturers Association, *Care and Service of Automobile Tires*, New York, 1972.

23. United States Department of Commerce, National Bureau of Standards, *Tires, Their Selection and Care*, Government Printing Office, Washington, D.C., 1971.

24. United States Department of Transportation, Federal Highway Administration, *Cost of Operating an Automobile*, Washington, D.C., Government Printing Office, April, 1972.

25. United States Department of Transportation, Federal Highway Administration, *The Effect of Speed on Automobile Gasoline Consumption Rates*, Washington, D.C., Government Printing Office, October, 1973.

26. United States Environmental Protection Agency, *A Report on Automotive Fuel Economy*, Washington, D.C., Government Printing Office, October, 1973.

27. Weiers, Ronald M., *Licensed To Kill*, Chilton Book Company, Philadelphia, Pennsylvania, 1968.